'Mangoana
Ka Bohaleng

■

My Life in the Struggle

Maggie Resha

For the memory of Robert,
for our daughters Nosipo and Masechaba,
and for the brave women in the struggle

and in memory of
the three most important women in my life:
my mother, Moselantja Mmamolise Tsiu
my grannie, Mmatau Mokhele
my aunt, Maelia Mokhele

'Mangoana Tsoara Thipa
Ka Bohaleng

∎

My Life in the Struggle

Maggie Resha

SA Writers
London

Congress of South African Writers
Johannesburg
1991

SA Writers

25a Greencroft Gardens, London NW6 3LN

Congress of South African Writers
POBox 421007, Johannesburg 2033

First published 1991 in Great Britain by SA Writers
and in South Africa by Congress of South African Writers

Cover photo: Sean Smith – The Guardian

Cover design: Andrew Lord

ISBN 1 872086 02 0 (SA Writers)

Set in 10/12 New Century by Robert Vicat Ltd, London
Printed and bound in South Africa by
Creda Press

Contents

Preface

Somebody once said that the printed word robs time, distance and death of their sting. These words kept ringing in my mind throughout the five years I spent writing this short story of my life, for it is the fulfilment of a wish I have harboured for more than thirty years.

The idea for an autobiography first came into my mind in 1958, shortly after my release, with many other colleagues, from our prison sentences for our participation in the dynamic Womens' Anti-Pass campaigns. But because of the unpredictability of my life in those days — as will be seen from the pages of my book — I was forced to shelve this idea. Perhaps the doings of fate? In a sense, yes, because in my view the experiences I gained subsequently certainly helped to enrich my story. Being forced to postpone also supports the rule that (unless one is a Bob Geldof) the twilight of one's life is the propitious time for recollections; so that when the curtain finally drops, friends and relatives might revive delightful memories to mollify their grief.

In 1983, when Kenny Parker reminded me of my late husband's influence upon his political development from their first encounters while working in the London office of the ANC in the mid-Sixties, and suggested that I write Robert's biography, my answer was unambiguous. Not only did I tell him that Robert should have written his own while he was alive, but that he should not forget that I have a history of my own to tell.

His reply calmly gave me a rope to hang myself: 'Go ahead and write it; I'll help you', he said. These words were a Godsend because, from 1958, when I first had the idea, I knew that I could not just make a plunge into the world of writing without help. Robert had known of my desire to write my biography, and had offered to help; my main worry after his death was who would have the literary skill, as well as the understanding of our deep feelings as victims of apartheid, to help me tell our story.

Before I festoon all the people whose contributions deserve my accolades, I should like to state how the writing of this book revived memories of my twenty-six years of companionship with Robert — as a person who believes in Fate, I doubt if the book could have been written, in the first place, had I not met him. Robert was a true democrat who believed in partnership and in equality. It was because of his insistence that I should come out as myself, and not live in his shadow, that this book is in his memory.

I wrote this book under difficult conditions. The loss of documents as a result of raids by the South African police is incalculable. It was because of this awareness of loss that, the moment we came to the ANC office in Algeria, we — Robert, Joe Matlou, Johnny Makatini and myself — started to compile and preserve the remnants of what we had salvaged. We also reminded each other of significant details while these were still fresh in our minds. On the whole, I think, following the traditions of our forebears, Africans are good at remembering: the majority of us hardly use a diary. But then, the life of an African in South Africa under apartheid is so full of traumatic events, which leave such permanent scars, that these remain forever vivid in the mind. Nobody can forget!

For material, I sent letters to friends all over Africa, who had been in the struggle, to remind me about significant details. Among these are Peter Ntite, former Secretary-general of the ANC Youth League, former Treason trialist, and former prominent member of the Sophiatown branch of the ANC and one of the leaders against the removals; Temba Mqota, who now teaches in King Saud University in Saudi Arabia, but who was formerly a member of the ANC National Executive Committee, a Treason Trialist and a prominent member of the Port Elizabeth branch of the ANC; his wife, Tozi Mqota, also gave me enormous help. Tozi had participated in the Defiance Campaign of 1952, while she was still in her teens, and later she fought fierce battles against the 'Africanists' in her ANC branch at Orlando. Tozi was an exceptionally efficient courier of messages to some of the most sensitive areas and persons; she finally escaped from South Africa, with her baby, as the police were on her heels.

I thank Bhut' Fikile Nobadula, founder member of the ANC Youth League and former chairman of the Benoni branch, former regional chairman of the East Rand region of the ANC, not only for his knowledge of the history of our struggle in that period, but also for help with Xhosa translations. I particularly thank his former wife, Tembi Nobadula, a founder member of the Federation of South African Women, and a prominent member of her branch at the time when her mother, the late Mrs Shange, chaired the ANC Women's League branch.

I regret that my sister (Mangoane) Susan Matu Baloyi, who helped me with the story of the campaign against the Sophiatown removals, in which she was a prominent participant, did not live to see the publication of this book.

I am also indebted to Mr Livingstone (Livy) Mqotsi for helping me with Xhosa idioms and spelling, and to Karabo Sello (Mrs Iweibo), formerly of the Port Elizabeth branch of the ANC; she, too, had participated in the Defiance Campaign while still in her teens, being later on sent abroad to join Umkhonto we Siswe.

My thanks also to the late Dr Allen Madolwana (Francis Meli, author of *South Africa Belongs to Us: A History of the ANC*) for the encouragement he offered me along the way, and for reminding me about my old school in East London, where he went as a student many years after I had been there.

I also want to thank our two daughters, Nosipo and Masechaba, and my son-in-law, Dr Jolimela Mkwananzi, for their encouragement during the long years of my writing; also my grandson, Mwelisi Mkwananzi, for typing some documents for me in the initial stages.

I owe an especial debt of gratitude to my two brothers, Professor M. Bolofo and Ntsukunyane Mphanya, whom I met by chance in Britain, where they are engaged in research on the history of the BaFokeng clan, to which I belong. It is to Professor Bolofo (whose research has revealed many distortions by white historians about the rise to power of Moeshoeshoe I) that I owe particular thanks for producing the chart of my family tree, which is included in this book.

My thanks also to Dr Rob Turrell for the readiness with which he accepted my manuscript, and for the care he took produce such a pleasing book.

Lastly, to Professor Kenneth Parker, who insists that helping to tell the story of our struggle is sufficient, all I can say is *ungadinwa nangomso* (the nearest literal translation being 'thank you very much; don't get tired, not even tomorrow!').

London, June 1991

1

■

My Roots

I was born and brought up in Matatiele in the Cape Province. Matatiele was, at that time, a very large district: it spread from the foot of the Drakensberg on the north and north-west (where it acts as a natural boundary between that part of the country and the neighbouring kingdom of Lesotho) to the northeast and the east, where it bordered on Natal province.

Today, Matatiele, like all so-called former 'Reserves' has a new map and new borders. Patches of it have been allocated to the Transkei Bantustan, while areas nearer to the Drakensberg and the surrounding hills remain part of the Republic of South Africa.

I belong to the BaFokeng clan ('Dew People', not 'Mist People', as incorrectly translated in some books!) The praise poets of the BaFokeng speak of the 'Secret rain which falls without clouds. It puzzles even the lion, king of the beasts, by soaking it to the skin on its way from the hunt, yet there had been no clouds overnight'.

As in all societies where writing came late, our history was passed on from generation to generation by elders in the form of word of mouth. According to what these elders passed down to us, the BaFokeng had been great kings of Lesotho and parts of Southern Africa. Even today, in places like Rustenburg and the surrounding areas, the BaFokeng are still rulers. While the heraldic sign of the people of these areas is *kwena* (crocodile), the heraldic sign of our family is that of the hare. We are called Bafokeng *bacha sefali sa kotoane baha tsatsi mpone ba'mutla ojeoa-tala* (who eat the hare uncooked). Among the Basotho it is accepted that the BaFokeng belong to the royal family. To this day, whenever there are customary duties to be performed in the community, a MoFokeng (singular of BaFokeng) is always given the honour of taking the lead.

My family, that of Tsiu, has blood relations with the Lesotho royal family. The story goes that Ntsukunyane, a powerful BaFokeng king in Lesotho, had two children: a son called Makakane (also called Ratsiu) and a daughter called Kholu. While the son Ratsiu had two sons, Tsiu and Mphanya, Kholu was married to Mokhachane, head of village of the BaKoena clan. Their son, Moshoeshoe, who later became the legendary king of Lesotho was brought up, according to custom, by RaTsiu. In other words, Ntsukunyane, the grandfather of Moshoeshoe I, was my great-great-great-grandfather, and his mother my great-great Aunt. (For these details, see the Appendix II: Family Tree of Tsiu.)

Of course, this was during the time before the whites came, when African clans fought many wars between themselves, which we refer to as the Lifaqane. But it was also a period when rich and established communities had existed for a long time. For instance, although RaTsiu had succeeded his father Ntsukuyane as king, it is alleged that he later said that he became tired of holding authority, especially because of the endless wars between the clans. In his view, what the clans needed was a brave young man who could unite these bickering factions into a strong nation. His nephew Moshoeshoe had already proved himself, according to the rituals of those days, as a brave young man, and he clearly had all the qualities required for leadership. So, RaTsiu overstepped his own son, Tsiu, and handed his authority over to Moshoeshoe as a necessity to save the Basotho nation.

2

RaTsiu, however, remained the young king's chief counsellor, or prime minister if it was today, and whenever the new king left his country to visit or make war with others, RaTsiu was once again left in charge of the affairs of the nation.

RaTsiu foresaw that the Boers from the Cape posed the greatest threat to the BaSotho. The Boers, fighting with superior weapons, were grabbing more and more land from the African people as they moved north, so that increasingly the people were forced to flee from these wars and the dispossession and starvation it brought. Tsiu himself had to flee. Later, his son RanTsiuoa lived at a place called Rapasi.

My great-grandfather, Rantsiuoa, had only one child, a daughter named Ntsiuoa. When it became obvious that she was to be an only child, the family took a grave decision about the future — it was decided that, instead of her getting married, *ho tsoanela hore a nyalloe monna*, a husband should be married for her. This was perfectly in order because of her royal status. It also meant that her children would be Rantsiuoa's heirs. Ntsiuoa's sons were my grandfather Malitse and his brother Mosoeu.

Later, the brothers crossed over the Drakensberg into Matatiele and settled at Ramohlakoana. From there, my grandfather said, they used, as young men, to travel to the diamond mines in Kimberley — a three to four month journey on foot.

It was at Kimberley that my grandfather became a convert. This event caused serious conflicts between him and his elder brother, who denounced Christianity as a madness, and something not fit for people with royal blood. They used to have physical fights, and, as he was small in stature compared to his brother, he tended to be dashed to the ground by his elder. But he would get up, he said, and tell his brother that there was only one kingdom, that of the Kingdom in Heaven. Of course, the irony was that his elder brother would, later on, himself also be converted. Later on, the two brothers would be seen, going from village to village, wearing their black cassocks, seeking to make converts. Thus it was that the Tsiu family became very religious, and staunch members of the Anglican Church.

3

A white Anglican missionary asked my grandfather to open a church at a place called Hankasele, about thirty miles from Ramohlakoana. The church was called St James. When my grandfather finally moved there, he already had three children — my father, Tsekiso; my aunt, Libuseng; and my uncle, Moeti. My grandfather's wife was one of the daughters of Maphela, a Hlubi who had lived in Matatiele for several years.

Then the missionaries wanted to help with fees to help my father to go to college, but he declined that offer. Soon thereafter he went to Johannesburg to work in the goods sheds of the railways. After his arrival, he joined the ICU that had been started by Clements Kadalie, and which was very powerful at that time.

My mother, Moselantja (dog's tail, a name usually given to a female child born after a dead child, which the BaSotho believe give longevity to the child) was the daughter of Raeti Mokhele, a well-to-do farmer and cattle-rancher of the Bataung (Lion People) clan, who had also been converted. He was originally from Kroonstad in the Orange Free State, while his wife, Motseoane-Mmatau, was the daughter of Malule, another member of the same Bataung clan. Being Anglicans, they attended the church at St James, which was where my grandfather, Malitse, spotted my mother, Moselantja, for his son, Tsekiso.

My maternal grandmother was the second wife of my grandfather, Raeti. She was chosen for him by his first wife, who was her cousin, when that wife found out that her health was failing. But, for that family arrangement, my grandfather was excommunicated for marrying my grandmother while his first wife was still alive.

After he had contacted my mother's father about wanting her for his son, it was agreed by the parents that the children should meet to see if they fancied each other. But then, after they had met, my mother's father made it a condition that his daughter could marry only after she had completed her industrial course which she was then pursuing at Mariazell College. The day the Tsiu family took the lobola-bohali to the Mokhele, they came with eleven head of cattle

4

and a horse. This infuriated my mother's father; knowing how poor they were, he asked my father's father what his daughter was going to live on if they brought so many cattle. He told them that he was not selling his daughter, that he had lots of better-looking animals, and that five or six head of cattle would have been sufficient to seal the bond of friendship and relationship between the two families according to custom. Indeed, the day my mother went to her in-laws after the marriage, she was sent with two fat cows for milk and ten sheep for meat as a present from her father.

My parents' first-born was a girl; she was named MaMakakane (mother of Makakane/Ratsiu). I was born second, and was given the name of Matebello (Hope). I was christened Magdeline after grandfather's elder brother's wife, but when I was still very young, many people in the village nicknamed me 'Lekhooanyana' (little European) because of my yellow complexion. However, when I grew older, I rejected this nickname and did not reply when called after I had seen what Europeans looked like and came to know more about them.

The first time I saw a white person I was about four or five years of age. I had gone to a shop with my elder cousin and there I saw this pink man with golden teeth, from which he got his nickname, 'Maziny'egolide' (golden teeth) I recall that his daughter was playing with a doll that could open and shut its eyes when it was tilted. I was so taken up with this doll that when we came back I asked my grandmother to buy me one. When she said that she had no money I started to cry, which made my grandmother so angry that she said something that I had never heard of before: 'You cannot cry for European dolls', she said, 'because these people have taken our country and they have money'. I kept quiet, but I was puzzled by these words about the country having been taken. Anyway, I went back to my usual dolls made out of pieces of rags. The game we enjoyed most, as children, was playing at *mantloane*, or miniature houses built with stones and mud. The intention was to mimic the adults. Every day we built new ones, if the ones built the previous day had collapsed.

5

My mother told me that she was lucky to have me because she nearly had a miscarriage when she was about three months into her pregnancy. She was taken, on horseback, to a herbalist about eighty miles from our home, and luckily his medicine stopped the bleeding. But, I was told, I was born a premature baby as big as an Ellis Brown coffee container, which, I think, was about a foot long. I was placed in a sheepskin hat for the first few months as it was winter. This sheepskin hat idea is still a useful incubator for rural people, even today, but after I was taught in nursing that a woman with a threatened miscarriage was to lie still in bed I realised how true mother was when she said how lucky she was to have me.

My parents in the end had nine children in all. Fortunately, a boy was born after me, and later still, three more were added. When I was one year old, my mother's elder sister, Maelia, who was a spinster, requested to take me in order to rear me. However, as she later took up work as a domestic worker for white people, I was really reared by my grandmother. Still, I used to call her (my aunt) by the name of 'Mother'. I loved her so much that I did not, at that time, have any idea that I had another mother. I had no real idea of my grandfather's farm which was called La Grange, which was about seven miles from St James, because I went there when I was about one year old. By the time I began to understand things we were living at a place called Klein Jonas, near the Drakensberg, ruled by a tribal chief, and inhabited mostly by peasant farmers.

The story I heard was that when grandfather became very old, he sold the farm and moved to Klein Jonas with his whole family — sons, daughters, grandchildren, but he died a short time after our arrival there. His last child had been born when the comet of 1910 appeared. So my grandfather must have been really very old when he died in the late twenties. Although he had made a will and signed it, his sons of the two houses fought long legal battles contesting it, particularly details relating to money in the banks. My mother never pardoned her brothers for that because she said that all the money ended up in the pockets of the solicitors; the only consolation left to my grandmother was the livestock. And, of course, all the children (including the girls who had married) had inherited cattle, sheep and goats.

When I was a few years of age, there was a rumour all over the locality that teams of mounted soldiers were going from village to village, arresting people who had not paid their khafo (poll tax). The poll tax was £1 for each male over the age of eighteen and 10 shillings for a widow. The aim was to force adult males to work on the mines, leaving their families behind.The rumours also claimed that many men had gone into hiding in the mountains, and that some of those who had run away had been caught and had been shot. Others had been forced to go to the cities and the mines to search for work. There was even talk that one or two had committed suicide. There was gloom all over the locality.

The day they came to our locality was a horrible one. It was my first encounter with red-faced soldiers, wearing heavy, green felt coats, riding on high horses, and accompanied by a black man who acted as interpreter. They stopped in front of our house. The soldiers stayed outside, still seated on their horses, shouting 'khafo', while the black man went into the house. We children were terrified. Since she was by now very old, my grandmother had great difficulty in getting to her steel trunk in which she kept all her valuables. So, whilst I tried to push that heavy object, she crawled towards it. Finally, having got to it, she emptied all its contents on the floor. There were many bits of papers, including old cheque books which had belonged to my grandfather. The problem was that she was illiterate, and so did not know which was the poll tax receipt. Being a small child, I could not help.

As the shouts of 'khafo' went on outside, she began to panic. '*Oo Molimo, lengolo la khafo le kae? masole a tlilo ntsoara*'. (Oh God, where is the poll tax receipt. The soldiers are going to arrest me.) I dashed to her, grabbing hold of her skirt; there was now real pandemonium in the house. Then the soldiers called the black man to come out to them. Then, after talking to them, he peeped in through the door and said: 'All right, old lady'. They then left and passed on to

7

other houses. At that my grandmother sat down, took her tin of snuff from the pocket of her apron, and, as she took it, said: *'Tanki, Molimo'* (Thanks God). Although I was still very young at that time, I really thought that I had seen the ugly face of white people. From that time on I hated them and regarded them as dangerous people. That remained in my mind for many, many years.

I started school when I was about seven years of age. I was sent to the local school, which was called Pontseng. My aunt had instructed me to tell the teacher that my surname was Tsiu and not Mokhele, like hers. She also told me the names of my parents, as it was the practice for schools to need to know those details. This was the time when it dawned on me that I had a real mother and father, like other children.

When I say that I was seven, I am referring to my estimated age. According to the law of those days, black children were not allowed to start schooling before that age. That delay caused a great deal of frustration to parents; they had to wait until they saw signs that the child could express himself or herself well enough. That was done by making the child repeat fables and fiction stories related every night by the elders. From there, the child was taught to count one to seven fingers, or to count seven stones. If the child passed that test, two to three years were added to the child's age in order to comply with the law. The child was then sent to school, where her or she were instructed to raise seven fingers to indicate his or her age to the teacher. The number seven was the first known and best known figure.

Some parents, especially those who were themselves illiterate, just did not know the age of their children. From within traditional African societies, age was associated with happenings — drought, the devastation of a crop by locusts, epidemics, heavenly events, like an eclipse, or the appearance of a comet. Even when, in modern times, births started to be registered, that did not happen in the rural areas. In any case, the education system for Africans was of longer duration than for white, but of less worth. Even in the days before Bantu Education, the Junior Certificate that white children completed in two years black children had to do in three. In other words, black children had a distorted age, which remained with them for the rest of their lives. It is out of that kind of experience that African people attach greater importance to physiological than to numerical age.

The school was about three miles away from our home. We had to pass through fields. In winter it was terribly cold, especially in the mornings when there was a lot of frost, while in summer we got wet from the dew as the grass was very long. We had no shoes. I cannot recall any child who wore shoes at school. I was one of the lucky ones who had a pair of white tennis shoes, but that was strictly for going to church. Many children, especially the boys, were shabbily dressed. Most of them wore khaki shorts which usually reached below the knees, with their shirts not tucked in. What I recall now is how strange it was that we did not seem to get hungry for the whole day despite the fact that we had nothing to eat between our breakfast of maize, bread and milk after sunrise and the next meal, which was in the late afternoon when we came back from school. No child carried provisions to school.

The school had two rooms. Classes from Sub-A, Sub-B, Standard 1 and Standard 2 shared the same room, with each class tucked into its own corner. Only Standard 3, which was taught by the Principal, had its own classroom. To ease some of the disturbance, classes were held outside when the weather was good. Inside, we used to sit on benches to listen to the teacher. But, when it came to writing, we used to kneel on the floor and use the benches as desks. In Sub-A we wrote with a slate pencil on black slates, while from Sub-B we used exercise books and pencils. Among the lessons we took were reading, writing, arithmetic, poetry, and music; we also learnt sewing, weaving mats and baskets, dictation, and mental arithmetic.

In those days, English poetry was my favourite subject — so much so that the day the Inspector (they were white in those days!) came, I recited my poetry so well, also acting it out with my hands and feet, that he smiled. Then, after he had left, my teacher praised me; she was so happy that she had picked me out of the whole class and had said that

'Magdeline is going to be a teacher'. I was in Sub-B then, and I think I did a lot of showing off. Some other children, however, were so much in fear of the white man (the Inspector) that they literally shivered.

What I noticed from that early age was that many families were pulling very hard. Some children stopped coming to school because the parents could not afford to buy the school books, while others, we were told, abandoned coming because they had no clothes. Although some of the fathers were working on the gold mines, the money they sent home did not stretch to cover food as well as clothing. Yet, despite these difficulties, which many people encountered, life was exciting for us as children. The only work we had to do when we came back from school was to fetch water from the well that was half a mile away. This we had to do several times to fill a big clay container we had at home to see that grandmother had enough water left over after we had washed before setting off for school the next day. We certainly did not go to bed early. After the evening meal, the whole family sat around the fire, sometimes roasting *lik hoahla* (hard) maize in winter, which is said to strengthen the teeth.

There was great fun about that: for us children, when your cob was roasted, you gave it to someone older than yourself to eat two or three rows from it. This was called *ho 'bula tsela* (open the road for luck!). We really believed that we would not be lucky if we omitted or refused to do that. It was during this period that the younger members of the family were gradually introduced to the ethos and ethics of African society, when the elders related stories of old, how the Africans lived before the arrival of the whites, about the wars which had been fought by our forbears. These were astonishing stories, which, at first telling, we found hard to believe.

Sometimes, when it was moonlight, we would sit outside, watching the heavens, and would be told the names of the various stars. Every night before going to bed, we helped grandmother spread her mattress on the floor. As this was an extra large mattress, all three of us (myself as well as my two cousins) found space on it with her. There was always a scuffle or rush getting into bed because each of us wanted to sleep next to grandma. But before we went to bed, grandma related fables to us. We used to listen with great attention to these; they acted like a sedative, so we were soon asleep. Then, the next evening grandmother would be expected to continue where she had left off.

But at dawn grandma would wake us up to kneel and say our prayers. She did the praying. She repeated the same prayers every day, and they were rather too long for our liking. She always prayed for people who were working in the mines, with dangerous instruments, and facing sharp stones and the dangers of Johannesburg. She also prayed that those who had been injured by sugar cane stumps in Natal should be healed, as well as for those bitten by dangerous snakes in the vineyards of the Cape, and for those in dark prisons. Finally, she prayed for rain. Sometimes we fell asleep during these long prayers and she would tell us, 'So and so, you were asleep because you did not say "Amen"'.

Many a time, when we were playing with other children, we would talk about grandmother's prayers, and wonder if it was true that Africans were working underground. And time and again, when news came that a mine had fallen, we realised that it was true. Also, some men would come back to the village, having been declared unfit for work because they had contacted the incurable disease called phthisis. I remember one man who had come back, having been given a compensation of £130. The relatives were very happy to handle so much money, but they soon realised how little it really was.

Similarly, with farm workers, who were simply discharged when they fell ill, though the ways there were discharged were always very phoney ones. The farmer just told the worker that 'mosebetsi o felile' (the work is finished). But that very same day the farmer would employ someone else to do the same job he had said was finished, for less money. African farm workers were very bitter about that, but there were no laws to protect them, and they did not know about trades unions. I remember a young man who was brought back from a farm; he had extensive wounds on the face and

11

chest after being kicked by a horse in the farmer's stables. His screams could be heard all over the village as his mother dressed his wounds. I never forgot those wounds throughout my youth. That boy was disfigured for the rest of his life, but there was no compensation paid for the injuries he had received at work.

All we knew was that these men worked from dawn till dusk, often for a salary of five shillings per month! Then, at the end of the month, their salaries would not be handed to them. The farmer would tell them that they would get their money after they had worked one month's notice, if they wished to leave — which meant that those who absconded because of the harsh conditions would lose everything. The farmer would give the men a ration of mealie meal, with neither meat nor milk nor vegetables — yet these men were looking after cattle, milking cows, growing vegetables. Most of those who stayed two or three years therefore contracted phthisis — we said a man was 'kicked by a dwarf' — because of coughing up blood. That is when they were told, 'work is finished'. They also never got holidays: they came home to be near their families when they realised that they were going to die.

This was particularly true with regard to work by women. When the villagers had finished their weeding and harvesting, hundreds of people, especially women and young girls, were recruited to do odd jobs on the neighbouring white farms. These farmers were well-known by their names; it was also known whether they were honest, cheats, or were cruel to their workers because the people refused to work for cheats and cruel ones. The work was mostly harvesting and breaking of stone in quarries, for which the payment was threepence for filling a large hessian bag with either maize cobs or stones. By the end of the day, many workers managed to fill up to two or three bags, coming back home with sixpence or ninepence. But others came home empty-handed. Those farmers who cheated would send their recruiters to the fields at about five p.m. to tell the workers that they had gone on holiday but had not left any money to pay them. That infuriated the workers, and they and their relatives would therefore leave the village at dusk to help themselves of as much of the crop as they could in order to teach the farmer a lesson. But no such thing was done to those farmers who paid what they had promised. At that age I could not realise that even the farmers who were called honest were indeed also exploiters of cheap labour.

What made life bearable was the spirit of community that was always very high in the villages. For instance, boys from families who had neither cattle nor goats helped with the milking of cows at their neighbours and were given milk to take back to their parents. Similarly, especially during the seasons of weeding and harvesting, people helped each other.

Many people, though, in those days, had good crops. I remember my grandmother had two huge grass barns outside the house: one for maize, the other for sorghum (which the whites called 'kaffir corn'). People also planted beans and peas — the soil was still fertile. Furthermore, when a beast was slaughtered in the neighbourhood, every family benefitted; all the men and boys of the village shared parts of the beast — like the head, feet or trotters — while the women and the girls shared the chest and breast. The rest of the meat was made into biltong (strips of sun-dried meat) so that it did not go bad. There was also no shame in asking for such items as tea leaves, sugar, salt, etc. from a neighbour.

This community spirit of sharing is very deep-seated in Africans. It descends from the very first mouldings of our human relations, and is part of our culture and traditions, and I imagine it is this that has kept the African people as a nation proud of its culture despite the hardships and humiliations that have been our lot since the arrival of the colonisers.

2

■

The Road To Holy Cross

When I was about ten or eleven years of age, my aunt decided that I should go back to live with my parents. One of the main reasons was that there was a better school, with classes up to Standard VI, near my parents' home at Ramohlakoana. By now they had left St James, but when that event took place I do not know. So here was my aunt preparing to send me to college, even though she was earning only fourteen shillings a month, working for a white shop-keeper as a domestic servant and seamstress, when the school fees for most black colleges in those days was between £14 and £28 a year.

By the time I got back to my home, my mother had four children. She used to complain that my aunt and my grandmother had spoilt me. Then, every school holiday I was on my way back to my grandmother's place, about 70 miles away. I used to walk all that distance to go to report to her about how I was doing at school and about how I was being treated by my parents. My grandmother used to get furious; she begged me to leave the school and come back to her, but my aunt disagreed with that; she was determined that I should go to college and become a teacher.

Ramohlakoana school had many children — some had come from as far away as Lesotho, others from far-away farms where there were no schools — and about six or seven teachers. The subjects taught were: English, SeSotho, Arithmetic, History, Geography, Physiology and Hygiene, Nature Study, Music, Sewing, Cookery. When the girls studied Sewing and Cookery, the boys engaged in sports. Girls also took part in sports after school. This was the time when I got my first pair of shoes and my first overcoat. Before that, we used to wear light-weight blankets, called lepae, which were not to be used for sleeping, and which we would wash every Saturday. The principal of the school, who was very old at that time, was Mr Ryne Thipa; it was said that he had taught my father.

In 1939 I was sent to study for my Junior Certificate at the Welsh High School in East London, where I took English, Xhosa, Latin, Biology, Physiology and Hygiene, Cookery, History, Geography. Music and sports were also done, but not as subjects. Here I specially liked English, Latin and Biology.

I was now sixteen years of age. Unfortunately, before I had completed my Standard VI, my aunt as well as my grandfather had died. Furthermore, on the insistence of the congregation, my father had to return to St James to take my grandfather's place as Catechist. Anyway, as father had been sickly since he had stopped working on the railways, and could not find other employment, this was a good idea, even though the stipend was very small. The mission, however, allowed him to hire four fields from its farm, and that was how he could maintain his family; the soil was fertile and produced good harvests.

My elder sister had, meanwhile, been sent to an industrial school, called St Margaret's; there she studied cookery, knitting and weaving. In those days, the most popular courses for girls were either industrial or teaching courses; the former was preferred because it was said to be useful, as it could be done at home. It was certainly going to be extremely difficult for our parents to educate the two of us. To do that they needed to sell grain and cattle, which my mother supplemented by doing a lot of sewing for people, often working well past midnight by candlelight or paraffin lamp. Luckily, when plans were well advanced, at the end of 1938, to send me to Mariazell College, my mother's sister of the senior house offered that she could pay for my schooling in return for what my dead aunt had done for them.

This offer was not well received by the rest of the Tsiu family, especially by my father's mother, who tried hard to influence my father to reject the offer. Her main argument was that I was too young to go to such a far-away place, and that they would never see me again. Although my father was inclined to agree with his mother, my mother did not want to hear a thing about such 'useless obstructions' as she put it. This was the time I saw the power of my mother. The arguments caused great tension in the family, and my father was torn between his mother and his wife. What was strange was that although we lived within a stone's throw of each other, my grandmother did not want to discuss the matter with my mother, but only with her son.

One day father came back from my grandmother with a new story. His mother thought, he said, that it was useless to send girls to school because they would soon get married without helping their parents. And, he said she had told him, Junior Certificate was 'education for boys'; no girl from our area had ever undergone that education! My mother's answer to that was that she wanted her daughter to be the first to take 'boys' education.

She was an extraordinary woman, my mother; not only was she an orator, but she was also very witty and hard-working. She was the power behind my father. Many people feared her because they knew she was a woman of no nonsense. The farmer's daughter had, I think, learnt a great deal from her father. One of her tricks was hardly ever to leave out the words 'the law says' from her arguments. She was outstandingly rational.

I must emphasise that both my parents were strict, but also gentle. I cannot remember either my elder sister or myself ever being punished. Both my father and mother disciplined us by explaining things to us thoroughly. The only one who was ever punished by my father was our brother

16

Rantsiuoa, and that was for dodging church services. What had made him dodge going to church was that, after three services including Sunday School, father that evening, after prayers had asked us one by one what had been said in church. My brother hated this so much that he decided not to go to church at all. This became such a big case that it involved my grandmother as well, because my brother had gone to tell her that father had wanted to kill him. So grandmother came from her kraal, holding her walking stick, shouting: 'Tsekiso, you must remember that Rantsiuoa is your grandfather. How dare you touch him!' Father would usually have no chance of explaining, because of grandmother's threats that she would take my brother to live with her. The custom that children should not talk back to mothers had the effect of cowing him.

When we grew older, we (my brothers and sisters and myself) used to talk a great deal about our mother. We all thought that we owed her a lot for the sacrifices she made and the love she gave to us during our tender years. We were thankful that, by the time she died in 1985 (when she was in her nineties) each one of us had tried in several ways to show how we thought that she was a 'Golden Mother'. I was very sad that I was the only one who could not be present to lay her to rest.

The day I left to go to school in East London, my father, together with two of my cousins, took me on horseback to the station. I was to take the railway bus to the town of Maclear, (where I spent the night sleeping on a bench in the waiting room) and from there take a train to Sterkstroom, where it would connect with another train from Johannesburg to East London. Although I was frightened at the thought of making such a long journey for the first time, I travelled in a motor vehicle and later, for the first time, in a train. Our main means of transport in those days was our own feet; for the lucky ones (who might be one in a thousand) there were other forms like horseback, ox-wagon, or horse-drawn carts.

The sound of the thumping of the wheels of the train on the rails enchanted me. I also looked out of the window the whole time to watch the engine or to count the number of carriages whenever the train took a curve. I really enjoyed it. I remember that I was given sixpence for pocket money, and this made me very happy. I also had with me two roasted chickens, two loaves of bread, and two bottles of home-made ginger beer and some peaches in my provision basket. Anyway, one of the chickens went bad and I had to throw it out of the window. It took three or four days (I cannot remember exactly) to get to East London. I do remember, however, that at Sterkstroom I slept in an empty carriage, waiting for the train from Johannesburg, which was due only the next morning. When I told a guard who had come to lock the doors about nine p.m. that I was going to East London the next day and that there were no waiting-rooms, he said that I should come to sleep in his carriage. This offer I declined; I did not trust this white man. The station was deserted, and I prayed to God to protect me that night.

The train from Johannesburg arrived early the next morning, while it was still dark. I had not slept well on the hard wooden bench, on which I had tucked myself in my travelling rug with one flap on the bench, with the other covering my body, fully dressed. I got up immediately and, taking my little suitcase, I boarded the train. This time the Third Class carriages had cushions. I was now feeling great — I was actually going to be travelling on the much talked about train from Johannesburg! The next station on from Sterkstroom and I could hear only Xhosa, no more Sesotho. So I realised that I was now in the land of the amaXhosa. I was fetched by two girls at East London station, it presented a bit of a problem; they knew not a word of Sesotho, and I understood only very little Xhosa. However, all went well. 'As long as I do not get lost', I said to myself.

I think I arrived in East London on a Saturday, because on the following day we went to church with the other girls. On the Monday, when I got to school, I had no problem about talking to the teachers; they spoke to me in English. However, as all the other pupils were Xhosa-speaking, I was soon the centre of attraction, everybody wanting to talk to me in their language. Every day there were groups of students around me, wanting me to talk, some actually laughing at my pronunciation of Xhosa words. But, they, too, could not pronounce Tsiu properly; some called me 'Tseo'.

The principal of the school was a Dr Wollheim, while our teachers were young black graduates from Fort Hare. The most senior was a Mr Ebeniza Majombozi, who had been Principal before the arrival of Dr Wollheim. In fact, I soon found out that Mr Majombozi had founded the school; it was said that he had started it by teaching (in his house) some pupils who had been unable to go to boarding school, but that he was soon overwhelmed by the numbers of pupils. The East London City Council then allowed him to use its large Peacock Hall for holding classes while a new school was built across the valley on a site about two miles away. Indeed, we moved into the new school building towards the end of that year.

On the walls of the Peacock Hall were huge framed photographs of four African men: Rev. Rubusana; Mr Mapikela; Mr Godlo; Dr Aggrey. Each student seemed to venerate these pictures; we were told that these were the men who were fighting for the liberation of Africa. This was the first time since my grandmother had told me, when I was a child, about how our country had been taken away from us, that I had heard that there were Africans who were fighting for the restoration of our land.

Before we moved to the new school, we had a meeting of all the pupils, at which Dr Wollheim asked us to choose a name for it, because it had had no name before. One student, Loli Jamela, who was in her IVth year, proposed the name of 'Majombozi High School' because of the work that teacher had done for the school. This was promptly seconded, but the Principal explained to us that we needed the name of a well-known person so that our school could get help from white people. He recommended 'Welsh High School'. I do not know if the majority of us were already brain-washed to believe that our prime interest was that the school should get donations from rich white people, but we all cheered the Principal for his proposal. Later on, we all started to blame each other for rejecting the name of the man who had taken the initiative to uplift his people with much devotion and under enormous difficulties.

Mr Majombozi left at the end of the term; later we learnt that he had opened another school somewhere in the Ciskei. Still later, when I began to take part in politics, I regarded Mr Majombozi as a hero, because in fighting for your country and your people education is a weapon as powerful as a gun. Indeed, the successes and failures of a country depend largely upon education. I still feel a sense of guilt that there was not even a reception or a card sent in his honour to this son of Africa, who loved, and fought for his people so much.

The opening of our new school building was a great occasion. For many months we had been feverishly practising entertainment activities such as sketches, music, poetry and folklore dances. Many personalities, both black and white, had been invited. The teachers all wore their graduation gowns, which were mostly black, except for that worn by Dr Wollheim, which was a brightly-coloured pinkish silk one — I think his doctorate was in Divinity.

An academic atmosphere filled the air as we waited for the guests to take the places reserved for them. Then, from a distance we could hear 'Kwete ... Kwete ... Kwete'. The sound became louder and louder, so that we were all attracted to the direction from which it came. Someone cried out 'Ah! Imbongi ye sizwe! (Salute the poet of the nation!) The atmosphere was electric when the poet S. E. K. Mqhayi appeared, walking slowly towards the stand. He wore a beautiful animal skin, thrown carelessly over one shoulder, while the other one was free. As he uttered golden words in praise of education and of the school, the people silently echoed his last words in appreciation. I remember very well, to this day, one of the things he said, and which I heard then for the first time: '*Uyavuya yena umtu onenyeke ngokuba xa ehleka uhleka nge nyama*' (Happy is the person who has a hare-lip because when he laughs, he laughs with meat).

When the next term started, we had three more white female teachers. I think that this was a time I enjoyed very much in my life. I certainly worked very hard, especially in Xhosa, because it was a subject which I had to pass to achieve my certificate. But the subjects I liked most were

20

Latin (for which I used to get passing marks of 90%), followed by English and Biology. We were taken on visits to museums, aquariums and many other places connected with our lessons. Because our school was not well-equipped, Dr Wollheim, a devoted man who wanted good results from the school, got permission from the neighbouring Selborne High School to do some lessons there. This was a boys school for white children, and we had to wait until after they had finished their lessons before we could go there for our lessons in Biology, Physiology and Hygiene. We also had sports matches, both home and away, with other black schools, but never with the whites.

Then, early in 1941, which was my last year in school, I had to visit the Frere Hospital because I was suffering from a severe toothache. It was the first time I had had toothache. In general, our teeth were good while we were at primary school; there were no children with either tooth decay or fillings. We scrubbed our teeth with white ash which we carefully scooped with a spoon from a fire that had been made with dry cattle dung called *lisu* (plural) or *sesu* (singular).

There at the hospital I was received by two smartly-dressed young nurses who were very kind to me. I also watched them very closely when they were attending to other patients. I was really charmed by their kindness, smartness and cleanliness. Thus it was that, by the time I left the hospital, I was debating fiercely with myself about why I should not take up nursing. My mother had, on several occasions when I was still at primary school, suggested that she would be happy if I took up nursing, but I had rejected the idea. The reports which were circulating in the community in those days were that nurses were cruel to their patients, that they beat them up when they refused to take their medicines. But my second reluctance to take up nursing was that I was too horrified to look at open wounds and extensive burns; it was just unthinkable that I should be able to handle such things — the image of the little boy I had seen at my grandmother's place, which I mentioned earlier, was still vivid in my mind.

I was helped in my decision by the knowledge that a few

21

other pupils who were, like myself, in Form III, had already declared their intention to take up nursing. I therefore wrote at once to my mother to tell her that I had changed my mind about taking up teaching, and that I had now decided to take up nursing. My mother took quite a long time before answering my letter. When her reply came, she made it clear that she, as well as my father, were delighted and that he had already contacted the Anglican priest, Father Wordsworth, to seek his advice. The priest, in his turn, suggested that I go to the Holy Cross Hospital, in East Pondoland, where he had missionary friends. Later, they sent me the full address of the hospital, in order that I should start making application.

My application was successful, and by the time I left East London in December 1941, I already knew the date on which I was to start at Holy Cross. That was July 1942. I was very happy to have a break of six months before I had to start studying again. Although all students were happy at Welsh High School, towards the end of our time there was much gloom and uncertainty because of the Second World War which had started. Every day, when the siren sounded from the city centre, everybody would stand still for a prayer for five minutes. During the night, the street lights were off, and we had difficulty going to our night studies. East London being a seaport, it seemed as if the Germans were about to land there at any time. Then, when I went home for good, the trains were really packed with soldiers, black as well as white. At every station the train passed there were men in uniform. It was a great difference from the time I first travelled to East London. But, in general, we pupils did not talk much about the war. I think the reason was that it was more important for us to get our education in order to improve ourselves.

In January 1942 the results of my Form III examination came, and I had passed. It was a great relief to me, because I was so worried about my Xhosa. My parents as well as the rest of the family (including my grandmother) were very happy and proud that I had been successful in getting 'boys education' as they called it. The family were even more pleased when my father came back from one of the quarterly meetings and reported that Father Wordsworth had told him that I would be getting a higher training in nursing, one that would enable me to work anywhere in the world. During those days in South Africa, several black nurses were often given only a Hospital Certificate, and not allowed to take State Registration, because their standard of education at entry was considered to be very low.

As I had six months in which I could do nothing, I paid a visit to my mother's mother, with whom I stayed for two months. She, as well as the rest of the family were delighted; it had been three years since I had last visited their place. When I told her that I was going to take up nursing, my grandmother's advice to me was that I should not lose my temper with people who were ill. As I went backwards and forwards in the next few days, nostalgia for my youth came back. I remembered the days when we used to run in the meadows, chasing butterflies and grasshoppers; I recalled how we used to ride on goats and how I used to practise balancing a clay carrier full of water from the well on my head.

Coming from a big city, I was now comparing traditional life with western civilisation. For instance, I saw a balloon for the first time in East London. When we were young, boys and girls in our village used to make balloons by washing out the bladder of any beast that had been slaughtered, inflate it, and tie the top with strong grass — the same grass that would also be used for making skipping ropes. We had copied this from children of two villages near ours; we had called those children *maqaba* (illiterates), and they had responded by calling us *makarammele*, which I think was a corruption of *makeresete* (Christians). They also referred to us as *mathisa*, meaning that we had not gone to initiation ceremonies. This remark was intended to hurt us, but as Christians we could not go along with that custom. These people, who neither went to church, nor used coffins for burial, also did not send their children to school. But we liked them: they were a peaceful people, who taught us a great many of the traditions of the past, as well as their language, which had remained pure and uninfluenced by contact with others.

Their men took more than two wives, and girls, like boys, were sent to initiation schools, at the end of which period a big feast would be held, where the girls would parade, well-groomed, with their breasts exposed and their bodies covered in red ochre and wearing v-shaped skin *sebeto* (skirts) very short in front to expose their thighs. As they marched slowly in a line, being seem for the first time in three months, young men would stumble over each other in their rush to plant feathers on the heads of those they wanted to marry, while the women would ululate as the older men beat the drums for the girls to march in step. Young men who could afford to do so, would festoon the girls they wanted to marry with beads, with colourful chiffons or flowers. On that day the girl would not even know who had planted the feather on her, because she would have to look down all the time; it was the older men and women who kept a close watch on the movements of the young men.

These people used to have large flocks of sheep, goats and cattle, but now, three years after, I found their flocks to be terribly diminished. The landscape, too, had changed; the grass and shrubs were all gone. But what I noticed were the great changes with the people. Many of the boys and girls with whom I had gone to school were no longer in the village; some had married, but most were reported to have gone to the cities — mostly Durban and Johannesburg — to seek work. I also noticed that only about six of us from our village and the neighbouring ones had managed to get to colleges; there were only two girls (their father was a teacher) who had taken Junior Certificate: the majority left school after completing Standard III.

As I painfully debated these matters with myself, I even thought how nice it might have been had Mr Majombozi come to Matatiele. I recall how, before I had left to go to Holy Cross, my grandmother called me one day and showed me a chicken which, she said, would be part of my provisions on my way to Pondoland, and had gone on to talk about the olden days when her father had had so many sheep and cattle that they ate meat every day; she blamed the increasing poverty of the people on the coming of the whites. That was the time I said to myself that, for an African child to get education, was like a camel passsing through a needle's hole. I left towards the end of the second month of my stay with my grandmother; by now she was sleeping with her great-grand-children. She died in 1954, having seen my two children.

In those days, only one train per day came to Matatiele; it arrived at about ten o'clock and left at four o'clock in the afternoon. So, from home I took the bus which transported migrant workers between Matatiele and Lesotho. For the first time I travelled Second Class, which meant that I could reserve a seat. But I still had to carry all my provisions, since there were no services on the trains for Africans; these were reserved exclusively for whites. From Kokstad I took a small railway bus to a small town called Flagstaff, which is in Pondoland. From there it was easy to get the transport going to Holy Cross because it was well marked, and had a regular route: after collecting the hospital post in the town, it would go to the railway bus stop to collect any passengers for the hospital.

Holy Cross itself was a conglomeration of all types of building set in an area of some thirty to thirty-five acres. The most conspicuous building was the church, with its spire that could be seen from a great distance. Then there was the hospital itself, together with the usual quarters for doctors, nurses, and domestic staff. In addition there was a post office, a primary school, and a boarding school for boys between the ages of twelve and sixteen. This boarding school was renowned for its discipline. The pupils were Pondo children whom the mission had offered to educate in order to equip them to help their people in the future. For recreation for the residents there were two tennis courts, as well as a hall for concerts and dances.

The atmosphere at Holy Cross was one of friendship and benevolence; people got to know each other very well because of the daily rubbing of shoulders at work, in church, at places of recreation. We also got to know people from the neighbouring villages, as many of us, especially the young nurses, used to pay regular home visits for chats when we were off duty. Perhaps staying at an isolated place, like a mission, for four years, made many of us homesick, but these village visits were helpful in that we learnt the Pondo dialect from its roots; that helped us to translate for doctors from abroad, several of whom did their housemanship at Holy Cross. There were no trained African doctors then, only African 'Medical Aids'. It was only in the final year of my training that the first African doctors to qualify at the University of the Witwatersrand came to do their housemanship at Holy Cross.

Although my enthusiasm to take up nursing was influenced by my visit to the Frere Hospital in East London, when I actually started, I found it a great challenge. For the first three months we all had to go through what was called PTS; this was a probationary period, during which all new nurses worked in the pantry. There we prepared special diets based on the request forms sent by the ward sisters according to what each patient was supposed to eat. At lunch times we were each allocated different wards in which to serve the meals and to feed those patients who could not help themselves. After that we had to take round bedpans and generally clean up the wards as we went along. In the afternoons we were trained in how to give bedbaths, to take temperatures, and in the art of bedmaking. All these things had to be done within an allocated time; it was stressed that conscientiousness, speed, and thoroughness were essential requirements for each pupil nurse.

Then, after the three months, the Matron called each probationary nurse for a friendly chat, during which she wanted to know if we were all prepared to continue with our course after what we had seen and done. She said that it might so happen that some of us might have discovered that nursing was not the right course for us. She would give us three days to think it over, after which each one of us could tell her, individually, of our decision.

From that time, after the end of our probationary period, each one of us accepted the challenge of nursing as a career. The theoretical level, as well as the responsibilities of the practical work, increased with each passing year. What I appreciated most was the attachment to the patients and the internal joy which followed when patients improved and got well. I also found that the Latin I had studied at Junior Certificate was very helpful in nursing as so many medical words originated from it.

Although there was hard work and studying to do at Holy Cross, I really enjoyed my stay there. The environment was superb: not only was there no pollution and noise like in East London, but what was even more gratifying was that members of the staff, from the Rev Dr Drewe — the Superintendent, who had been trained at St Thomas's in London, the Matron Miss Tracey and the Sisters, who were all from Britain, were sympathetic to all the nurses, and devoted to their work of teaching us and seeing to our welfare and that of the patients. Once a week Dr Drewe had organised visits, by medical teams from the hospital, to the remote areas around us to attend to those people who could not reach the hospital. I really appreciated his work and always thought that if successive white governments in South Africa had created such a machinery in all parts of the rural areas, many African lives could have been saved. In Matatiele the people had to depend on traditional medicine; although there were two white doctors in private practice, nobody could possibly afford them because they were too poor.

Although our stipend was only thirteen shillings a month for the first year, and £1 in the second, I always saved, and so was able to find the fare for the return journey for my holidays. I felt that my parents had done enough for me and my elder sister not to ask them for the fare; besides, they were still faced with the education of my younger brothers and sisters. Going home to see my family was wonderful, but at the same time it was an agonising and depressing time for me when I looked at the state of health of the people. I would find that whole families had been wiped out by TB, by child mortality from pneumonia, from whooping cough, measles and generally from malnutrition, which had reached alarming proportions. The more I learnt and knew about these diseases and how easily these could have been prevented, the more I realised the suffering of my people.

27

It was at Holy Cross that I began to understand more about the Second World War. There was an Englishman, Mr Houghton, who had fought during the First World War who used to come to the Nurses Home with maps twice or thrice a week to explain the war. As everybody was aware that thousands, perhaps hundreds of thousands, of Africans were being recruited, we believed that things might change for the better for our people after the war. But others amongst us recalled the sinking of the Mendi, during the First World War, in which hundreds of African soldiers on their way to Europe had perished. Yet there had been no change after that. Anyway, we lived in hopes.

In 1944, a friend of the family who worked in Kokstad had subscribed to weekly copies of *The Bantu World* for me as a Christmas present. It was in this paper that I first read about the African National Congress, whose president, at that time, was Dr Xuma. Many nurses read the paper because it reported mainly on African affairs; it was the first newspaper I ever read. It was the pictures in this paper that reminded me of the men that I had first seen in East London at the Peacock Hall. Some nurses from Natal said that they knew of a man called Champion who was also a leader of the ANC. However, the talk would end there as nobody really understood much about the subject.

We left for Durban early in 1946 to sit our final examination at the King Edward VIII hospital. It was my first visit to that city. We were lodged at the McCord Zulu Hospital, which was also a missionary hospital, where the Superintendent, Dr Taylor, was also a friend of Dr Drewe. What struck us in Durban was the huge Indian population.

The results of the examination came towards the middle of the year. I was in charge of the male medical ward when Rev. Norton, who was in charge of the church, walked in and embraced me, after which he broke the news that I had passed. I just stood there motionless; it was only after he had gone that the joy for my parents flashed through my mind. I was to stay on at Holy Cross for a further three months to complete my contract. In the meantime, having abandoned the idea of taking midwifery immediately, I made

28

an application to work at the Pretoria General Hospital. My brother was doing his final year at the primary school, and I thought that it was time for me to help my parents after their hard struggle. I made up my mind to work for at least five years before I could think of getting married.

At eight o'clock on the eve of my departure, like all other nurses who were leaving, I went to see the Matron for the presentation of my Hospital Certificate and to bid farewell to her. After I had taken my seat facing her, she handed me my Certificate, which was written in red letters. (I received my State Registration later, when I was working in Pretoria.) She then explained that after all my reports since my probationary period had been scrutinised, they had decided that I merited a First Class pass. I heaved with astonishment. She went on to say that the doctors, sisters and herself (she was an anaesthetist) had all thought that I was one of the best theatre nurses they had ever had. Amazing! I just could not believe my ears. Then, finally, she unwrapped a paper and took out a brand new navy blue and red nurses' cape and gave it to me. She went on to say that she usually presented either a pair of scissors, or a torch, but she was giving me the cape as a mark of distinction so that I could wear it during my work; she then wished me all success in my career.

As I left the office I still could not believe it. During my training I had tried hard to do what I was capable of doing, but I had never expected so many words of praise from the Matron. Miss Tracey was well-known for her strictness all round; we used to shiver when she came to take rounds — she was such a perfectionist that she was nicknamed 'Colani' (Pick Up!) because, as she went round the hospital, she would ask staff to pick up even the smallest piece of paper or rubbish she saw. Actually, she got to know her nickname later on, because she learnt to speak Xhosa; she would say, 'I know Colani is my name, but I want the hospital so clean that I can eat in it'.

I spent a month at home before going to Pretoria, where there were already a few nurses from Holy Cross. I was going to the Transvaal for the first time but I was somewhat apprehensive because of the stories, which were commonplace, that we heard about the Boers .

3

■

Marriage and Politics

I joined the Pretoria Hospital in 1947. The first thing that struck me, on my arrival there, was the segregation then in operation — nothing in my training had prepared me for this discovery. Although the hospital was under one central administration, it was divided into two sections: one for 'Europeans', another for 'non-Europeans', but with the added oddness, however, that all matrons as well as all doctors in the so-called 'non-European' section were white, and that the 'European' section was staffed exclusively by whites as well.

The majority of trained nurses commuted to work by buses from the townships. This meant that they had to be in the bus queues by 5.30 am in order to report to work at 7.00 am. Those who did not have homes in the townships were accommodated at the hospital. They paid a monthly rent. Four nurses usually shared one room. Although the place was kept clean, because there were cleaners, it was disgusting. It had no ceilings, no floorboards, no carpets, and it had horrible steel doors. We usually had our meals in the quarters reserved for pupil nurses, which was a stone's throw away from the hostel. Our food, which was different from that of the patients, was sufficient, but it was terribly unappetising.

But what astonished me even more, as I settled into work, was to discover the gap between the salaries of white and black nurses —a staggering figure of 4:1 in favour of the former. Yet we all had the same qualifications, we all nursed in the same way. Differences stretched even to our uniforms —while these were all white for both sections, the capes were different. One of the consequences was that I could not now use the brand-new cape which I mentioned had been given to me by the Matron of the Holy Cross Hospital when I left there because it was the colour of the cape worn by the white nurses in the 'European' section. What on earth was this? Yes, the sharp knife of apartheid was right at my heart.

Depression and discontent started to set in. I felt so discouraged and unwanted that I even thought it was useless for a black person to bother to be educated. When I discussed this with other nurses, I found that everyone felt the same way: our disillusionment had been rapid. Psychologically, I felt hopeless and helpless; life seemed to me to be losing its meaning after all the joy and pride in my success as a student. From then on I was, from time to time, so bitter that my face wore a perpetual invisible mask to cover my discontent. Yes, every black person wears that mask in order to survive.

Apartheid has devastating effects on all black people — it stifles and throttles talent and initiative, it leaves one like a tree which has suddenly stopped bearing fruit. Here I was, a young nurse, fresh from training, full of enthusiasm and energy, wanting to prove my worth, plunged into despair and disillusionment. Only a few months before, when the Rev. Norton had broken the news that I had passed my examination, I was a delighted and proud woman, one who had climbed to the top of the first ladder. At that time the plight of many boys and girls who were my classmates at primary school, but who could not reach where I was, had been wiped from my memory. But suddenly I thought that they were better off for having not bothered themselves to go further. I was choking, and I felt that I needed a very high ladder to take me out of the enclosure. However, the thought of my duty to my patients brought my senses back. The promises I

31

made to my parents that I would help to educate my brother also came back. Well, I said to myself, since all the nurses feel the same, I better carry on like everyone else.

Twelve days after I started working, a patient by the name of Robert Resha was admitted to my ward, which was for male surgical cases. The ward was overflowing with patients: some were sleeping two to a bed, others were lying on mattresses on the floor. Soon after coming on duty at 4.00 p.m., and after taking my report, I hurriedly went round to give injections before supper time. Robert also was to have an injection, because he had cellulitis of the cheek sustained during a rugby match; the abscess had been excised that afternoon.

Robert had been brought into hospital, as a consequence of an accident sustained while playing rugby, by Dr William Nkomo, who was one of the founders of the African National Congress Youth League. Actually, I found out afterwards, Robert had been advised by a Johannesburg doctor that he should have the thing excised. That advice had been rejected because Robert said that he did not want to be operated upon. The next thing that had come into his mind, he related, was that he should take the next train to Pretoria to see his friend, Dr Nkomo, thinking that he would receive treatment at the surgery. It was therefore a great surprise to find that the doctor, immediately he saw him, decided to drive Robert to the hospital, insisting that serious complications might result if the operation were to be delayed. In later life, Robert never stopped thanking Dr Nkomo for that action; he certainly did not realise, at the time, how serious his condition was.

As I came to the bed, I pulled the screen around it. Half of Robert's face was covered by a bandage, so I could not see the whole of it properly. But when I pulled the screen back, my eyes landed on his legs, and I remarked inwardly: 'What lovely shaped legs and clean feet!' I could see his legs quite clearly because black patients were not allowed to use their own pyjamas —they all wore khaki shorts and shirts which was the hospital uniform issue. I then passed to the next patient, noting only that Robert already was having visitors, and that his locker was full of books and newspapers.

Robert stayed in the hospital for ten days. During that time I found him to be polite and soft-spoken; he occupied himself with reading. Because he was in a ward with more than ninety patients, we spoke to each other only a few times during his stay. The first thing he asked me was whether I could lend him a book to read, but I had to explain that I had none, since I had but recently arrived in Pretoria. On another day, when he had been transferred to the verandah, he tried to talk to me about Matatiele, saying that he knew some people from there; he asked me if I knew a Mr Mda, whom I found out later, was one of the leaders of the ANC Youth League. I did not know him.

On the day of his discharge, he came into the dressings room (a place forbidden to patients) to say goodbye; he thanked me for the good treatment, and said that he would come to visit me at the Nurses' Home in two weeks' time, after seeing his doctor as an outpatient. On the appointed day I found him in the nurses' home sitting room. He greeted me cordially and reminded me that he had said that he would come to visit. He then switched smartly from health matters and the weather and started to woo me. I told him that I had a boyfriend at home in Matatiele. His reply was that he would be stupid to think that I had no boyfriend. The 'patient-nurse' syndrome flashed through my mind, so, in order to put him off, I said 'God will see'.

'Well', he said, 'since it is not God who is courting, I will see.'

Then, typical of a country girl, I looked down, scratched my foot on the floor like I was making invisible drawings, and I became bankrupt of words. I then became restless, stood up and said I had to prepare myself for going back to work. We then both walked towards the door. Before we got there, he came close to me, and kissed me. I did not resist. That was when I felt I loved him, but, being a girl from a peasant background, I felt guilty for having allowed him to kiss me on the very first day he came to see me. However, Robert teased me about this for the rest of our lives together.

In the rural areas of Matatiele in those days, young men

33

had to court girls for months and months before they were accepted. The young men also enjoyed it because they felt they were conquerors, and that the girls were not cheap. Sometimes, during the long chase, one of the young man's friends would go to the girl to test whether or not she really loved the man who was wooing her, by asking her, in a playful way, to choose which people she loved. But the whole exercise was a trick; it was called *senyamo* (choose). First the friend would call senyamo to the girl on a number of peoples' names before calling his friend's name, like this:

Friend: *Senyamo* (choose)
Girl: *Semang?* (who?)
Friend: (pretending to be thinking) *Se ...e ...e* (eh ... eh ... so-and-so). The name called was not of the wooer
Girl: *Thlotse* (I don't love him)
Friend: *Senyamo* (choose)
Girl: *Semang?* (who?)
Friend: *Se* (This time he calls the name of his friend)
Girl: *Kashoa* (I am dying for him, or, I love him)

The friend has now clinched the clue on the wooer's standing; he meets him without delay to tell him, '*Moreso, metsi a ka tlasa mangoele*' (brother, carry on, the waters are below the knees; or there is hope). The onus is now on the wooer to redouble his eloquence when he meets the girl again; either on meeting her on the way to fetch water from the well or river, or going to the fields. Had the girl replied: '*Thlotse*' (I don't love him) the messenger would have told his friend: '*Monna —ke koetsa*' (man, the waters are too deep; or: Forget about it).

I would say that for Robert and I it was a case of 'love at first sight'. He had a wonderful figure, and the day he was discharged he looked immaculate in a dark blue suit and a grey hat with a narrow brim, the fashion in those days. So, when he said that he would come to see me at the Nurses' Home, I worried because I knew that, as a single man, he might woo me, and that I would have no way of refusing him. In fact, on the first night we went out together to the

34

cinema he did propose marriage and I accepted him.

But there were obstacles. From my very first salary, I started paying for my brother's school fees. My brother, whose name was Clement, was then at a college in Natal, called Lourdes. I told Robert about my responsibilities and that I would not be ready for marriage for at least five years. He said that my responsibilities would not be abandoned.

I did not like Pretoria Hospital because of the environment. There was too much Afrikaans, which I did not understand. The consultants used to address the medical students in that language during their rounds, and I could not follow what was being said. So I made an application to the Coronation Hospital in Johannesburg, and moved there after five months in Pretoria.

Robert came to fetch me to take me to Coronation Hospital. As the train entered the West Rand, I was dumbfounded by the spectacle of the mine-dumps. I was debating with myself what sort of mountains they were, with neither rocks nor grass on them, when Robert told me what they were. As he told me, my mind started to imagine the depth of the mines, and the time it took for the dumps to be built. It was a remarkable scene, and I don't think anyone who comes to Johannesburg for the first time did not have the same feeling I had.

One weekend, when I was off duty, Robert invited me to his elder brother's place in Alexandra Township, where he was then living. After that trip he told me that his brother was going to write to my parents to inform them that he wanted to marry me. As much as I loved Robert, I felt that my life was getting disorganised; all the plans that I had made when I left Holy Cross were being pushed aside by a person who was in a hurry to get married.

A few days after the visit to Alexandra, I received a letter from my parents, telling me that the relatives of my Matatiele boyfriend, with whom I had been in love since our schooldays, had sent his parents to them about their son wanting to marry me. Actually, from the time I was in Pretoria, I was no longer writing to this chap, although it was a foregone conclusion on his part that one day we would

35

get married. My decision not to marry him created some bitterness on the part of his family towards mine.

Well, things were bad for me, because I had just given the address of my parents to Robert. This was the time I was beginning to feel the pressures of adulthood, and I just geared myself to sorting things out once and for all. I therefore wrote a letter to my parents, telling them that I did not want to marry the Matatiele guy. In a separate note to my mother, I told her that they should expect a letter from the chap I wanted to marry.

Robert was a Xhosa of the Thembu clan. At an early age, Robert lived with his grandparents in Bholothwa, a rural area near Queenstown, where he was a herdboy. He joined his parents in the Queenstown location when he was ready to go to school. Because his parents could not afford to pay for his education after he had completed his primary schooling (his father earned very little in his job as builder's labourer; skilled building was at that time a job reserved for whites) Robert was recruited for the mines when he was sixteen years of age — he pretended he was eighteen.

He left the mines after about two years to work as a bus conductor. It was during this time that he took correspondence courses in Personnel Management and in Journalism. When we met, he was Personnel Manager at a big firm near Pretoria, called Knights, that employed thousands of Africans and whites. He soon left this job in order to concentrate upon journalism as a sports reporter, and to devote more time to politics. He became Sports Reporter for the African newspaper, *Umteteli wa Bantu*. Later on he was Associate Editor of *IGoli*, which reported extensively on the Defiance Campaign aimed at resisting laws regarded as cornerstones of apartheid. Later on, he became a reporter for *New Age*.

Robert used to say that his awareness of, and interest in, politics was fired by the Industrial and Commercial Workers' Union (ICU) of Clements Kadalie, in whose honour my brother was named. Robert was fourteen when he first heard Kadalie speak at a meeting in East London; by that time he had already been taken by his uncle to clan meetings in

36

Bholothwa — in the rural areas boys accompany their elders to these meetings at an early age, in order to be instructed into the arts of public speaking and of how to handle the affairs of the community and the people. Created in the 1920s, the ICU was the first major trades union that was open to all races as well as all industries.

Robert joined the ANC in 1939, having been inspired by a speech made by J. B. Marks at an open-air meeting at Western Native Township, where he asked people to join in the struggle for freedom.

Robert had by now moved, with a friend, to Sophiatown, to Bertha Street. I invited him to come with me to meet my Gertie Street relatives, who liked him, and my maternal uncle, whose name was Tsubathi Malule, started addressing him as *mokhoenyana* (son-in-law). Since I had hinted to mother about the new chap in my life, their reply to the Resha request was positive.

The customary talks proceeded smoothly between the Resha family and mine, with my uncle and aunt in Sophiatown playing a leading role, because they were near. Robert and I had already opted for a quiet wedding because I had to see to my brother's education at Lourdes. We were married on 18 March 1948, with just our relatives and witnesses present. The first ceremony was at the offices of the Native Commissioner, followed by a church service. We were married by Rev. William Molikoane of the African Episcopal Church in Soweto. Ten relatives and friends came to join us at my uncle's place later that day. It was at that ceremony that the Resha's announced the name they had chosen for me. I was named 'Nobantu' (Mother of the People).

The year of our marriage was the year in which the Nationalists under Malan won the white elections. The majority of people were apprehensive because the Nationalists had fought the election on a ticket of more oppression of the black majority; people expected a raw deal. But, at the same time, Africans do not regard the Boers as thinkers and as people who have any vision for the future. We know them as a hateful tribe. Many people (even those not in politics) were saying that the United Party of Smuts, when it was in

37

power, had done nothing for Africans. People were also still bitter about the treatment of African ex-servicemen, who had been fooled into joining the army during both World Wars, but who were told, on the day that they returned, to go and collect their passes at the pass office. Africans knew that there was no difference between the Nationalist Party and the United Party when it came to the so-called 'Native Question'.

At about this time Robert's friend moved to a house in Soweto and Robert took over the bedsit they had been sharing. At the same time my brother was writing frantic letters to say that he did not like Lourdes. We therefore prepared for him to continue in one of the Johannesburg secondary schools.

Then, in 1949, a few weeks after my mother had reported that he was very ill, my father died. I was very saddened by this, because I knew that mother had not only lost a companion but also a man with whom she formed a team to rear us with great affection, and to keep us together as a close-knit family unit. Together, they had surmounted the irksome deprivation Africans suffer in the country of their birth. When we returned from the funeral, Robert and I decided to help mother as best as we could with the other children. Mother moved back to her old home at Ramohlakoana since another catechist had to take over father's work.

* * *

1948 was the year my life in politics began. Robert asked me to go with him to a meeting of the ANC Youth League at the Western Native Township Municipal Hall, which was in walking distance from Sophiatown. I was still a bride, very shy, and had not really attended any meetings, except for the debates we used to have at the Welsh High School. The Youth League was very militant. The speakers made fiery speeches which demanded action against the white government's oppressive laws. After that meeting, I felt so happy and relieved to hear Africans talk of fighting for their freedom; I suddenly found I had something to live for after

38

all my depression and bitterness while I was at the Pretoria Hospital. Robert and I talked and talked after we came back home, because I had suggested that Africans must stop talking and fight physically to get their land back. He tried, patiently, to explain the ANC policy of non-violence.

From then on I never missed a meeting. At that time many areas did not have branches. Members of the ANC from Sophiatown, Western Native Township and Newclare all attended the same meetings at Western Native Township. Later (in 1953) when branches were formed, each area had its weekly meetings, with regional meetings once a month.

In 1949, Ida Mtwana, who resided in Western Native Township, was elected Provincial President of the ANC Women's League at the ANC National Conference. Other Provincial Presidents were Mrs Florence Matomela (Cape Province), Mrs Bertha Mkize (Natal) and Mrs Mohlakoana (Orange Free State). The essence of the ANCWL was to mobilise women to play a more meaningful role in the liberation struggle, and to watch for and resist any racist legislation directed against them as women. Ida Mtwana was a very militant person and an immensely eloquent speaker. She soon called separate meetings of the ANCWL. At these meetings we decided to organise as many women as possible to join the ANC. Ida had a wonderfully melodious voice, and she soon taught the women many freedom songs.

During those days in the ANC we had a Freedom Song which went: 'Vuma silibale igama lako' (Agree that we write your name!). When that song was being sung, people would flock to the stage, holding their subscription fees of two shillings and sixpence to join the ANC. People were proud to be members of Congress, since it gave one a sense of mental liberation, because of being engaged in doing something about apartheid.

When the Sophiatown branch of the ANC was formed, Robert was elected to the branch Executive. Later, when the Women's League was established and had its branch executive, I was elected first as secretary and later as chair. This meant that Robert and I were, once a month, present at joint meetings in our respective capacities as officers of these bodies. Both Robert and I were, at first, uneasy about this. Although we were elected to these positions, we were always aware that tongues could wag when, by coincidence, we shared the same view. Human beings have a tendency to think that 'one is pulling the other by the nose' no matter how independent a married couple may be. I always felt deeply wounded when some married couples who are in politics together are slighted in this way. To me, marriage is a partnership, where self-assertion and not subordination is the key to harmony. I recognise that clash of interests is one of the causes of family strife on many occasions.

In Sophiatown, when the women started to organise women into the ANC, they told all men to bring their wives to the meetings or the women would not vote for them. Men like Patrick Molaoa and others actually thanked the women for this action. Men came with their wives, and what cream of militancy would otherwise have been left idle! Many women, who had used to complain that their husbands had been neglecting them or were not supporting them because of their politics, saw the light when they started to be active in the organisation. The WL warning to the men in Sophiatown was so effective that dozens of men bought the green ANC blouses from Lilian Ngoyi, who had designed and sewed them, as presents for their wives.

Robert was co-opted on to the National Executive Committee in 1954, and elected to it in 1955; he was also National President of the Youth League and Transvaal Provincial Secretary — all this meant that he could no longer serve the branch. Yes, Congress was fast moving away from its elite image to the grassroots. The late Mr Simon Tyiki, who was elected chairman of the Sophiatown branch for six successive years, and who was one of the thirty who constituted the last batch in the Treason Trial, about which I write in another chapter, never went to school. He was not only a very effective and skilled politician, but would amuse us at meetings by mocking his own inabilities as well as the lies in the newspapers, by saying: '*Abafana bandixelela ukuthi amaphepha athi namhla nje* ...' (The boys tell me that today the papers say ...).

The Women's League became stronger and stronger, and

by the early Fifties it was a powerful force within the ANC nationally. Women organised house parties every month to raise funds for the organisation, since its only form of income was from membership subscriptions. But, chiefly, they began to arouse women to be involved in campaigns to fight against racist legislation which directly affected them as women, disabilities which eroded their progress as African women. Thus, by the time the ANC launched the Defiance Campaign of 1952, thousands of women across the country joined in the campaign; they served terms of imprisonment on the same basis as their menfolk, as there was to be no bail, no defence, no fines paid. The consequence was that, by the mid-Fifties, the preponderance of women in ANC rallies, conferences and campaigns was obvious.

After the Sophiatown branch was formed, the success of the M Plan was soon obvious. The M Plan, or Mandela Plan, was devised by Nelson Mandela in the immediate aftermath of the Defiance Campaign; it was intended to be the method whereby the Congress Alliance would be able to continue the struggle in a future when it would have to operate clandestinely. This Plan, the outcome of quite remarkable foresight on the part of its originator, was based on a discrete as well as discreet cellular structure at mass level, which communicated with the national leadership via intermediaries structured on the same cellular principle.

Regular mass meetings were held every Sunday at a place in the centre of the township; that place became known as 'Freedom Square'. These Freedom Square meetings were always big and very lively. National leaders, like Nelson Mandela, Walter Sisulu, Chief Luthuli, J. B. Marks and Lilian Ngoyi, were amongst those who addressed these meetings. From the Congress Alliance, leaders like Yusuf Cachalia, Stanley Lollan, Helen Joseph, Ahmed Kathrada, came to speak. Every Sunday morning, at about 8 o'clock, Mr Nkalimeng, whom we referred to as 'Re' (Father) Nkalimeng, would hoist the ANC flag on the Square, to let the people know that there would be a meeting. This, I think, also attracted the Special Branch, because they would always be waiting there, in their cars, before the people arrived.

41

Between 1950 and 1952, on Sundays ANC speakers used to address people passing along Victoria Road by standing on a rock in a little open space between Victoria Street and Gertie Street. This resembled something like Speakers Corner at Hyde Park; a few people would stop to listen for a few minutes. But this was but a step towards bigger things to come, when the branch was formed, in 1953, and it became necessary to hold branch meetings in a hall, and to have the much larger square for Sunday meetings. That was how Freedom Square came about.

The upsurge of stiff resistance by the oppressed was also triggered off by the new rash of racist legislation which the Nationalist government hastened to implement. Laws introduced included the Group Areas Act of 1950, which provided that ownership, as well as occupation of residential as well as business land, should be reserved for specified racial groups. The operation of this Act had at least two effects: firstly, it led to the forcible removal of Africans, Asians and 'Coloured' people from spaces designated as 'white'; secondly, it offered the opportunity for largely poor-white Afrikaners to acquire property as well as protection against incursion and competition.

The so-called Abolition of Passes Act of 1952, notwithstanding its name, had as its intention the consolidation of all the separate bits of identification papers that African men over sixteen had to carry with them at all times, into one single document, called a reference book'. It was also under the provisions of this Act that African women were, for the first time, forced into carrying Passes; I chronicle their resistance to that imposition in another chapter.

The Bantu Education Act of 1953 transferred the provision of education for Africans from the control of the provincial governments to central control — however, not under that of the Department of Education, but under that of the Department of Native Affairs. While the Act itself contained virtually no details about programmes or pedagogy, the debates in the white regime's parliament made it clear that the intention was to keep the 'Bantu' as Africans were also called, in their place. The then Minister of Native affairs, later to be the Prime Minister to be assassinated by a deranged Greek, made several classic statements, including the following: 'racial relations cannot improve if the wrong type of education is given to Natives ... There is no place for him (the Bantu) in the European community above the level of certain forms of labour ... what is the use of teaching a Bantu child mathematics when he cannot use it in practice?'

These racist laws were outrageous; they touched every single aspect of our lives. No wonder there was resistance from everywhere: towns, rural areas, schools and professions.

* * *

At the end of 1954 I decided to stop working at the Johannesburg General Hospital, and to devote myself to private work as a midwife, since I had acquired my professional qualifications in this specialism after training at the Bridgman Memorial Hospital. It was really during this time as a midwife that I discovered the hardships and misery of location life as I went in and out of houses. In the 'Golden City' of Johannesburg there were many people who went without a meal for days on end. Many of the patients I attended to were not calling for private doctors or midwives because they had money, but because of the paradox of the vicious circle stemming from the lack of cheap and easily available medical facilities for the poor.

Many women who had small children could not attend clinics because these were far away and overcrowded, leading to lengthy waiting before being seen. With menfolk, as well as women, away at work in the city or in the houses of the white society, finding someone to supervise toddlers at home was difficult. Many of the women would call a midwife also because their newborn babies had to be registered. Failure to register a birth could mean that children could be sent to the 'Reserves', if there was no document to prove that they had been born in Johannesburg.

To work among people who are so deprived is a heartbreaking thing for a midwife. For instance, we had been taught that a pregnant woman must drink at least two pints of milk per day, but I was in agony to find that many could not afford even one cup of milk per day! Soon, whenever I delivered a baby, a thought crept into my head: 'How will this little one fare, whose mother did not get proper nutrition?' There were times when I found myself having to bring a pint of milk for the mother, and thereafter tell them that they need not worry about paying me until the baby was 4-6 months old. The result was that some never paid me, but that did not worry me: at least, I had registered the baby so that it should be entitled to live in Johannesburg.

One of the things which I found out during my work, and which I found frustrating, was the psychological trauma caused by the Pass Laws. Many a time, after delivering a baby, and especially after telling the mother and other relatives that it was a boy, they would say, 'Oh! he is going to carry a pass'. When it was a girl, they would say, 'Oh! her husband will carry a pass; he will be sent to Bethal'.

'Bethal' has gone down in the history of oppression as a particularly sordid episode. Mostly recollected because of the discovery of pass offenders buried in shallow graves in the potato fields in which they had worked, and which led to the potato boycott of 1959 (since which date Robert never again ate potatoes), it is well to remember that already in July 1947 the Rev. Michael Scott had detailed the atrocities committed by Boer farmers against their. labourers. That was not the first time: Ruth First, later to be one of the regime's victims by assassination by letter-bomb in Moçambique, chronicled much of that history, noting events going back to 1929. It is important to remember, also, that 'Bethal' simply brings to mind for Africans a system of cheap labour whereby our people are channelled into farm jails or forced contracts with such farmers who would otherwise be unable to find workers.

Having been brought up in a rural area, where, in those days, the masses of the people knew very little about organised politics, my joining of the ANC was a real eye-opener. My thoughts always went back to the place of my birth. I could now quite clearly picture the plight of African women in the Reserves, those perpetual grass-widows who brought up their children single-handed; they were the ones who were directly faced with the hungry mouths and stomachs of their children. They were also faced with the gruelling task of having to till the most inhospitable soil with the most primitive implements in the most primitive ways in order to keep the wolf away from their doors. And when their young ones died of malnutrition and other diseases that could have been prevented, theirs was perpetual agony and weeping, as they dug the graves of their children.

In Johannesburg, location life presented itself as another extreme, to say the least. The daily mass early morning rush from dark, muddy or dusty streets (depending on the season of the year) in overcrowded trains or buses, to brightly lighted houses and tarred city streets is like going from one country to another. The stresses and strains caused by this environmental change is most damaging, and each hour of the day is clouded with deep resentment and hatred for the privileged white race. One of the most disturbing features of this life is the destruction of families through the hostel system for migrant workers, and by the beer halls which are built near the locations. Naturally, because of this proximity, single men and husbands who have been forced to leave their wives and children in the 'Reserves', get mixed up with location women. Illegitimacy amongst Africans in South African urban areas is therefore very high; we are being destroyed from the first and most important unit, because the family is the beginning of the nation. How the African family has survived this onslaught is one of the miracles of our times.

African women have been the worst victims of apartheid. All over the world where there is national oppression, women are always at the lowest step of the ladder. That is why the women have rallied to the call of the ANC to join the liberation movement in such large numbers, to fight side by side with their menfolk, for the restoration of their basic human rights; they see in the ANC their only hope for themselves and for their families. Indeed, it is encouraging to the women to see that the ANC has recognised the important role that women have to play in the struggle. Several women have taken up the highest positions in the organisation. During the fifties, Lilian Ngoyi was the first woman to be elected to the National Executive; it was during her period of leadership of the ANC Women's League and of the Federation of South African Women that twenty thousand women invaded the grounds of the Union Buildings on 9 August 1956, to protest against the extension of the Pass Laws, as well as against all racist laws against women, about which I will write in a later chapter.

Lilian, whose Sepedi name was Masedibe, was born in Pretoria in 1911. She did not have a high academic background. Although she had been to Kilnerton College, she really learnt her politics from the trade unions; she was at one time secretary of the Garment Workers Union in Johannesburg. It was because of her prowess and sincerity in the struggle that she found herself elected to the ANC National Executive. Many of those who worked closely with her were greatly inspired by her determination, and were ready to face any odds in pursuit of our goal. We certainly benefitted a great deal from her courage. The success of the Union Buildings march depended upon really hard work on the part of the leadership of both the Federation and the ANC Women's League, with planning in the hands of Lilian as president, and Helen Joseph, as secretary of the Federation. Of course some men helped to go round with the women, especially to the farms and to the rural areas, but effectively it was a campaign organised by the women.

Lilian was not only very brave and hardworking, but she also had a neat sense of humour. I remember a story she related to us after she and some other women had been released on bail after their arrest in the Treason Trial. As they were sleeping in their cell in the early hours of the morning, Dora Tamana, one of the stalwarts of the ANC in the Cape, suddenly called out from her cell, 'He Bafazi! mna ke ndibanjelwe ntoni' (Women! Just tell me, what exactly am I arrested for?). Someone answered from another cell: 'Have you forgotten that you went overseas with Lilian, without a passport?' Then, after that, there was laughter from all the other cells. With this, as well as other amusing stories, Lilian was trying to show us to be strong, because such arrests were to come to many women as the struggle gained

46

momentum. And, indeed, it was not long when, in 1958, the jails in all the provinces were overflowing with women resisting and protesting.

Another story she told was how she felt when, with Dora Tamana, she was removed from a ship in Cape Town, bound for Europe, to attend an international conference of women in Lausanne, together with Helen Joseph. After they had boarded the ship at Cape Town, they had locked themselves in the toilet, because they did not have passports, hoping that they would not be returned should they be discovered on the high seas. Their plan backfired, and they were forced to come out before the ship sailed. As they came out, Lilian said, she was more angry than afraid. Because of her anger, she said, she felt cold sweat rolling down her temples as if cold water had been splashed on her face. But, because of the harassment that followed from the Captain and his assistants, she could not even wipe her face until they were ashore. But they returned to Johannesburg, determined to leave for Switzerland to attend the conference, which they managed to do, going by air a few days later.

Abroad, Lilian was political dynamite; she made a tremendous impression on women from both East and West, who treated our representatives as friends and equals. In China, where they were invited after the conference, they met women who had been on the 'Long March' and who had endured the hazards of the revolutionary years. She recalled how, in Shanghai, they had been shown places which, before the liberation, had signs which said 'No Chinese and dogs allowed', and how that reminded her of South Africa. She also spoke to us about the heroism of the Algerian women, who were fighting side by side, gun in hand, with their menfolk, for liberation from France. In England, she told us, she had addressed a mass meeting in Trafalgar Square. It was there that she made her famous speech about African women being like chickens whose eggs are taken without their permission to end up on someone else's table.

Lilian was one of those people who had a great deal of charisma; even those people who did not like her as a person were nowhere, because she was the queen bee with the masses. After she lost her first husband, Lilian got married again, but that second marriage did not work. It was at that time that she played a leading role in the trades union movement. At her house she was modest; she kept a lot of souvenirs which she had collected during her travels. As she went around, addressing meetings and rallies all over the country, she called on women to be in the forefront of the struggle, in order to secure a better future for our children. Women, she said, had a duty to protect their offspring, to preserve their dignity as mothers, who produced the future leaders and workers of the country.

During all this political activity she lived from hand to mouth, caring for an aged mother, for her daughter Edith and her children, and later, for her sick brother, who died in his late thirties. The first time I saw her mother at her place, we took a liking to each other. She teased me by call-ing herself the 'Senior Wife' of my husband, Robert, and from that time on we called each other Khalitso (women married to the same man).

It was during my frequent visits to Lilian's house that I thought I discovered the source behind Lilian's bravery: her mother. Crippled with rheumatoid arthritis since her teens, she told me how people had mocked her husband when they got married, by saying he was marrying a coffin. However, her husband died before her, but not before she had born him two children — Lilian and her brother. This brave woman was very proud of her daughter, and my interest in her was fanned by the devotion and steadfastness of the daughter in pursuit of the ideals for which she stood. At times, I observed, relatives and friends viewed their situa-tion with great concern, especially when the regime hit hard at its opponents — arrests; banning orders, banishments, and frequent visits by the SB.

In some cases, people in the movement have lost their jobs because employers are intimidated by the SB, who claim that they are hiring dangerous communists, and even rela-tives and friends bleakly advised their next-of-kin that poli-tics is for rich people. I remember, on my visit to London in 1972, that a friend told me to leave politics to my husband, as other women had done. But my first warning had come from my mother as early as 1961, just before Robert went into exile. She came to Soweto unannounced, and we spoke tete-a-tete. She said that she had been told that my husband and I were in serious trouble because we were Communists. (Mother was opposed to communism, because she said, she was told that Communists say there was no God.) I failed to get the source of her information, because she said: *batho-bare* (People say!).

However, knowing that my mother knows nothing about Communism, and I, too, knew very little about it, I told her that we were members of Congress, and then explained to her what we stood for. After that she said, she was not against Congress, because she knew Congress was fighting for our land. She at once gave us her blessings.

Now, Lilian's mother was not the type who would tell her daughter to lay off; rather, she encouraged her in her political work. She rejoiced with her when, through hard work, she climbed to senior positions both in the trade union and in the ANC, and during hard times, when the regime pointed its sharp knives at her, trying to stop her from campaigning against the injustices towards black people, her mother was there to comfort her.

Lilian could not properly do her dressmaking, which was her livelihood, during the four and a half years of the Treason Trial, because she was amongst the last batch of thirty accused. Still worse was to come when she was detained, with many others, for five months during the 1960 State of Emergency, which was declared to cope with the wave of pass-burnings, strikes and stay-at-home campaigns launched by the ANC in mourning for the dead of Sharpeville and Langa and other places. The regime detained some 2,000 prominent people in the Congress Alliance, the Pan Africanist Congress, and even the all-white Liberal party; a further 20,000 plus Africans were arrested and sent to work camps and prison farms.

Then, after the Treason Trial ended in 1961, Lilian was under perpetual banning orders, followed by house arrest, and frequent visits from the SB during the day, as well as at ungodly hours during the night. All this kept some of her

49

customers away, and through all these stresses and strains she developed heart trouble. At the same time, her mother's condition deteriorated rapidly, and she died in the early Seventies. In the letter she wrote to me about her mother's death,. she wrote: 'Your khalitso was a cushion where my tears could drop on'.

We continued to correspond with each other until the end. I recall particularly one letter she wrote during the 1976 Soweto uprising in which she told me how the migrant workers had invaded her area, Mzimhlope; she recorded how women and small girls had been raped, and that they knew who was behind it all. During the late sixties and early Seventies, when informers were all over the place, she used to write and tell me all about it. These letters were written in a code only the two of us could understand. She was a great woman. I heard that hers was a simple funeral; her colleagues at home had all agreed that she should go to rest in the modest way that she had lived. The women of South Africa are proud to have had such a leader; today we can see that her work was not in vain —there are now millions of Lilians who have come up to take over the flag from where she left off.

Lilian finally succumbed to her illness in 1981, not having shifted a centimetre from her convictions. Her plough remains deep in the furrow of the field which was begun by ANC women pioneers like Charlotte Maxeke, Mrs Mapikela, Mary Mqwetho, Ida Mtwana and many other (some unknown) names. And the ploughing will go to the last acre of the field. Young women of today have already taken over from the departed, for struggle is our heritage.

4

■

The Struggle For Sophiatown

What was Sophiatown? Sophiatown was a sprawling township, with a population of about 130,000 inhabitants, a few miles from the centre of the city of Johannesburg. Most of them were a deprived community, who lived from hand to mouth. But they were a settled community, with established homes, a people who wanted to live a decent life. It was this community that the recently-elected Nationalist regime destroyed by forcibly removing the people. For that there were several reasons. The first, and foremost reason for the removals was that Sophiatown was one of the oldest townships in which Africans and other black people had the right to freehold ownership of land and property. This was unlike the more usual situation, where Africans, deprived of their rights to own land by the Natives Land Act of 1913, were tenants of the municipalities, in pockets on the outskirts of towns, segregated from so-called 'white areas'.

With the passing of the Group Areas Act of 1950 and the Natives Resettlement Act of 1954, the regime had empowered itself to remove black people from any place it deemed fit. The regime chose Sophiatown as its prime target, and indeed, as a test case, knowing well that if it succeeded there, other places would be a walk-over. With its obsession with colour prejudice and appeasement of the white electorate that had brought it to power, the regime introduced a new phrase — that of 'Black Spots', by which it meant that all pockets of black residence, especially in city centres or near white residential areas, had to be removed. It was the resistance of the people to this removal that explains the world-wide prominence of Sophiatown, because in the end it took the regime seven long years to complete its pledge to its electorate. An indication of the tenacity and courage of the people is that, on the first day of the removal, it brought in 2,000 paramilitary police, but managed to remove just 100 people! It is that story that I now want to tell.

Soon after the Group Areas Act and the Resettlement Act were passed, the regime formed the 'Resettlement Board', whose task was to conduct the removal, from beginning to end. Members of the Board went from house to house, collecting the names of members of each family, while at the same time ordering the landlords to sell their properties to the government.

The ANC, from the outset in 1953, mobilised the people, emphasising co-operation between the tenants and the landlords. The ANC argued that, if the tenants co-operated with the regime and left, the landlords would be left with empty houses, which they would not be able to keep. On the other hand, it argued, if the landlords sold to the government, tenants would have nowhere to go.

The battle for Sophiatown had started. Huge slogans appeared on walls: *'Asihambi. Ons dak nie'* (We are not moving). A Freedom Song was composed: *Sophiatown likaya lam asihambi* (Sophiatown is my home; we are not moving).

Several landlords went to their lawyers for advice, but with little success. Dr Xuma, who had become aloof and isolated since his loss of the leadership of the ANC, formed an organisation of landlords, called The Anti-Removal and Anti-Expropriation Ratepayer's Association, to fight the removal. That, however, soon fizzled out, as the majority of landlords drifted towards the ANC. The ANC leaders in Sophiatown saw Dr Xuma's organisation as divisive and a danger to community solidarity and unity. Dr Xuma had already held one or two meetings of the landlords, but before they could hold the next one, it was leaked to the ANC where and when the next meeting would take place. About ten or twelve ANC leaders, including Joe Matlou (Joe was one of the founders of the Youth League and one of Robert's great friends; as a result, his wife Violet and I became close friends), Simon Mahopo, Peter Ntite and Robert decided to gatecrash the meeting.

Actually, I did not know of this gate-crashing until Robert gave me the report when he came back from the meeting. He was in a jovial mood and asked me: 'I wonder why a man who was president of the ANC, like Xuma, should try to fool the people. Anyway, we put him in his place'. From there, Robert related, step by step, what had happened at the meeting, which had been chaired by the old man, Mr Lethoba, the quasi-Mayor of Sophiatown. One of Robert's gifts was that he was a graphic narrator. He could recount his or other peoples' speeches in an astonishing manner — and was very good at imitating people. He had a very sharp wit and a deep reservoir of recollection.

They had listened to three or four speakers when Robert asked for the floor. When the chairman called him, he first asked for the number of his property. Robert said he mentioned 41 Bertha Street, which was the number of our house, but then someone shouted from amongst the public: 'E! E! Monna re batla nomoro ea Mobu eseng ea ntlo' (No, man; we want the number of the soil, not of the building). Robert said he got stuck, because he did not know the number of the property. By not knowing the number of the stand, he betrayed the fact that he was not a ratepayer, and therefore not a member of the AARPA. Thus, according to the rules, he should not have been allowed to speak, but the Chairman permitted him to do so because he wanted to hear what he had to say. So Robert told me, he continued his speech, as if he had not heard the interjection. 'Mothers and fathers of Sophiatown', he told me, he said:

the message from the tenants to you is that they are not moving. They have sent us to tell you that they are sons and daughters of the soil, which you bought with sweat dripping from your brows. They have sent us to tell you that they stand shoulder to shoulder with you in the fight against removal. All that is needed from the landlords and tenants alike is unity. The tenants will be dumped in an open veld if you co-operate with the government; but by the same token, the landlords will be left with empty houses they cannot maintain if the tenants decide to leave. Many of you today own several properties. Many more have extended their houses. You did all this because of the support of the tenants. You were able to earn your living and to pay your rates. Today some of you are no longer young enough to be able to work. You bought these properties because you knew the phenomenon of ageing is unstoppable. In other words, you made an investment, and signed a guarantee for a happy and secure future. That is why your sons and daughters, the tenants, are standing with you. United we stand; divided we fall.

Robert said that there had been spontaneous clapping of hands throughout the speech, followed by rapturous applause after he sat down. He could hear some landlords asking: 'Whose son is this ? Where does he come from?' One of the landlords, named Mr Lepitse, who spoke after Robert, praised his speech so much that he said: 'This man's name is Makhonatsohle (Cure-all) because he had come with a message which has cured the horror I have had since the government mentioned the removal of Sophiatown. Now we know we have heroes in our midst. Let us die fighting, people of Sophiatown.'

It was after that meeting that Xuma's organisation died a rapid death. The majority of landlords drifted to the ANC campaign. In those days, when I walked the streets during my work, I could hear the people whispering: 'Yes! this is Mrs Resha'. Some old ladies would stop me to give me messages for Robert of how they had struggled to get their properties. Others gave messages of the words Robert should use when he addressed the next meetings, and also to quote their names. This revealed to me the deep shock people were having; it affected the elderly most of all. Mr Lepitse actually called me 'Mrs Makhonatsohle.

Huge crowds attended mass meetings every Sunday at Freedom Square, where local leaders like Peter Ntite, Patrick Molaoa, Joe Matlou, my husband and many others addressed the meetings. ANC leaders from other areas also came to address the meetings. I still remember the day that Nelson Mandela spoke at one of the meetings. He was loudly applauded when, in his speech, he said 'the day is not far off when the forces of progress and the forces of reaction will meet, and the forces of progress will triumph'. Nelson was banned for five years in the same week, after that meeting. But he and Walter Sisulu would unexpectedly arrive at our home on different Sundays, in the early morning, for briefings with Robert. Father Trevor Huddleston would dash to Freedom Square straight from the nearby St Cyprian's church to address the meetings.

The people of Sophiatown were united; they did not co-operate with the Resettlement Board. Even small children knew the slogans 'Africa' and 'Asihambi'. One day I heard a little boy aged about four shouting 'Africa' as two white policemen were passing his home. The police were furious; they shouted back, in Afrikaans: 'Afrika se moer' (Africa's mother).

The Resettlement Board's task of collecting the names of people was a Herculean one, in so much that they took to the tactic of intimidation. The day they came to my home I refused to fill in the form, and told them to come when my husband was at home. The official was so angry that he hit the table with his fist, saying: 'You people don't see that we are helping you'. What! Helping us move against our will?

However, some people did fill in the forms, though the majority gave wrong names and wrong numbers of people in each house. This created enormous problems for the officials. It took about two years (from 1955 to 1957) for the Resettlement Board to complete its unpopular task of collecting names, and still with virtually no co-operation. Many people never filled these forms until they left. The Board told the landlords that, if they did not sell, their properties would be bought for the original sum they paid for it, or would be expropriated. Some landlords, because of this threat, sold their property. Mind you, some landlords did not live in Sophiatown; they were people who bought houses in order to let them. Others were staying in the Protectorates (Bechuanaland, or Basutoland or Swaziland). I know, for instance, that there was a property which belonged to the King of Swaziland, who used to come to Sophiatown for his holidays.

Late in January 1955 the regime announced the day of removal as the 12 February, two weeks away. A big protest meeting was held on Freedom Square. The shock and anger of the people that day was evidenced by cries, at the end of each speech, of 'We want arms to face the Boers'. The crowd was so big that the square was overflowing with people; some were on top of the roofs of houses near the square, others were in trees. The voices which called for arms mostly came from the edges of the meeting. Youth Leaguers and Volunteers usually stood there to control the crowds and also to guard people and to see that they did not lose their tempers in case of provocation by the SB and the police. Mass meetings like these, where the majority of the people were not members of the ANC, needed a watchful eye from the Volunteers against agents provocateurs, whose actions could lead to disaster.

Robert was one of the speakers at that meeting. When he climbed to the platform, the masses shouted '*Asihambi*' (we are not moving). I still remember his words because, even myself, I felt very touched that day. He began by singing '*Sophiatown Likaya Lam-Asihambi!*' to the tune of a well-known Anglican or Methodist hymn. Today the same tune is sung with the words '*Senzeni na*' (What Have We done?).

Then he went on:

'People of Sophiatown. Twelve days from now, our mothers and fathers who worked hard during their youth, and who made Sophiatown what it is today, are going to be robbed of their properties. They are going to be robbed of their title deeds and of the right to own land.

All of us here — man, woman and child — are going to be

57

dumped on a meadow without shelter or roof over our heads [a
reference to the area, Meadowlands, to which people were to be
relocated] — a place where even grass would not grow.

'I want to ask all of you, when you leave here, to go to your
homes, take your calendars, and mark all the dates from today
to the 12 February with red ink. I want you not to forget the 12
February. Because on that day the people of Sophiatown will
give their answer to this government, which is a thief. We say
we are not moving. Asihambi!'

To this speech the assembled masses responded, '*Asihambi.
Ons dak nie*. We are not moving'.

Before we left the meeting, Robert called me and said that
someone had just told him that Oliver Tambo, who was a
banned person and could not come to the Square, was at
some corner, and that he wanted to see him. As we drove
through the streets, after picking up Oliver and Joe Matlou,
he asked Robert how the meeting had gone. Robert told him
about his speech, and about how the people were united.
'War has been declared', Oliver said. I did not say anything,
but, inwardly, I felt that Oliver was right. The cowardly government had declared war on the unarmed people of
Sophiatown. Nevertheless, the worry was always there,
because nobody knew exactly how we were going to be
moved, although we could sense and expect force from such a
government.

On the evening of the 8 February, a young man came running to our house from Toby Street. He told us that black
policemen had been to two or three houses, telling people to
pack up their belongings for removal the next day, the 9
February. This was three days before the date the government had announced for the removal. There again, the government was not only moving people by force, but by stealth
as well. Robert left immediately, after asking me to tell one
chap in our street to contact all the Volunteers according to
the machinery of the M Plan. Within one hour, everyone in
Sophiatown knew that people were to be moved from Toby
Street the next day.

Toby Street was the first street of Sophiatown. It faced,

58

and marked the border with the poor-white suburb of Westdene. Within no time, hundreds of Volunteers, young men as well as women, were assembled in Toby Street to move those people who did not want to go to Meadowlands. People were really intimidated, because they said that the policemen had told them that they would all be arrested if they did not move the next day.

During this time, other leaders were going around the township asking for permission from people who owned empty halls to allow the asihambis to stay the night. It was a difficult task, furniture having to be transported by hand, on heads, in wheel-barrows, and nobody was sure that the police would not suddenly be on the spot.

It was a frightful night. Then, at about 10.30 pm, a terrible thunderstorm broke out. But, thankfully, since Sophiatown (unlike most other places where Africans live) had street lights, people could see where they were going and what they were doing. Some Volunteers removed their jackets and shirts, and went with naked chests in the storm. As I looked out from our bedroom window, I remembered the words of Julius Caesar in Shakespeare, on the morning before his assassination: 'Nor heaven nor earth have been at peace tonight'.

Robert returned in the early hours of the morning. He reported that all the people threatened with removal had been accommodated in halls and in private schools. Because I had had a nap, I got up before my husband did, about 6 am. I then went to the gate to see the effects of the previous night's storm. As I came to the gate, I was horrified. About 200 to 300 black policemen were occupying the corner of Victoria and Bertha Street, and white para-military policemen were patrolling Bertha Street in army trucks, speaking on walkie-talkies. I ran back into the house and told Robert. I was really shaking. Robert just said, 'Don't worry; they are doing their work!' All the black policemen were armed with knobkerries (short clubs with knobbed heads)

By 9.30 am scores of women were already in Toby Street, led by Ida Mtwana, who was from nearby Western Native Township. Ida was sobbing quietly; so were many other women. Later, although I had not seen them arriving, Robert was standing next to Father Huddleston. They both looked very angry. Robert's face looked like the raised head of a puff-adder; I had never before seen him so angry. As for Father Huddleston, his tight-lipped face showed his contempt for the authorities. We were all standing there, helplessly, about twenty to twenty-five yards away from the place where lorries were being loaded. But, time and again, the Special Branch came to Father Huddleston and to Robert, to tell them to 'move on!' They appeared most provocative when they gave these orders. Perhaps they were angry to have found so many places empty of their inhabitants.

After the lorries were gone, we all went back to our homes, leaving Toby Street quiet. But, strange enough, the police did not leave immediately. That attracted more people to come and watch. Police were now concentrated about a stone's throw from our house, while Robert was having some tea with Mr Vundla, a senior ANC member who was from Western Native Township. He was later to join the Moral Rearmament. Then, at about 3 pm a boy came to report that some Youth Leaguers had been arrested in Victoria Street; they had been carrying placards which said, 'Rise up, People of Sophiatown'.

We all followed the boy to the corner of the street. As we were standing there, the Special Branch man, Colonel Spengler, dashed to us and, pulling Robert by the arm, said: 'Resha, I told you that I am going to arrest you!' Someone in the crowd shouted, 'What has Mr Resha done?' He, too, was pulled towards Spengler by a black policeman. Robert, together with the Youth Leaguers, were bundled into a police car and driven to Newlands police station; the man who asked about Robert was left behind. Can anyone understand how the South African police work? Perhaps Spengler realised that there was no possible charge against him. But there was to be no charge against my husband either — he had just arrived there, with his hands in his pockets, yet Spengler tried to have him arrested in terms of the Riotous Assemblies Act. Together with the boys who had carried the placards, Robert slept in the cells that night; they were released the following day, without facing a magistrate. This case of wrongful arrest was later taken up by Nelson Mandela.

Many people were now coming to the house to ask why Robert had been arrested. Father Huddleston also came later to ask what the charge was. The whole thing was so ridiculous; but people were angry when I told them of what had happened.

After the first people were moved, a reign of terror was unleashed on the residents of Sophiatown by the Resettlement Board. The Board distributed leaflets, telling the people to acquire residential permits at their office, in order to remain in Sophiatown. What was strange about these permits was that not a single person was given a permit that entitled them to stay in the township. With the men, it was easy for the Board to get them out. They endorsed all passes with a red stamp, which said 'Out of Sophiatown'. But the men could not go, and leave their families behind. So, every night, scores of policemen, both black and white, invaded the township, asking people to produce their permits. Then, those people who were arrested during these raids, whether men or women, were told that if they were found in Sophiatown again, the whole family would be locked up. This meant that people who were released and had been warned to get out, had to move from the house where they had been arrested before. People were therefore moving up and down the township in order to avoid re-arrest, but that was a tedious and impossible situation for working people, moving household goods from place to place.

The day they raided our house, in 1957 to search for our resident's permit, the police broke the kitchen door. They did this to all residents. There were three of them, two black policeman and one white one, with the rank of Commandant — I did not get to know their names. They got into the childrens' bedroom. We just heard the children screaming, knocking on the walls, calling, 'Mama! Mama!' As we rushed into their bedroom, police torches were flashing all over the house. After Robert had put on the light, the children rushed to us, crying 'Mama, we were sleeping, and the police came in'. We tried to comfort them; they were trembling. Robert was furious. 'How would you like it if your children were to be woken up like this, in the middle of the night. You people are sick!' he said. But, with no apology whatever, the white policeman said, 'Resha, if you leave Sophiatown, these people will move'.

Robert was, at that time, one of the Treason Trialists. Perhaps it was that that saved us from being arrested, because the police left without even asking for the permit. This episode strengthened our assumption that the police had been given instructions not to detain or arrest Treason Trialists who had to appear in court every day; their detention would have disrupted proceedings. The police never arrested any of these people, even when they had no passes on them. Indeed, not one of the trialists carried one during the trial. So, how could they arrest me for a permit, and leave Robert out? Further proof was that even after Robert had been 'endorsed out' of Sophiatown in 1959, and the police came on permit raids next door to our house, they never asked him for his resident's permit.

The ANC Youth League soon learned a trick about how to confuse the police in their search for permits. People were to be warned when the police were coming into the township. A few of the boys would hang around an area near the police station, to watch the police convoy depart. They would then run back into the township, where they would start to bang on the electric poles with stones or other objects. This made a ringing noise which would sound all over the place. When people heard the noise, even if it was two o'clock in the morning, as many people as possible would leave their houses, some in their night-dresses and pyjamas, others wrapped in blankets. They would then start walking up and down the streets. The not-so-old would move to a nearby hill, which overlooked the township, where they would remain until the police had left. In response, the Resettlement Board, seeing the possibility of hide-and-seek with no end, started to demolish all houses that had been vacated.

From 1958 Sophiatown looked like pictures we had seen of some European cities after the last world war. It was in ruins, with the thick walls with beautiful decorations and smooth, shining steps at the entrances, all that remained to show what had been. Some people were actually squatting on pavements with their belongings; others were collecting the bricks after their houses had been demolished. People were by this time drifting to Meadowlands, while others preferred to move to other locations, where they would buy houses on ninety-nine year leases. This could have been perhaps a quarter of the former tenants, with the rest going to a place called Emdeni, which is about twenty-six miles away from the centre of Johannesburg. A few landlords moved to Dube, where they built nice houses, but they, too, were buying on ninety-nine year leases. Even fewer people bought stands in Evaton, where they, too, built houses of their own choice. But, within a few years, Evaton also fell under the axe of 'black spot' regulations, and these people were again removed, still further from the city. The majority of landlords had moved to Diepkloof. Under the Resettlement Board scheme this was the original plan for the landlords, as prepared by the government. All these places form part of what is generally known today as Soweto; it is not an African name, but a government shortening for 'South Western Townships'.

Meanwhile, reports were coming in of the hardships of people in Meadowlands. The women who were Fah-fee runners were coming to Sophiatown daily to continue their work because there was no way of earning a living at Meadowlands. They reported that the houses were so bad that they were not fit for human beings to live in. The walls of these houses were made of unbaked brick, and were unplastered; these were so thin that the rains could pass through them. The houses were moist and cold. Dust came in because there were spaces left open between the walls and the roof (there was no ceiling), which was of asbestos, a health hazard. The houses also had no inside doors, so that there could be no privacy for the family, who had to make curtains for the doors. Unlike the houses in Sophiatown, which had wooden floors, the floors of these houses was of cement. There was no water in these houses. A few people had taps and toilets

63

outside, but others could get water only by going to queue at the tap at the police station. That tap was opened only at certain times of the day for the use of the residents. For those who worked, it was impossible to get water, because the tap was usually closed by the time that they came home. People had to ask for water to wipe their faces or make a cup of tea, from the neighbour next door.

But, above all, the transport costs were much higher, because Meadowlands was 23 miles from the city. Today, Soweto has stretched more than 30 miles from the city, and with low wages for black people, life is still a nightmare. In medical terms, the removal from Sophiatown claimed many lives. Several landlords dropped dead from heart attacks as their houses were demolished. Mr Lethoba was one of the victims; he died of a heart attack in 1958. Others became psychiatric cases. When you met some of them in the streets, you could stand for half an hour or more, as they related how they got the sites and how they built their houses. Others still talked in terms of the government changing its mind. Personally, I don't think I'll ever forget this, because I saw it with my own eyes.

The resistance of the people of Sophiatown against removal marked an unprecedented spirit of solidarity amongst all the inhabitants. Throughout history, and in many countries of the world, it was an unusual phenomenon for property-owners and landlords, on the one hand, and tenants, on the other hand, to fight, shoulder to shoulder, because of the difference of the social status between the groups.

During the campaign against the removal, the impossible happened: *tsotsis* (street fighteres) made a truce between themselves; they started to attend ANC meetings at 'Freedom Square'. The atmosphere in the township changed, and people could walk at night without fear of being robbed or molested. Some newspapers even reported that the police station at Newlands had revealed that crime had dropped dramatically in Sophiatown. The spirit of solidarity amongst the residents was outstanding, because the people fought against the removals as a community and the divisions of social status were buried. The unemployed youth, in particular, were worried about the 'removal', because of a regulation which stipulated that children over sixteen or seventeen, boys and girls, should not be allowed to live with their parents in the new 'locations'; they were to be sent to hostels. This was un-African: our custom has always been for our children to care for their parents when they get old. The whole thing was a trick intended to deprive children of the right to claim houses when their parents died — so much for the security of a family!

To many ordinary people in the street, the removal of Sophiatown evoked the Two Hundred Years Wars, when our forbears fought for their land against the European conquerors. It evoked the 1910 formation of the Union of South Africa between the British and the Boers, which excluded the Africans from taking part in the political life of their country. And, finally, it evoked the 1913 Land Act, which allocated 87% of the best land for the white minority, leaving 13% of the eroded parts for the black majority. Every African in South Africa supported the resistance of the people of Sophiatown, because they knew that it's fate affected all black people everywhere in the rest of the land.

For us, who are former residents of Sophiatown, it is important that we write the story of the township, so that coming generations should not be given distorted history about the resistance of their people. The whole history of South Africa has been so distorted that one cannot be surprised when, in a few years time, the white regime, which is well-known for its deception, will be writing books that Sophiatown was moved because the Africans wanted to move, like they have said that African men like to live in compounds without their families, and that they want to carry passes. We want the younger generations to know of the sacrifices and sufferings of men, women, and children who woke up one morning to find the township looking like a place under siege.

In 1957 the people of Sophiatown also joined the boycott of PUTCO buses, which were being boycotted by the people of Alexandra Township and Pretoria, because of its excessive fares. Owing to the solidarity of these three communities

65

(Sophiatown, Alexandra, Pretoria), they won the battle and the employers had to pay the extra penny that was demanded by the bus company. In other campaigns too, like the strike for a minimum wage of £1 a day, in Sophiatown the strike was solid. In the end, the regime had to send armour-plated Saracen light tanks into the streets of the township to intimidate the people.

The strike had been planned to last for three days, but because of the patchy response in other areas, as well as the concentration of the army and police on Sophiatown that morning, the ANC National Executive Committee called the strike off in the late afternoon. This decision baffled the people. We had thought that other places might pick up on the second or third day, especially when they got reports of success in other areas. Many people were also angry that the calling-off of the strike was being reported on Radio South Africa; people argued that it was one of the regime's misinformation tactics. The result was that the ANC had to send Oliver Tambo, who was at that time the Secretary-General, to the Sophiatown branch to explain the dangers which the National Executive Committee saw if the strike continued.

During all these activities, my husband stayed out until the early hours of the morning, or was sometimes called to emergency meetings at night. But I always used to get up before him to go to the bus rank to see if there were police and if people were boarding the buses. Robert always used to tell me to be careful; the police could arrest me and charge me with picketing. Actually, I continued to picket, although I continued to deny to my husband that I did so. I would walk as far as fifty yards away from the bus rank, and when I saw the police there with red faces, and holding sten guns, my blood would boil, and I would turn back, shouting 'Azikwelwa' (Don't take buses).

During one stay-at-home I met one of the Youth League pickets in a side street. (His nickname was 'Action', because he always shouted 'We want action!'. While in exile, as a member of Umkhonto we Sizwe, he was called 'Bushie'; he died a few years ago in Tanzania.) Just then, a man was hurrying to the bus rank, carrying his tin of sandwiches. 'Hee,

66

ndoda, uyapi?' (Hey, man! where are you going?) he asked. The man replied, *'Emsebenzini'* (to work). 'Haven't you heard that there is no work today?' *'Unyoko'* (your mother!), replied the man. 'All right', said the Youth Leaguer, 'we'll see if you will get a better pay for defying the strike'. The man stood for a while, thinking, then turned back, saying: *'Mfo wetu unyanisile'* (you are right, my brother). Others of course did not turn back. The so-called police protection was a real farce, because when people returned from work, the police were nowhere to be seen.

Police intrusion into the privacy of African homes and harassment is standard practice. On one evening, in 1958 for example, my husband and a few friends, white and black, were having a friendly discussion, as well as a few drinks, at home. The friends left at about 11 pm I then went to collect the glasses and tidy up the sitting-room. As I came out, going towards the kitchen, carrying the glasses and one empty beer bottle on a tray, a white policeman came rushing at me and said that he was arresting me for selling European liquor. He grabbed my arm and pulled me outside the house. He then ordered me, still carrying the tray, to get into the police car. I was really baffled, because when I heard the banging of car doors outside I thought that it was the friends who were leaving. Fortunately, not all of them had gone. Patrick van Rensburg, a former South African Vice-Consul in the Congo (now Zaire), who had resigned his post in 1957 in protest against apartheid, and who was at that time the Organising Secretary of the Liberal Party (he had to flee from the police into Swaziland in 1960, and later started a famous and excellent non-racial school near Serowe in Botswana) who was still there, asked them not to take me, as my husband was coming back soon, but they ignored him. When Robert returned, Patrick, who had waited, explained the episode. Robert thereupon jumped into the car, with me, although it was already in motion. We were driven to the police station.

Newlands police station, where I was finally taken, was about a quarter of a mile from our place, and to the west of it. But the bossy, arrogant young constables drove first towards the city, in the south-east. As the flying squad sped away on a quiet road, Robert and I did not say a word to each other, since I was now a prisoner. Suddenly, an idea came into my mind. I gently removed the corkscrew and the few corks on the tray, and put them in the pockets of the apron I was wearing. Then, about a mile further on, at Brixton, the police stopped and got out, rushing at two African men walking on the pavement. Well, as it was curfew time, we thought that they would be arrested. As soon as the policemen left, Robert took the bottle of beer from the tray, got out and went behind the police car, and put it down on the ground. He immediately came back, sat himself down beside me before the police returned. Meanwhile, I was busily polishing each of the glasses with my apron. By the time we came to the police station, they were sparkling on a spotless silver tray, although I was now smelling strongly of alcohol because my apron had become quite soaked from the cleaning. I followed the policemen into the charge office, still carrying my tray and glasses. However, I was a bit worried that they might find the corkscrew and the corks if they searched me. But they didn't.

The policeman who arrested me said, 'Bring the bottle of malt with you'.

'What bottle of malt?' I asked. He went back to the car, but there was no 'bottle of malt'. The black policeman at the desk wanted to know what the charge was, because he saw only nine empty glasses on a tray. The white policeman repeated that I was illegally selling European liquor. I was then taken to a cell, where I was given neither blanket nor mat, but the policeman told me to wake up some people who were sleeping on the floor and ask them to put me under their blankets. As I did not know these people, I just stood there. It was cold in the cell, so I decided just to fold my arms in my armpits and kneel on the floor. It was a cement floor; the smell in the cell was horrible. At four o'clock in the morning a policeman came to the cell to tell me to get out. Robert had asked Nelson Mandela to intervene, and he had got me out on bail.

On the day the case was to be heard, we waited and waited; the time for the hearing of the case had passed. Nelson finally came out and told us that the prosecution witness had not turned up, and that the case had been dismissed. I reminded Nelson that I wanted my tray and glasses, and he made the police go and seek for it. I particularly did not want to lose my tray and glasses, so I insisted, since I knew that the police usually tended to confiscate exhibits such as containers or anything else they find when they arrest people. You can imagine how I felt about being dragged out of my house in the middle of the night, locked up in a stinking and cold cell, only to be told that there was no case. Nelson, too, was angry, and he kept asking, 'How could anybody be arrested for nine empty glasses?' Well, it was obvious that the policeman who had arrested me was not expecting me to be defended, especially by Nelson Mandela. White policemen feared and detested him because he had messed up many white people during his cross-examinations in the courts. Most of them lost their cases, partly because they could not tolerate being cross-examined by someone they regarded as a 'kaffir lawyer' — a subhuman being to them. Had it not been for the ineptitude of these young Afrikaner policemen, obsessed with the notion that black people are inferior, and whites superior, the case would not have been dismissed so unceremoniously. Many whites, especially those who know our languages, claim that they 'know the native'; as if we do not know them!

5

■

Outside The Drill Hall

Immediately after the successful conclusion of the Congress of the People, which had adopted the Freedom Charter, in 1955 (about which I will write in the next chapter) there were leaks and rumours that the regime was preparing to arrest certain people and charge them with high treason.

When this rumour first circulated amongst people in the movement, a very grim picture was given about the fate of those who would be arrested. Amongst other things, it was said that those who would be charged would not be allowed to engage lawyers to defend them; they would not be allowed bail; and they would be sentenced to death, or to imprisonment for life, on Robben Island prison.

For most of us, in the movement, our expectation was that only a few top leaders would be arrested. But, with the bungling and unpredictability of the South African regime, the actual number charged was 156. Apparently, the regime's intention was to whip up panic and fear amongst the population, as these arrests were carried out across the whole country. In other words, it meant that, in each area, people would be scared because of the arrest of people known to them, and so turn their backs on the struggle. But, on the contrary, the arrests had an opposite effect on the masses. Overnight, the Treason Trialists became the heroes of the people. The masses rallied their support behind their leaders, whom they regarded as champions of their struggle for liberation.

It was at about 6 o'clock on the morning of 5 December 1956 that there was a knock on the door. When we opened it, there stood four or five white members of the Special Branch, who said that they had a warrant to search the premises, and a further warrant for the arrest of my husband on a charge of high treason.

We were still in our nightclothes. While my husband read the warrant, the policemen searched the house. My husband started to dress, then waited for the search to be finished. I think it took something like two-and-a-half to three hours. The police scrutinised every paper and book around the house, put them all in a hessian sack that was full to the top. One book which they took was a copy of *The Pilgrim's Progress* in a Sesotho translation. In it was a picture of Father Huddleston, carrying an African child in his arms. I had put the picture in the book some time back, when I had been reading it. The police also took away ANC pamphlets, bulletins, documents of meetings and conferences, and all copies of liberation newspapers like *The Guardian*. They rummaged through wardrobes, the dressing table, the sideboard; you could think they were looking for a murder weapon or a blue-print document advocating a coup d'etat. One policeman climbed on top of a chair in the kitchen and found a few books on the very top shelves. These he hurled down on the floor of the sitting room, baaha! in front of another SB man, who checked them through and passed them to a third, who put the names down on his list.

One of the books was *The History of the Communist Party of the Soviet Union*. I was the last to read this book, and I thought that I had hidden it safely, particularly since Robert had warned me to be careful since it was a banned book. To say the least, my stomach rumbled from fright, when the policeman threw the book down on the floor. I could not look my husband in the face when it was found. But, at the same time, where else could I have kept it? These people combed the house with the finest comb and touched everything that was paper. Still, for them to take the *Pilgrim's Progress* was astonishing — perhaps the book became treasonable because of the bookmark in it, which was of Father Huddleston holding a black child; perhaps to them that was treason as well!

The place was, by now, in a mess. The pockets of each of my husband's suits in the wardrobes were turned inside-out. Robert, who had in the meantime got dressed, and I, in my morning gown, sat on the edge of the bed, while the children and my sister sat on the couch. There was not a word from anyone, except for the rustle made by the turning over of pages. What a morning it was to be woken up in this manner and left in a house looking like it had been struck by a cyclone! Finally, they searched Robert personally, going through all his pockets. Then, after he had sponged himself over, they took him away with them. At the door he just said, 'See you, darling!'

When I came back from the toilet, to which we all rushed, in turn, after the virtual imprisonment, I phoned Helen Joseph to break the news. 'Maggie, I am also under arrest, and the police are searching my house!' she said. I had phoned her first because she, together with Lilian, were among my oldest colleagues; we had worked together from the foundation of the Federation of South African Women in 1954, and particularly during the campaigns during the turbulent years of the Fifties, when the women were in the forefront of the struggle. She is a woman of wonderful wit, but besides that, she has something very unique about her — her modesty. To work with her is a great pleasure, because you feel equals in every respect, which is surprising considering her background — born in England, teacher in India, officer in the South African Air Force during the Second World War, then from involvement as secretary of the Medical Aid Fund of the Garment Workers Union, to a life of distinguished radical politics, which led to her being put under house arrest in 1962, and to being one of the star accused in the Treason Trial.

Helen is extraordinary in the manner in which she gets

thorough enjoyment from her work, and what is noteworthy about her is that she never loses her smile even under the most difficult conditions.

She can also be persuasive, and once she has made a decision, she tries and tries until she has turned mountains to get her way. An example of that tenacity was when she persuaded the police to remove roadblocks during a demonstration outside the Baragwanath Hospital during the campaign against passes for nurses. But, when there is success, Helen is not a person who wants to be piled with praises or take credit and glory for it. Many years later, when she was one of the few to whom I whispered that I would be leaving the country, she was happy for me. She told me 'go and represent the women and tell the world about the plight of the African women and of their heroic struggle'. We have remained in close contact since that time, even if some of the letters we have written to each other have not reached their destinations. But we have nothing to hide.

I now realised that the anticipated day had come. My fears were confirmed when, about half an hour after my talk with Helen Joseph, Mrs Ethel Ntite, a militant member of the Sophiatown branch, who lived in Toby Street, walked in to say that her husband, Peter (elected Secretary-General of the ANC Youth League at Durban in 1958) had also been arrested. An hour after that, Mrs Beauty Makhoti, another militant member of the Women's League, came to report that her husband, Henry, a former President of the Youth League — he had taken over from my husband — had also been taken. The three of us were shaken; our first reaction really seemed to want to know who else had been arrested. But Mrs Ntite (who sadly passed away in 1958) was a bit brave. She told us that, when her husband went out, she had said 'Darling, I am proud of you!'.

As we slowly recovered from our shock, we decided to go to the homes of other ANC leaders to find out who else had been arrested. Some of the homes to which we went were those of Simon Tyiki, who was chairman of the Sophiatown branch of the ANC; of Joe Matlou; and of Patrick Molaoa, National President of the ANC Youth League from 1958.

Their wives confirmed that each of them had been taken.

The day became gloomy. We could neither eat, nor do any work. We did not know where our husbands had been taken. And, with what had been previously rumoured about no bail for people accused of treason, we held out no hopes of seeing them in the near future. It was only when the late editions of the newspapers came out that we began to realise how many people had been arrested all over the country that morning, and that more and more people were being flown to Johannesburg by helicopters and military planes.

For the next two nights, Mrs Makhoti slept at my house. She said that she felt better in company, because she lived in Bernard Street, which was on the other side of Sophiatown, beyond Freedom Square. Later, we went to the ANC branch office, where we were soon joined by Mrs Mokhofe, a teacher whose husband, a trade-unionist, had also been arrested. By the look of it, it seemed that the police swoop had come at the same time in all the homes of the arrested. Towards mid-day there came news from Western Native Township that Ida Mtwana and Mr Moretsele, ANC President in the Transvaal, had also been taken.

It was only after about the third day that we were advised by ANC officials that all the 156 arrested people were being held in the Johannesburg Fort prison. I don't remember after how many days it was, but at last we were told that visitors would be allowed to see those arrested. They were also allowed to have a change of clothes. So, several of us rushed to the shops to buy corduroy shirts and trousers for our relatives, since, it was said, corduroy clothes were the best for prison conditions.

The accused stayed at the Fort for sixteen days before bail was granted. During those two weeks, scores upon scores of relatives and sympathisers gathered outside the prison to see them. The place was like a madhouse; each visitor had to shout the name of the person he or she wanted to see, and the police or other inmates would go in to call them. When the accused came out, they were made to stand about twelve yards away, separated by mesh wire, from their visitors. They then had to conduct their talk with their visitors

74

against the deafening noise of the shouting by both visitors and accused; it was a real circus. But still, it was a relief to see them.

Mrs Matlou's baby was very small at that time, so she could not go to the Fort. I asked her about her husband's size of clothes, and bought him a pair of corduroy trousers and a shirt at the same time that I bought the same for Robert. Although Mrs Matlou was very sad that she could not go to see her husband.

At the Fort I first called for my husband, and after I had spoken to him, called for Joe, gave him apologies and greetings from Violet. The parcels that we brought were passed on to them by policemen, who stood in a passage between the two wire mesh walls. It was really difficult to talk to each other because of the noise. However, I managed to tell Robert about the mood of the people and their reaction to the arrests. For instance, the Sunday after their arrests there was a huge meeting at Freedom Square, which was addressed by the ANC veteran, Mr Ngakane, who lived in Soweto. In his speech, he made a passionate appeal to the people to keep calm, and also not to prejudice the case of those arrested. I told Robert that, from what we had seen, people were very angry, but very proud of them. In the streets, on the trains and buses, people talked of nothing else but of the leaders arrested for high treason.

For the first day of their appearance before a magistrate at the Drill Hall they were transported to the court in prison vans. The Drill Hall, we had heard, had been used for Army drilling, but because of the large number of people appearing, it was changed into a court room. However, things were not properly organised, and only a handful of people could go in. So most of us that day saw only the waving of hands from the prison van windows; we did not come near the accused.

Outside the Drill Hall, on the first day, there were hundreds and hundreds of people, some from places very far away from Johannesburg. In the crowd there were people like Dr Moroka, the former President of the ANC, who had come, with many others, from the Orange Free State. There were people from all the other provinces, and from remote parts of the country, which gave many of us the chance to gauge the mood of the people and the support they gave to the accused. What I saw outside the Drill Hall that day was one of those happenings which becomes engraved on one's memory for ever.

What I saw was not a matter of ANC members having come to attend the hearing of a charge of high treason against its leaders, but that of the African nation come to give their full support to their heroes. People from all racial groups stood outside the court for the whole day, without food, until four o'clock, when the court adjourned. The atmosphere was one of sadness and of anger, particularly because of the non-admittance of the public into the courtroom. Although many people knew that the accused were now represented by lawyers, the idea of 156 people being hanged was in the minds of many people. One could hear, for instance, from a distance, someone making a passionate prayer. He called upon the names of Moshoeshoe, on Chaka, on Hintsa, on Sekhukhuni, and on Makhanda

There were emotional scenes; people were worried about the fate of their leaders. What surprised me most was the presence of several male and female *dingaka*, referred to as 'witchdoctors' by Europeans.

To Africans, these *dingaka* could best be referred to as soothsayers, or psychics. Many of these people are genuine diviners, who get their power of divining from their dead ancestors, who may visit them in dreams or by means of omens; even the herbs and medicines they use for healing people are revealed to them in their dreams. These practices have nothing to do with European witchcraft; *dingaka* have been part of African society for as long as the African people have existed, and they are trusted in healing many diseases. In the olden days they were reliable in forecasting the weather, especially impending hailstorms. They are said to have had medicines to break these storms, thus saving crops in the fields when these were at a delicate stage of growth. They could also protect people and houses from being struck by lightning. Some could cure the dreaded syphilis brought from Europe. However, many Africans are skeptical about *dingaka* these days, because, as in all professions, charlatans have invaded these roles. It is like in religion, where the apostles themselves warned against false prophets. Nowadays, the invasion of the *dingaka* profession by charlatans is economic, pure and simple, hence the mistrust of people in them. But, even with these charlatans, the *dingaka* do not necessarily become witches. In Europe, in the past, we hear there were witches, but they were not referred to as witchdoctors. *Dingaka*, who are really genuine, should not be lumped together with witches. In African societies we also have people referred to as witches. They are said to go about naked at night riding on a broom. They are called *umtakati-moloi* (ostracised from society). No one wants her or his child to be married to a witch's child.

Now, my point about the *dingaka* is, why should they have been there, at this political trial, supporting the leaders. Outside the Drill Hall, that morning, even those people who thought little of them, could not pass by without gazing at them in some bewilderment. Some were dressed in animal headgear, with tinkling bangles around their arms and legs; others were waving white goat-tail fans in the air, and sprinkling small drops of medicinal waters on the crowd. And everyone of them had an expression of anger and defiance, in support of the arrested men and women, on their faces. Yet they were not paid to come, or for what they did; their presence in front of the Drill Hall was a sign of the extent to which all sectors of the people had become involved in the freedom struggle, especially after the Congress of the People.

Dingaka are ordinary men and women — Africans who suffer in the same way as any other black person does under apartheid. But, although they do not take part in politics, they also want to be free. The widespread coverage of the treason arrests was such that it could not have been possible for them not to know about it, at least, as individuals. I do not, in the least, think that they came as an organised group, although I know that they have an association which is registered. I think I am right in saying that the regime miscalculated by making these mass arrests, because what it considered as treason was heroism to the masses. For *din-*

77

gaka to offer their services uninvited was unprecedented. The ANC had held big gatherings, like the Congress of the People, but there had never before been such a show of solidarity from that particular group. That is why everybody was so amazed at their decision to be seen not to be standing idly by when the leaders of the people were in danger.

Prayer sustained me during the four and a half years during which my husband was on trial. Then, when the trial collapsed with the acquital of all the accused, in 1961, my memories switched back to that first day. I recall, for instance, that another group that attracted the attention of the masses outside the Drill Hall that day were members of the Zionist Church of Lekhanyane. The late Edward Lekhanyane was a very influential man. When he used to travel from Pretoria to Johannesburg, it was in a convoy of Cadillacs, with an escort of speed cops (provincial traffic policemen) clearing the way for him. He was said to have been one of the richest religious leaders in the country.

The Lekhanyane group were distinctive in their green and silver badges on the lapels of their coats, and by the green skirts and yellow blouses worn by the women. Since I had never seen the Zionists pray before that day, I found it very interesting. During their prayers, which was said in words which I could not decipher, they gesticulated with their hands, and finally dropped to the ground in something like a fit or a trance. It is, they say, during this period that they are filled with the spirit of God. Their church is very big in the Transvaal, but since I had never seen them at ANC meetings before, this was another sign of the scale and breadth of the involvement of all groups.

On day two of the trial the crowds were even bigger. Volunteers lined the streets outside the Drill Hall, displaying huge placards, which read: 'We Stand By Our Leaders'. As on the previous day, the crowds were very orderly and well-behaved. Still, the trigger-happy police started to shoot into them. Though, fortunately, no-one was killed, several people were injured. Several arrests were made, including some of the ANC activists holding the placards. Once again it was largely provocation by the police. No charges were laid against those arrested; they were kept in the cells overnight, and returned to their homes the next day.

That second day nearly ended in catastrophe, but for the bravery of the Anglican Bishop of Johannesburg, Bishop Reeves. He had been standing, with another priest, near us at the corner where Colonel Pienaar had said all those who had parcels of clothes for the accused should wait until they were called in. I think there were about twelve to fifteen of us there. Suddenly we heard shots; the police (just like at Sharpeville later on) had panicked, probably by the sheer size of the crowd, and had opened fire. The Bishop rushed to Colonel Pienaar, shouting 'Stop the shooting!', which order was given, but it was followed by indiscriminate arrests of bystanders. One of those arrested was my sister, who comes third after me; she had been staying with us since 1955; she, too, had taken up nursing; she died in 1989.

We were allowed in at an interval or recess. We all rushed in, rashly thinking that, at last, we would be allowed to shake hands with the accused, especially after the madness of the Fort. But the shock of seeing them placed inside a cage was so much that the excitement I had simply evaporated as quickly as it had come. 'Hmm! *Amabulu*' (the Boers!), one of the visitors remarked loudly, at the door, '*Intoni le*?' (What is this?). As we moved forward to the cage, I said to myself 'these people are not going to live!'. I had seen animals caged in the zoo, but to see human beings caged is quite another thing. My heart was so heavy that I felt like dropping down dead. I don't remember looking around the building to see the arrangements of the court, only that the accused were seated on benches in the centre of the cage, and facing east, towards the magistrate's chair.

While we waited, those of the accused whose relatives had come, stood up and came to the edge of the cage to talk. Unable to shake hands, most of us resorted to passing kisses by pressing our lips on the cage. The whole thing was so frustrating, because human lips are not shaped like beaks, and the mesh wire would allow only the width of one finger to pass through. The Makhoti family were standing not far away from us, and I heard Beauty Makhoti say 'Oh!, Sis

79

Maggie, I did not know that people could be caged as if they got leprosy!' Everyone, visitors as well as accused, were obviously angry. Indeed, not even during the Nuremburg Trials of Nazi mass murderers were accused treated in that manner.

The court attendant came round to us and took the parcels we were carrying to hand these to the accused. Anyway, during that short period I told Robert about what had been happening outside the court during these days. He told me that the lawyers were battling for bail, and for the removal of the cage. Although I was not certain if these battles would be successful, the information did pump some adrenalin into my system. But we could not stay long in the court, because there were no arrangements made for the public. So we were marched out as soon as the case was resumed. Later on, arrangements were made, and benches were placed against the wall behind the accused, and the public started to come to the hearings. Throughout the length of the hearing, there were always members of the public who were present.

Bail was granted after the second week of the hearing, which was to go on, in the Drill Hall, for another year. The problem was that most of us could not go to the court every day, since we had now become the bread-winners. Still, the day the accused were bailed, there was great joy and relief from all the relatives. Since some were far away from their families, the ANC had asked the Women's League to get Volunteer families to accommodate people who came from other areas. Many families were happy to do that. Indeed, many families who were not members of the ANC, volunteered to keep at least one trialist at their homes.

I had also offered to take one Treason Trialist. Of course, they all got food vouchers from the Treason Trial Fund, which had been set up. But, in the end, because the case lasted four and a half years, there were more Treason Trialists spending their weekends and eating at our place than the one I had agreed to accommodate. In Sophiatown, I organised two or three private doctors, who agreed to attend to the medical needs of the accused, free of charge. That was a great service to the accused, as well as to their families. The Treason Trial Fund also organised distribution of second-hand clothes for the accused and for their families. Much of that came from overseas. This, too, was highly appreciated by many families, especially in those cases where there were children of school-going age.

The name of the Treason Trialist who stayed with us was Lungile Kepe, from Port Elizabeth. He was unmarried, in his mid-twenties, and thus one of the youngest of those on trial. Lungile was a lively young man. Before his arrest, he had won the championship in jive dancing in the Eastern Cape. After his acquittal, he was arrested again in the mid-Sixties for alleged underground activities of the ANC, for which he served a long prison sentence on Robben Island; he died a short time after his release, in the Seventies.

Mrs Kopo, our next-door neighbour, invited Vuyisili Mini to stay at her place. Mini was a renowned singer and composer of music. It was he who composed one of the most famous of our freedom songs, *'Nantsi' ndod' emnyama Verwoerd, Basopa'* (Verwoerd, be careful! There's a Black Man!). Mini, together with Kayinga and Mkaba, were hanged in the early Sixties for ANC underground activities. He left a wife and three children. These three heroes were reported to have gone to the gallows, singing freedom songs.

Milner Ntsangane also stayed in Sophiatown. He was one of the accused who gave evidence from the witness-box (not all accused did so, but that may have been by arrangement between the prosecution and defence lawyers) in Pretoria. When asked by the prosecutor what his occupation was, he replied, 'Butcher-boy'. He was a highly intelligent person, with a great sense of humour, hence his telling the judges that he was a butcher-boy, instead of saying that he worked at a butcher's. But, his argument was, that was how his boss addressed him. Milner, too, later served a long prison sentence on Robben Island; we heard that the dust from the breaking of stones with a hammer damaged his eyes. He died a few years ago in the late Eighties.

Dr Conco, another of the accused, also stayed in Sophiatown, with relatives. He managed to open a practice there, and treated his patients when he came back from Pretoria in the evenings, and during the weekends. Yet another accused,

Dr Letele, Treasurer-General of the ANC, who was from Kimberley, did the same in Soweto. Some accused stayed in Soweto, but most of these came back to Sophiatown at weekends to be together; they usually ended up at our place to play cards.

Sometimes they really amused us, because they reenacted the proceedings of the hearings. There was a moment when the prosecution produced a man from prison, called Solomon Mgubasi, to give evidence against the accused. This Mgubasi was serving a long prison sentence for criminal offences. The defence lawyers publicly called him a first-class crook and liar. He claimed that he was a BA, BSc and LLB, yet he had gone to school at Cradock only as far as Standard Three. He claimed that he was one of those who had drafted the Freedom Charter, together with Professor Matthews, but he could not identify the professor. Kepe told me that there was absolute consternation in court among the accused. During his evidence, Mgubasi was to identify Robert. As he walked towards Robert, Robert looked at him with such disdain that Mgubasi began to tremble. The prosecutor, having noticed the tense atmosphere, asked the witness if anybody said anything to him, to which the man replied, 'No, Your Worship!'

Mgubasi told the court that Dr Letele and Walter Sisulu had told him that they were preparing a 'Chesa-Chesa' (burn-burn) army to burn down white farms. In order for us to understand what happened in court, one of those present acted the part of Vernon Berrange, one of the defence lawyers, and another one took the part of Solomon Mgubasi. From this re-enactment I could capture clearly how Advocate Berrange demolished Mgubasi's evidence. I really cannot understand why the regime brought a well-known criminal from jail to come and give evidence for the state. Perhaps Mgubasi was promised that his sentence would be reduced if the 156 were convicted. Although his evidence was crushed, one can not stop asking about the regime's moral principles. Of course, birds of the same feather flock together. There were many other witnesses, including that of the Special Branch, whose evidence was a disgrace. But the case went on and on for four and a half years, until it finally collapsed, like a pack of cards, in 1961.

Several accused depended upon their working relatives to keep their homes going. Their difficulties were increasing by the day. Very few of the accused were able to continue with their jobs at odd hours in order to pay their debts. The hire purchase system is very popular in South Africa. It is used very widely by Africans because, with low wages that is the only way to acquire possessions. Many accused found their furniture repossessed because of the hardships caused by the Treason Trial. And even, at the end of it all, when they were acquitted, many found that they did not get their jobs back. The Special Branch had a sinister method of going secretly to the employers, warning them that they should be careful of giving jobs to trouble-makers and to communists. And many employers were scared of taking on anyone who had been charged with high treason.

My husband was one of those who managed to keep his job as a part-time reporter. And my practice as a private mid-wife was doing well until the late fifties, when the destruction of Sophiatown was completed. So, when we were finally forced to leave Sophiatown, we, too, were forced to apply for help from the Treason Trial Fund.

This Fund was started by Canon John Collins of St Paul's Cathedral, who operated Christian Action in England. The formation of the Fund was announced a few days after the arrests, and it became very popular right from the start, with donations pouring in from many countries and individuals. I recall that it was mentioned in the press that Seretse Khama, later to be President of Botswana, had sent a donation of £200. Bishop Reeves formed a Fund committee in Johannesburg, which included some of the trialists. Monies collected were used for bailing out the accused, for payment of defence lawyers, and for help with living expenses. The formation of the Fund was one of the greatest slaps in the face for the regime, and an enormous morale booster for the accused. At the office of the Fund, accused were given vouchers for their food supplies, as well as a small amount towards the payment of rent. The food vouchers could be used only at a Chinese grocery shop in the centre of Johannesburg, called Yenson. Later, second-hand clothes were issued according to the needs of the accused and their families. During long adjournments of the court, train tickets were bought for those who were from other provinces, so that they could visit their families.

At the conclusion of the Preparatory Examination, ninety-one people were committed for trial, the charges being withdrawn against sixty-five. Among those released were Chief Luthuli, Oliver Tambo, Rev. Calata (former Secretary-General of the ANC, from Cradock) and the Rev. Gawe, an ANC veteran from Queenstown, who had been one of Robert's teachers at primary school. Some of those discharged, who could not get their jobs back, continued to get help from the Fund.

Later, the defence were successful in having the entire indictment withdrawn. But that was only temporary, since the regime soon thereafter produced a new indictment on the single charge of High Treason, levelled against thirty. The Crown's case was a shambles from beginning to end. In fact, because of the regime's bungling, the liberation movement got advantage from disadvantage. Some of the ANC leaders had been banned and restricted to their areas of residence for years. But when they were arrested and put together, it was an opportunity handed to them on a plate. No more were decisions of the NEC delayed by being sent from province to province. Because the entire NEC had been arrested, they were in direct contact with each other. It also meant that they got to know each other better. It was out of these meetings of the NEC that the National Action Committee, composed of some members of the ANC NEC, together with some co-opted members of the Transvaal ANC, was formed. Nelson Mandela, Oliver Tambo, Walter Sisulu, Moses Kotane, and my husband were some of the members of this National Action Committee.

Another advantage of this situation was that leaders, militants and activists from other provinces were able to share their techniques of organising with their Transvaal comrades. The comrades from the Eastern Cape, where the ANC was strongest, had a lot to teach us, because they had mas-

84

tered the M Plan long before the Transvaal had done. I remember Kepe and others telling us how they were able to call meetings under the noses of the SB, whom they confused by saying: 'Tonight we are meeting — Kwandawo'. There is no precise English translation for that, but indawo means 'place', so, properly speaking, kwandawo should mean 'at Ndawo's place'. The SB, they said, became so confused that they combed the Eastern Cape locations, asking people if they knew anybody called Mr Ndawo.

The Treason Trial put the ANC on the map. The trial became another rallying point, just as the historic Congress of the People at Kliptown, where the Freedom Charter was adopted in 1955, had done. Never had the leaders of the ANC been so much talked about by ordinary people in the streets. The newspaper industry also gained a great deal, because many people who had not read newspapers before that, now bought them daily in order to follow the court proceedings. I recall the day the press reported the death of Pirow, the former Cabinet Minister, who was the Chief Prosecutor at the trial. The bush telephone in the townships said that he had collapsed in court, while cross-examining one of the Treason Trialists; yet he had died at his home. It was a way in which the masses wanted to display their absolute solidarity with the accused. In churches, like in the Anglican Church, prayers were regularly said for the accused. My daughter came home from church one day, very excited, telling us that the priest had made prayers for the release of the trialists.

Although the money from the Treason Trial Defence Fund was small, it kept the wolf away from the door. One of my brothers was still at college in Natal, and we had to help to see him through that. I also received a small donation from the Journalists' Association because of Robert being a journalist. But there were those who never recovered financially from that long trial, because the regime continued to haunt them for one thing or another. Lilian Ngoyi, for instance, lived in poverty, until she died in 1981. Ida Mtwana and Florence Matomela, two of the pioneers of the Women's League, died just after the trial ended. Frances Baard, the distinguished trade unionist and leader of the Women's League in the Eastern Cape, was banished to a remote place in the Transvaal. Other people had to go to neighbouring countries to get started again, because their responsibilities to their families were so great that these could not be carried on under the continuous harassment by the regime. But, on the whole, I think everybody coped well, especially as we began to realise that the Crown case was becoming weaker and weaker. Of course, one could never know, but the horror that everybody had during those first days, had subsided. The day they were committed for trial was one of great anxiety for many, because we knew that the regime was being serious. The defence team became very popular; many children born during those years were named after Maisels, Berrange and Bram Fischer, who were at the head of the defence team.

Having said that, I do not want to give the impression that these people, whose lives changed for the worse after the trial, the detentions and banishment, should have lived in comfort. What I am saying is that joining the struggle is a great sacrifice, and that these men and women, who pioneered our struggle that all black South Africans should live and not just survive, should not be forgotten. That their pioneering was an heroic effort can be shown by looking at the relations, at that time, between the ANC and some of the other organisations, and it is to that story that I now turn.

6

■

Alliances and Discords

The ANC is one of the oldest liberation movements in Africa; it was founded in 1912, when the whole of the continent was still held in the colonial cocoon of bondage by several Western countries. Many younger liberation movements, which were formed long after the foundation of the ANC, in different parts of Africa, have waged struggles — sometimes bloody ones — which have liberated their countries to nationhood.

The ANC was the inspiration for the formation of several of these liberation movements. There were Congresses in Lesotho (then Basutoland); in Zimbabwe (then Southern Rhodesia); in Zambia (formerly Northern Rhodesia) and in Malawi (formerly Nyasaland) as well as in Tanganyika: all these adopted, as well, the tune of the ANC National Anthem, 'Nkosi Sikilel' iAfrika'.

In Europe and America the ANC was also known, but was not taken seriously at that time. The leaders of the ANC of the time had sent deputations to London and to Versailles both before and after Britain had given independence to the white settlers in 1910; but they had come back empty-handed each time. Britain, under a Liberal Party government,

87

was guided by self-interest and a continuous flow of wealth as well as by allegiance to the Crown by the white settler regime. At that time, the black majority in South Africa had harboured high hopes that the Western countries, which prided themselves so often about their democracy, would remedy the anomalous situation in our country, but alas! no the British and the Boers came to an agreement — no change in the status quo; there would be no power sharing with the black majority. Even as late as after the end of the Second World War, the then President, Dr Xuma, had gone to the United Nations to present the case of the African people; he was snubbed, and once again, a leader had to come back empty-handed.

White minority regimes have been violently opposed to the ANC right from its foundation. Until recently it was labelled a 'terrorist' organisation, yet for over fifty years it had gone out of its way to wage a non-violent and constitutional struggle. Still the regime must have known that, even if it had finally closed all channels for peaceful means of struggle, it would not be able to destroy the will of the oppressed to fight for freedom. It must have known that, by outlawing the ANC, it would drive it underground. And that is exactly where it went, until very recently when it was forced to unban it. There can be no doubt that it speaks on behalf of the majority of the oppressed.

Apart from being opposed by the regime, the ANC has had, at one time or another, its own internal squabbles. These ranged from petty political rivalries within itself, to breakaways. But it has managed to soldier on, never allowing its flag to lie on the ground — the ANC is referred to as 'the shield and spear of the oppressed', and that is not just a slogan.

From the mid-Fifties (that is, from after the Congress of the People, which adopted the Freedom Charter) the word 'Africanist' started to catch the ear of the ANC membership. 'Who are these Africanists?' the members asked. Nobody knew exactly who they were, but for some time, actions of some ANC members at meetings and conferences showed that there were some malcontents. These people kept up a

88

systematic attacks against the ANC leadership, whom they accused of having abandoned the 1949 Programme of Action.

In Soweto, people like Peter Raboroko, Peter Molotsi, Rosette Ndziba, Potlako Leballo and Mlomzi kept the branch on its toes with arguments around interpretations of the 1949 Programme. These debates often lasted into the early hours of the morning. At conferences, they were joined by people like Joe Molefe from Evaton, Dr Peter Tsele from Pretoria, and Nana Mahomo, as well as a few others. It was increasingly becoming clear that these comrades were going over the top.

During 1957 and 1958, Josiahs Madzunya made frequent visits to the Sophiatown branch office. He would hang around there for the whole day, discussing with Todd Siwisa, the treasurer of the branch, and other people. Later, Dr Tsele would also be a frequent visitor — all the way from Pretoria. When asked about the reasons for these visits, Siwisa would say 'No! this chap passed here after seeing a friend near here.' Later on we found out that this was the time they were recruiting people to join the Africanists. Oh, it was terrible! The membership could not stand it any longer, because definitely many members felt that there was something going on from these visits.

It was from that time on that we heard the term 'Charterist'. That, too, puzzled us for a while. We soon discovered the term was used by the 'Africanists' against all those who did not agree with them in denouncing the ANC leadership and the Freedom Charter, which, they said, was from Moscow — which was exactly what the white regime said!

It was at this same time too that the rumours were rife that the regime was planning to make arrests connected with the Congress of the People and the Freedom Charter. That caused much pain to ANC members, because it should not be forgotten that these self-same 'Africanists' had played their part in the organising of the COP and in the adoption of the Charter. Many people suspected that the rumour of arrests for 'treason' might have been responsible for the turn-about of some of the 'Africanists'. There was now so much animosity between former comrades that many were not on speaking terms with some of these 'Africanists', particularly when some of them resorted to abusive language and insults instead of cool political debate on differences.

The ANC, however, closed ranks, and became stronger because of the attacks and threats from the regime; the propaganda of the 'Africanists' attracted only a very negligible number of people.

Preparations for the Congress of the People had started in 1954, two years after the end of the Defiance Campaign. When the Defiance Campaign was called off, after the passing of the Criminal Law Amendment Act and the Public Safety Act of 1953 (the former laid down quite severe penalties, including lashes, for the breaking of any law as part of political protest; the latter made it possible for rule by decree in an emergency) some 8,000 people had been arrested for defiance and breaking of apartheid laws. Although the regime had banned several top leaders, the liberation organisations decided to call for a Congress of the People to draw up a Charter that would reflect the wishes of all the people on how the country should be governed, because, as far as the people were concerned, there could be no turning back until all South Africans had an equal say in the laws that governed them, and the Freedom Charter was one hope for a new South Africa. The idea for a Freedom Charter was the brainchild of Professor Z.K. Matthews. Since he was not a communist, the accusation by the government, as well as the PAC, that the Charter is a communist document is inaccurate.

The structures created to organise for the Congress of the People were elaborate, with members of the Congress Alliance embarking on a mass mobilisation of the people in all spheres of life. At the summit was an ad hoc National Action Committee of the ANC, which liaised with a sub-committee with representatives of the Congress Alliance. Below that were the Provincial and Branch Committees. These, in their turn, created numerous sub-committees for real spadework among the masses. Volunteers visited people in their homes, at their places of work, in their churches, youth and sports clubs, womens organisations, factories, etc. All political parties, including the ruling Nationalists, were invited to participate, but not only did all of them decline, they attacked and showed great hostility to the very idea of a Congress of the People. The oppressed masses, for their part, received the news of the COP and of the Freedom Charter as a milestone; there was so much excitement and determination to participate that many people who could not be included in their branch delegations because of limited numbers, decided to go to the venue anyway, and watch from outside the sports ground where the COP took place in Kliptown.

Judging by the demands collected from the many local and regional meetings, the preparations for the COP had raised the expectations of the oppressed to levels never before experienced; offices were piled with pieces of paper, which finally reached the apex — the Alliance sub-committee, which, after careful study of these demands of the people, drew up a draft Charter to be presented for discussion and adoption by the delegates at the conference on 25-26 June 1955.

There were other committees chosen. One was for housing the delegates from other provinces. Many were housed in Kliptown location, where the local people felt honoured to do this job. The sports field had low stools for the people to sit on — a bit uncomfortable, but great things have been born in unknown and insignificant places. To the oppressed people, Kliptown is our Bethlehem, because the Freedom Charter is the gift of hope for peace, harmony and justice for all South Africans.

The morning on the 25 June, when the delegates filed on to the sports field, was one of unimaginable pageantry. Each delegation hoisted an ANC flag and a huge placard showing the name of the place from where it came. Other people carried smaller placards, with slogans such as: 'Houses For All'; 'Votes for All'; 'Education Not Indoctrination'; 'Peace and Friendship'; 'Down With Pass Laws'; 'Jobs For All'. The wave upon wave of people entering the sports field resembled Olympic teams filing into the arena. Since each delegation walked in singing a freedom song, the place was soon filled with a humming sound — as if there were thousands of beehives in the area. Each delegation, on arrival, was ushered by a Volunteer into an unoccupied area, so that, by about eleven o'clock, the 3,000-odd delegates were all seated.

The platform which had been prepared for speakers was about fifteen to eighteen feet high; it had a huge spoked wheel, representing the Congress Alliance. The meeting started with a prayer, followed by the reading of messages of support and solidarity. After that came one of the high points: the ANC gave awards to three personalities for their contribution and steadfastness in the fight against apartheid. The awards were to Chief Luthuli, to Father Huddleston, and to Dr Dadoo. The award is called Isitwalandwe; it is the highest award for bravery within African custom. Unfortunately, because of their banning orders, neither Chief Luthuli nor Dr Dadoo could be present, and their awards were accepted on their behalf by, respectively, Chief's daughter and Dr Dadoo's mother.

On the second day, ten different speakers, each in turn, introduced the ten articles of the Charter, and spoke about these. Each speaker was applauded vociferously by the crowd, both inside and outside the fence. One after the other, each of the Articles of the Charter were adopted. Then, at about 4.00 or 4.30 pm, when the indomitable Helen Joseph was reading the Ninth article: There Shall be Houses, Security and Comfort, and the crowds were cheering, the SB walked in with stern and flushed faces, accompanied by police with sten-guns. The crowd remained seated, but there can be no doubt that it was surprised by this invasion. Handing a search warrant to the chairman, the SB said that they were investigating 'High Treason'. They then proceeded to carry out a thorough search of officials on the platform, at the same time confiscating many documents. But, even while they searched, speaker after speaker carried on addressing the people on the Charter. The mood, at the time, was one of defiance and anger. Although the Nationalist Party and other white political parties had been invited, they had made it clear that they did not want to come. Furthermore, there was no secrecy. The Congress of the People was being held in broad daylight in full view of the public. Is that how treasonable acts are usually planned? Of course not! The regime invaded this peaceful meeting only because the people were speaking about fundamental human rights, equality and justice for all South Africans.

Having completed their long search, the SB left the meeting. But, an hour later, when the meeting dispersed, to our dismay, we found them blocking the gate. They had apparently brought tables and chairs, and were now seated on both sides of the gateway, taking the names of all the delegates. Because of the huge crowd, this name-taking lasted until well after nine o'clock. Because Johannesburg people had hired combis (closed vans) to take them to Kliptown and back, transport was not a problem, but even we did not reach our home until between eleven and midnight, because each delegate had to be delivered to his or her door.

What was annoying about these 'Africanists' was that they were calling for action, but when action came it was obvious that some of them got shaky knees. This became clear when Madzunya and Leballo issued a statement condemning the 1958 strike, which I mentioned earlier.

So, when Madzunya and Leballo, joined in this all-out campaign against the people, they were hailed in the daily Press as 'the most responsible and powerful Native leaders', although overnight (as Walter Sisulu wrote so accurately in *Africa South* Vol 3, No. 4, July-Sept 1959), they had become heroes to the upholders of white supremacy, overnight they had forfeited whatever small respect or confidence they might still have enjoyed within the ranks of Congress.

It must be remembered that, during its long history of struggle, not one single ANC leader had been showered with praises by the Herrenvolk and its Press, that not one of our leaders had been referred to as 'responsible' and 'powerful' by successive white regimes. In fact, had they been praised along those lines, the people would have suspected them, not trusted them.

The NEC promptly expelled Madzunya and Leballo. It is noteworthy that this action was warmly applauded by branches throughout the country.

In the Western Region (that is, in Sophiatown, Western Native Township and Newclare) the presence of the 'Africanists' was not detected until 1958. Here they had adopted a different strategy — that of working from within, in order to capture the whole region. To show how they operated, let me start with a regional meeting that was held in the Balansky cinema in 1957. That meeting was chaired by John Gaetsewe, a prominent trades unionist and a leading member of the Western Native Township branch, who worked closely with the former Transvaal President, Mr Moretsele. During the course of the meeting, Mr Z. T. Siwisa, who was Treasurer of the Sophiatown Branch, moved that, since the leaders had been arrested for High Treason and were no longer able to do their job properly, new leaders should be elected in the NEC and in the Province. That motion was rejected. Speaker after speaker pointed out that our leaders had been banned and arrested by the regime, and that if we removed them from their positions, we would be supporting what the regime was doing to them. After all, it was pointed out, the banned leaders continued to play active roles in decision-making; they were as busy as ever, doing political work, despite the risks. Furthermore, if this kind of resolution had succeeded, delegates from these three branches would have gone to provincial and national conferences to support the removal of the arrested leaders because they had agreed to the move in their own branches. Recall that every member of the ANC NEC, as well as many of the top provincial leaders, had been arrested, while the bulk of 'Africanists' like Madzunya and Leballo had not been arrested, and were, at this time, still members of the ANC. Still, even after this incident, nobody suspected Siwisa, and the few who supported him, of being 'Africanists'. Although Siwisa and my husband had been friends even before our marriage, he did not tell us of his new beliefs. He did not show the outright hostility against the leadership.

Later, at a meeting of the Sophiatown branch, Siwisa suggested that the ANC should form its own church so that all marriages, christenings and burials should be done by it, instead of by the orthodox churches to which many of us belonged as individuals. This, too, was rejected; the ANC was not fighting against the Church, but against the state, speakers said. And, it was pointed out, the suggestion was not in keeping with the policy and programme of the ANC; it

94

was a deviation.

Unfortunately for the ANC during this time of the 'Africanists', there was also trouble in the province because of maladministration. That had angered all the branches. Delegates came to the Transvaal Provincial Conference, held in the Donaldson Hall in Orlando in 1957, thinking that the problem would be thrashed out properly with the provincial Executive. Mr MThembu was Acting President because Mr Moretsele was one of the Treason Trialists, and was banned from attending meetings. But nothing was solved. The conference had started badly because there were two delegations from Alexandra Township — that branch had already split! When the chairman called out the number of delegates submitted to him by the Credentials Committee, he called out the number from the Alexandra branch. That included T. X. Makiwane and Florence Moposho, among others. Next, he called out the number of delegates from what he called 'Madzunya's Group'. Like a flash of lightning, Madzunya jumped on the stage and tried to snatch the credentials document from the chairman, shouting: 'There is no 'Madzunya Group'. I am leading the delegation from the Alexandra Branch of the ANC!' He had to be restrained and removed from the platform by Volunteers. The credentials document, which fortunately was not torn, was recovered.

At that conference the 'Africanists' seated themselves strategically. One or two were seated right at the back, near the door; two were in the centre (that is, on the right and the left sides of the hall); two or three sat in the front few rows, also on both the left and right sides of the hall. It was at this conference that I first saw Robert Sobukwe. He was tall and dark, a bit hefty, and with a scholarly appearance. When I saw him, I immediately whispered to the person next to me: 'Who is this chap?' It was from this neighbour that I found it was Sobukwe. I took long to know him, because at that time he lived in the town of Standerton.

Because of the way in which they had seated themselves, the 'Africanists' had an advantage of taking the floor one after the other. From the chair it did not look as if they were together, yet they all spoke on how the 1949 Programme of

95

Action had been abandoned. They all also attacked the
Freedom Charter. So the meeting started to get rough,
because the other delegates wanted to follow the agenda.
Leballo, who was seated next to the door, then took the floor
without the permission of the chairman. That was enough
for most of the delegates. Mrs Walaza, a tall and hefty
woman from Orlando, stood up and went straight to him.
Grabbing him by the lapels, she started to shake him, and
said: 'Leballo, either shut up, or get out!' The Volunteers
stood next to him, ready to throw him out. But he sat down.
Mrs Walaza and her husband both later joined the Pan-
Africanist Congress, when it was formed, although at this
time we fought together against the 'Africanists'.

Surely this was not the way the ANC conducted its meetings. It was not only annoying but it was also depressing the
delegates. We just did not know how long such behaviour
could be tolerated. Clearly, some of the 'Africanists' were up
to disrupting the meeting when they saw they could not get
the support they wanted.

A week or two after the conference, some Youth Leaguers
from Sophiatown, led by Steven Sekhale, removed all the
furniture and documents from the provincial office, and
brought these to Sophiatown. The Sophiatown office was
part of Mr Siwisa's tailor shop, so he was really administering the office as well. The upshot was that the NEC took
over the administration of the Transvaal province. It ordered
the Youth Leaguers to return the furniture, and that was
done. Perhaps the Youth Leaguers had acted unwittingly,
because of the anger of the people against the provincial
maladministration. But that was hardly the correct thing to
do. It caused a great deal of embarrassment to many people
in the branch, including the perpetrators, when they came to
their senses.

At the next branch meeting, the crypto-Africanist, Mr
Mani, was acting chairman because the chairman, Mr Tyiki,
was still involved in the 'Treason' trial. To that meeting
Siwisa had, of his own accord, invited Mrs Ellen Molapo to
address the branch. Mrs Molapo was a beautiful woman and
a good speaker, who had been a member of the ANC in the

early Fifties, but who then ceased to belong. The majority of people who had joined the ANC after the Defiance Campaign of 1952 did not, therefore, know her. It was clear that she was seeking to make a come-back through the 'Africanists'. So, after she had been introduced by the chairman simply as 'Mrs Molapo', she stood up to address the meeting.

Before she could start, both Kate Molale and myself sprang to our feet. We both asked for a point of order. Although we were not sitting in the same place, our action was simultaneous. Because Mrs Molapo was already on her feet, the chairman hesitated for a moment, then leaned towards Siwisa, after which he asked : 'Yes, Mrs Resha, what is your point of order?' My response, calmly outside, but angry inside, was: 'Mr Chairman, never has a branch meeting been addressed by an outsider who is not a member of the organisation'.

'All right, sit down!', said he.

Although I remained standing, he now turned to Kate and asked: 'And you, Miss Molale, what is your point of order?' I repeat, word for word, what Mrs Resha has just asked', said Kate; she was clearly angry — her voice was choking. The top table whispered to each other again. They, too, were now standing. The masses started to be restless; we could hear them say: 'Who is this woman?' Soon, therefore, there was uproar in the hall. One of the members of the top table asked Mrs Molapo to take a seat; the executive were clearly divided. By now some of the masses were shouting: 'Chuck her out!' Wow! I would not have liked to have been in Mrs Molapo's shoes; she gazed this way and that way, but nobody came to her rescue. Some people were now starting to walk out, but Simon Mahopo, one of the Executive, asked them to stay behind for the meeting to be properly closed, as was usual, with a prayer. This was readily agreed, because Mr Mahopo was a very respected member of the branch, who had played an important role in the successful bus boycott; he, like Mr Moretsele, spoke in Sepedi.

When I got home, I related the episode to Robert. 'That one!', he said. 'I warned you people to be careful not to be used by people who are using the problems of the province for their own schemes against Congress.' However, thanks God, the worst had not happened. And the regular Wednesday meetings of the next two weeks were quiet. Then, in the third week, the acting chairman announced that the meeting scheduled to be held in Pretoria at the weekend was still on, and that everyone should make an effort to attend. I do not know, to this day, who had called that meeting; what I do know is that the NEC, who were then administering the province, had not called it: in fact, the NEC had written to branches to call the meeting off when they heard about it. But, in Sophiatown, this message was not delivered to branch members. The letter had been opened by Siwisa, and he had not told the Secretary, Jerry Mbuli, about it. So, that third Wednesday we went to the branch meeting for final preparations for going to Pretoria.

During the meeting, someone came in to tell me that my husband wanted to see me outside. When I came out to him, he asked me if a a letter from the NEC had been read at the meeting. When I replied in the negative, he asked me to call Mbuli, who also said that he knew nothing about a letter from the NEC. Robert then asked Mbuli to ask Siwisa where the letter was, because it had been sent, with great urgency, by the NEC. Siwisa's reply was that he had left it at the office, since he did not think that it was urgent. The letter was fetched, and read. In it, the NEC made it clear that no member of the ANC should go the Pretoria meeting on the Sunday. After the letter had been read, the members said: 'Congress has spoken; we are not going.' It was on this day that the Sophiatown branch found out who were the 'Africanists' in their midst. Siwisa stood up, and said: 'Everybody who is an Africanist must follow me out of the hall.'

The atmosphere was now very tense; everyone wanted to see who these 'Africanists' were. Siwisa had, meanwhile jumped down from the stage. He looked very smart in his navy blue suit, white shirt with gold cuff-links and maroon tie. When he got near the door, he was joined by four Youth Leaguers. One of them was Patrick Letlalo, son of Old Man Letlalo who had joined the ANC in 1917. (In exile, Patrick rejoined the ANC and studied printing in the GDR, where he qualified; he died about two years ago in Zimbabwe.) Mr Mani followed as they went out. So, there were only six of them in a hall which contained between 250 and 300 people. These six stopped coming to meetings. Mr Makhoane was elected acting chairman, and all ANC property was moved to his place in Morris Street. It was a great relief to the members, because (although the 'Africanists' behaved in a gentlemanly manner in our branch) people were getting tired of sabotage and daily dirty tricks on the part of two people out of an executive of eleven.

The ANC showed great tolerance in dealing with the 'Africanists'. That was because of its adherence to democracy: all its members are given a chance to voice their opinions, and are allowed to defend themselves if they are accused of violating the Constitution. But it will not tolerate sabotage or treachery, as in the cases of Madzunya and Leballo, who were expelled in 1958. Madzunya, even after his expulsion, announced himself as a candidate for the presidency of the province at the 1958 Transvaal conference. Yes, moles had been going around, whispering to ANC members that the 'Africanists' intended to take over the leadership of the organisation by force at that conference, which was chaired by Oliver Tambo, and at which Chief Luthuli was present.

The first day was pretty bad. The 'Africanists' had come with a large number of men armed with a variety of weapons including sticks and knobkerries; they pushed their way into the hall, refusing to have their credentials checked. That day, the SB stayed in their cars outside the fence — almost as if they had been warned! The meeting itself was very noisy; there was no progress at all as the 'Africanists' hurled insult upon insult at the leadership. They even shouted at Chief Luthuli to go back home in Groutville. In the afternoon, the Volunteers had to escort Chief Luthuli and Oliver Tambo out through a back door for their safety.

That night, the Youth League in Sophiatown called as many Youth Leaguers as possible to come to Orlando, fully armed, to face the armed gangs which had forced their way into the meeting the previous day. It was now a matter of saving the ANC from being taken over, by force, by the

'Africanists'.

Other delegates were already settled in the hall by the time the Sophiatown delegation arrived. The delegates walked in front of the non-delegates — everyone was singing 'Sophiatown likaya lam'. The SB were in their cars, outside the fence, exactly like on the previous day. A group of 'Africanists' stood outside the hall, near the fence; there may have been ten or twelve of them. Outside the gate also stood some of the Treason Trialists: Patrick Moloao, Peter Ntite, Wilton Mkwayi, Milner Ntsangane, J. Mokhofe, and Robert. Although the bail conditions did not allow them to be at the meeting, that did not prevent them from being outside the fence, bail or no bail, they were there to defend their beloved organisation, if need be. As the Sophiatown delegates checked in at the door, the non-delegates walked round the hall, singing 'Sophiatown is my Home!' The effect was that the atmosphere inside the hall suddenly changed from being tense, as on the previous day, to one of daring. Chief Luthuli took off his coat and rolled up his sleeves — the old man was indicating that he was ready for anything! Nobody was prepared to see the ANC hijacked.

The meeting started at once — enough time had been squandered on futile arguments the previous day. Nobody knew what the 'Africanists' were planning. They did not come to the meeting, but sent Rosette Ndziba to deliver a letter to the conference. Although the Volunteers at the door took the letter, the messenger left on wheels as the Volunteers raised their sjamboks to give it to him on the body. Oh, yes, that day the 'Africanists' realised that they were outnumbered.

So, the moment of the parting of the roads had arrived. After all, what good purpose does it serve in remaining in a body into which one does not fit? Amongst other charges the 'Africanists' said, in their letter, that they were breaking away from the ANC. Furthermore, they asserted, they and not the existing leadership, were the custodians of the traditions of the ANC.

It was therefore inevitable that a few months after the break-away, there should be formed the PAC. There were persistent rumours that it was founded at the American

Cultural Centre office in Johannesburg. Shortly after its foundation, the PAC held its inaugural conference in the Donaldson Hall in Orlando, where the National Executive, under its President, Robert Sobukwe, and the Secretary-General Potlako Leballo, all had titles in the American style: for instance, Peter Raboroko was Secretary for Education. Interestingly, Josias Madzunya failed to get a place on the NEC; perhaps his antics had gone a bit too far for even his colleagues. Anyway, he kept on supporting this new organisation in whose foundation he had played a leading role.

The split was inevitable and unavoidable. The ANC has always believed it politically correct to co-operate with other sections of the oppressed, and for several years the Congress Alliance had taken heroic joint actions in the fight against racial discrimination and white supremacy. Thus, for the ANC to abandon the alliance would have been to abandon its own principles and objectives.

Then, in 1953, these allies decided to assist in the formation of an organisation to help to combat adverse and anti-African propaganda among whites. That body, the South African Congress of Democrats (COD) included people who had belonged to the Communist Party, as well as other white people who had not belonged, thus widening the opposition against the minority regime. The regime, in its turn, behaved towards this organisation and its members in the same way as it did to the others. Many COD members were placed under house arrest, or banned, or imprisoned and their lives, too, were turned into hell by the SB, until many of them had to go into exile.

But these joint campaigns against the common enemy did not stop the PAC. Thus, the annual conference of the ANC in 1959, which took the decision to launch the Anti-Pass Campaign from 31 March, 1960, was followed a week later by the first annual conference of the PAC. According to reports of comments by some PAC members, that conference determined to launch a 'Status Campaign'. That meant, we were told, to force whites in shops, places of work, to address Africans in a conventional way: Mr, Mrs, or Miss instead of the insulting form of 'boy' or 'girl'.

But, two months after the conference there were still no reports, neither about the campaign, nor about police responses to the leaders of the campaign. Then, in the middle of March, the PAC, without announcing either the suspension or abandonment of this 'Status Campaign', suddenly announced at a press conference that it was launching its own Anti-Pass Campaign on the 21 March — in other words, ten days before the date long before chosen by the ANC! What was even more puzzling and insulting was for the PAC to extend an invitation to the ANC to join its campaign! Strange! It had not invited the ANC to join in its 'Status Campaign'. Duma Nokwe, the Secretary-General of the ANC, quite properly rejected this cynical invitation in an open statement.

The only picture that could be drawn from this was that the PAC saw the momentum aroused by the ANC campaign, and decided to jump the gun. The press took up the ANC rejection of the PAC invitation and the result was confusion: only the oppressor had a laugh to see the two organisations at loggerheads at such a critical time. During the few days remaining before the date of the PAC campaign, the ANC set out to warn the people about this confusion. The result was that, except for the events at Sharpeville in the Transvaal, and Langa in Cape Town, the PAC campaign went unheeded — especially in the hottest political areas like Johannesburg, Port Elizabeth, and Durban.

On the eve of 21 March, groups of young men went around the townships, telling people to join the campaign. Four or five of them came to our house in Mofolo. When we answered the knock at the door, the young men said: 'Congress says all men must leave their passes at home tomorrow and present themselves at the Orlando police station for arrest — no going to work!' After they had left our house, we went outside to see if they were going to all the other houses; and, indeed, although Soweto has no streetlights, we heard them repeat the same message from house to house in our immediate vicinity. Now, 'Congress', as I have said several times earlier, is the name used for the ANC by all and sundry, and for the PAC to hide its identity behind the name was another calculated move to sow even more confusion.

In the morning, I left with my husband to catch the eight o'clock bus that transported the trialists on their daily trip to Pretoria. We were expecting that transport might be disrupted, as it usually was during strikes and stays-at-home, but people were queuing for buses as usual. There was also no sign of the army or police, which was another usual feature during strikes. At Dube, we picked up Patrick Molaoa, who reported to us that people were streaming to trains and buses as usual. At Phefeni, which is the busiest bus stop (it serves people from West Cliff Extension, Dube, Meadowlands, Phefeni itself, and Killarney), the pattern was the same: people were going to work. This was the spot at which the bus stopped to pick up Duma Nokwe. While we waited for him to get on, we could see, on the left-hand side of the road, Robert Sobukwe, the PAC President, and six or seven other people, walking slowly towards the Orlando police station, about 1.5 miles away. Incidentally, since Sobukwe lived in Mofolo North, which was about 4.5 miles away from the Orlando police station, he had a very long walk indeed, passing big stations like Dube and Phefeni.

I really cannot explain the reaction of the people towards the campaigners. Whether people noticed them or not I don't know, but people did not seem to care about what was happening; they simply carried on with their daily rush to work. Along the route, we picked up other trialists: Sisulu, Mkwayi, Ntsangane, Lilian Ngoyi. Because I was going to Diepkloof, I got off at Orlando East (which is where Leballo lived). Here, as well as at Diepkloof, it was an ordinary working day. On my way back, in another bus, I noticed a group of men at the Orlando police station. Although I could not estimate their number because of the speed of the bus, it was clear that it was not very great. All the time, the atmosphere was normal, as if it was just another working day: unlike the events like the Treason Trial arrests, or the Sophiatown resistance, or other major Congress campaigns, people in the buses did not talk about this one.

The early afternoon editions of the evening papers carried a statement from the PAC President Sobukwe (I think he must have spoken to the press in mid-morning, before he

103

was arrested) saying that he was disappointed with the response of the people to the campaign. Then, towards late afternoon, reports started to filter out from radios that the police had opened fire on a crowd of pass protesters at Sharpeville township police station, and that many had been killed and wounded. Later on, it was established that at least 67 people had been killed.

When my husband came back that evening, he had with him a late edition of *The Star*; that gave a bit more details than the radio reports about the event. That story was beyond anyone's belief: sixty-seven unarmed people killed protesting peacefully against the Pass Laws! What else is there for us to do? I went to bed with a heavy heart, after asking myself that question; I believe that each and every African was outraged.

At seven o'clock the next morning I went to Cross Roads to buy a copy of *The Daily Mail*. Wow! Had I delayed I would not have got hold of a copy; people were snatching papers as if they were hot cross buns. 'Sharpeville 67 Dead 160 Injured' screamed the posters. The front page pictures were horrific: photographs of bodies of human beings were strewn on the veldt; they resembled carcasses of animals that had been overcome by a ferocious bush fire. They lay on the ground, stretched in all directions and one could see that some bodies had had their limbs either torn off, or hanging on by a thread of skin. There was blood all over. Oh! what a massacre. In one picture, a child of about 4-5 years stood looking dazed, crying next to the dead body of a woman. Another woman lay on her side, still wearing her apron. That showed the hurry with which she had left her house, having heard the call — 'Congress calls upon all residents to march to the police station to be addressed by the Police Commissioner on the Pass Laws' — that we were told was the message the campaigners had spread. A man in his late thirties or early forties, looking bewildered and dejected, stood next to the body of a woman lying on the ground, his arms outstretched towards the body.

From the pictures it was clear that people were running away in horror and panic from the boom!-boom!-boom! of the deadly weapons. How so many escaped is a miracle. In another corner of one of the pictures the police stood proudly by, carrying their weapons of murder; they had carried out the instructions of Robert 'Blackie' Swart, the then Minister of Justice, who had told them to 'shoot first, ask questions after'. This man was later given the post of 'State President' for the good job he had done as 'Minister of Justice'.

I don't recall how long I stood scrutinising these pictures. All I know is that, walking home, I had a sense of weakness at the knees. The amount of blood I saw in the pictures gave me an imaginary smell of blood in my nostrils. Amabulu!

Robert perused the paper for some minutes before he left; I had told him that I would not be going with him on the Treason Trial bus, as I used to do. After he had left I was not even sure if I would go out at all, because of the way I felt. But, at about 9.30, I decided that I had to go to Diepkloof. I went via the shorter route, which is via Baragwanath Hospital. The bus, when it came at last, was quite full, but nobody said a word. Then, just before the bus pulled out, a woman boarded. She looked quite agitated. 'People,' she said, 'I must get to Sharpeville. I just pray that my mother and my daughter are not among the dead or injured. Because. according to what I read in the paper, hundreds of people are dead because Congress called people to go to the police station.'

There being no comment from any of the people on the bus, the woman went on: 'I really don't understand how Congress can do this, because we all know these Boers.' She went on and on, attacking Congress for exposing people to the Boers. At one stage I wanted to explain to her about the new organisation, but I saw that it would be futile: after all, she was from my area, where young men had gone from house to house, telling people that 'Congress said ....' In any case, I was now nearing my stop, and would not have had enough time to explain it all to her. So, instead, I got off at the Baragwanath Hospital, from where I crossed to Diepkloof. But my heart was sore that I was not able to tackle the lady about the name 'Congress.'

Shortly after the PAC leaders and activists went to jail after their defiance of the Pass Laws, we learnt of the death of Mr Siwisa at the 'Blue Skies' prison in Boksburg. The police explanation, which they gave to his family after they had buried him, was that he had died from pneumonia. When we got the news, his family were (with the help of the PAC) fighting hard to have the body exhumed to establish the cause of his death, and also to give him a decent and proper funeral. It took a great deal of effort to get permission for the exhumation, but the police then buried the body again immediately after the coroner's examination. So, again the family had to go to lawyers to force the police to release the body for decent burial.

Personally, I was very grieved about Siwisa's death. He had left Sophiatown before we did, and it was only after his death that I learnt that they had been living in Orlando East at his daughter's place. To me and my husband, Bhut' (Brother) Todd, as we addressed him, was our big brother. When Robert and I got married in 1948, I found them already close friends, and Sipo Siwisa, Todd's nephew, shared a bedsitter with Robert. Todd was so close to us that, even after he had left the ANC for the PAC, we could not stop talking to him.

During the high days of Sophiatown, Bhut' Todd would come to our house. where he would play his accordion for us: he played that wonderfully well, and used to belong to a band at one stage. The children loved it so much that they regularly used to ask me if 'Grandpa', as they called him, could be asked to come to play for us on Sundays. Todd's daughter, Nkunkuse, also called Sybil, whom we all loved very much, grew up in front of us until she got married. Bhut' Todd was a devout Christian. He went to church every Sunday, and even preached at times. Soft-spoken and polite, he was respected and loved by many people. Moreover, as a tailor, he helped many people by sewing and altering for them. Many never paid him. During the Defiance Campaign we had planned to defy in December, but the Campaign was called off before we could do that, because of the vicious laws which were passed to suppress the campaign.

So, when I received the message about the day of the funeral, I asked Mrs Makhoti to accompany me to our brother's funeral, which was held in a small church in Orlando

East, and which was conducted by Rev. Dlepu, a close personal friend of the deceased. 'My people', said he, 'you all know that our late brother Siwisa was a short person in stature. But look at his coffin: it is so big it looks as if it contains a person nine feet tall. This shows that, although he looked small in this world, he is big in the place where he has gone.' In fact, I had never before seen such a large coffin: someone later said to me that they place the body in a double coffin after exhumation. The reverend's voice was breaking at this stage; he was bidding farewell to a dear friend whose sudden death in a South African jail would never convince anyone that it was by natural causes.

The funeral was attended by many people, but I think Mrs Makhoti and myself were the only ones there who knew him from his ANC days in Sophiatown. It was very difficult to communicate with people elsewhere about the details of the funeral, because of the problems of the exhumation I had mentioned earlier. Furthermore, although no political speeches were made, because of the state of Emergency, PAC members did form a guard of honour around the coffin throughout the service. The service was wound up with the hymn which the Reverend Dlepu said was one of Siwisa's favourites: '*Warazula Ngenxa Yam Liwa Laphakade*' (Rock of Ages).

In August, when the State of Emergency was finally lifted, there was rejoicing all over. I had been under such stress during the whole period that, the Sunday before it was lifted, I asked for help. I was at home, looking outside through the front window, from which I saw two men from the Salvation Army knocking on the door of the house opposite ours. After they had been inside that house for some minutes, they came out. Although they could not see me because of the lace curtains, I thought they would come to our place, because they were going from house to house. They did approach, but then I noticed they hesitated after they had read the sign outside that said 'Midwife'. So they passed to the next house. I just did not know how to call them, although I needed a prayer so much because of the stress.

So I went outside and stood on my stoep so that they could see me when they had finished their prayers at the house next door. Indeed, when they came out and saw me standing there, they came to me and asked if I would allow them to come in and pray. I welcomed them. I told them why I stood outside; they, in their turn, told me that they had hesitated to knock on my door because of the placard outside. Before they prayed, they asked me if there was anything that troubled me which they should mention in their prayers. I told them of my husband's detention and of the Treason Trial to which he had now been going for four years. Finally, I told them, I had recently spent three weeks in the Fort, and had only been released during the amnesty.

After the prayer, I felt as if the heavy burden that was pressing me down had been removed —my strength and hope came back. I gave them each a cup of tea, and thanked them. Three days later I was in the kitchen when I heard a banging of a car door outside. When I went to investigate, Robert was just being delivered to the door by a friend. I was ecstatic — the last time I had visited him at the court in Pretoria, nobody had the slightest idea that the Emergency would end.

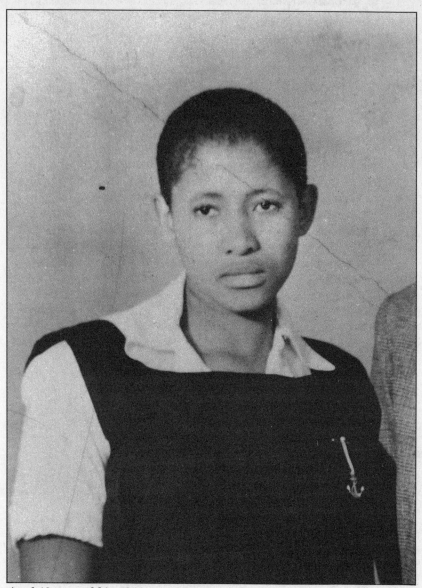

Aged 19 years old in 1941

On training at Holy Cross Hospital 1947. I am on the right with Albertina Masuku and Tembekile Mkhize.

My grandmother, Motsewane MaTau Mokhele in 1953, a year before she died.

My husband, Robert Resha, when he was associate editor of Egoli in 1952.

My eldest daughter, Nosipho, now a fashion designer.

My youngest daughter, Masechaba, now Dr Resha.

My mother and my brother's children. My sister-in-law, the niece of Archbishop tutu, is on the left.

Women protesters from Sophiatown surrounded by police at the Pass Office in Market Street, 1958. The police barred me from joining these women.

Members of the Pan African Women's Organisation Presidium receiving government and FNL officials outside the conference hall, Algiers, 1968. Left to right: Mrs Resha, Chair of the Inaugural Session; Mrs Jeanne-Martin Cisseé, Secretary General of PAWO; Dr Neffisa, President of the Union of Algerian Women.

Maggie Resha presiding over the inaugural session of Pan African Women's Organisation, Algiers, 1968. On the left is Mr Khalid Ahmed, former Secretary General of FNL.

Pan African Women's Organisation seminar at Brazzaville Congo Centre. Former President Ngaobi and Jeanne-Martin Cisseé, Secretary General of PAWO, on the left; Maggie Resha on the extreme left, back row.

Tenth anniversary of Pan African Women's Organisation, Dar es Salaam, 1972. (Mrs Makiwane, South Africa; Mrs Chesson, Liberia; Mrs Resha, South Africa; Mrs Madengwe, Tanzania.)

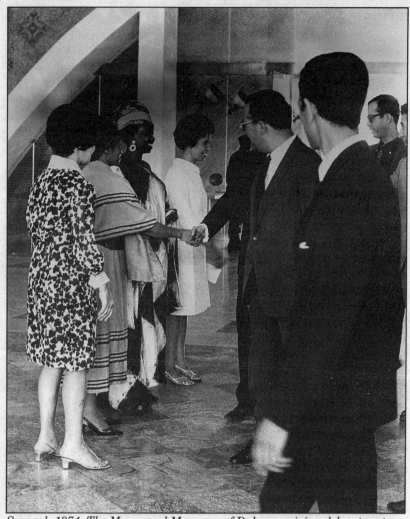

Senegal, 1974. The Mayor and Mayoress of Dakar receiving delegates at a reception.

7

■

Women's Resistance Against the Pass Laws

During its long history of struggle, the ANC has always been in the vanguard of the struggle against racism, today known by the name 'apartheid". Some of these battles were won by the pioneers of the movement, others were lost, but all left a heritage of struggle upon which the younger generations could build.

When the ANC was formed in Bloemfontein on 8 January 1912, the ink had hardly dried on the paper on which the two white races, the British and the Boers, had signed the 1910 Act of Union. In other words, the formation of the ANC was a direct response to the nefarious act which alienated the black majority from power sharing. According to ANC documents, the gathering in Bloemfontein was an extraordinary one; it brought together people from every stratum of life and from every part of the country, including the then Protectorates of Bechuanaland, Swaziland and Basutoland. Former foes, who were still suspicious of each other, because of internecine and fratricidal strife between their forefathers, sat around a table and faced one another. The founders of the ANC made an appeal to the different groups to unite, in order to fight against the common enemy, which had turned black people into aliens in their own country, by forming the whites-only Union.

The ANC has stood the test of time because its roots, from the start, went very deep. It was formed by the masses, and the masses are its power. There are thousands of men and women whose names are unknown, but they are the ones who carried out its policy, who took part in its campaigns, who elected their leaders, who became the spokespeople for their cause. When I look at the ANC in retrospect, I appreciate how the organisation makes each and every member a valuable and indispensable part, so that the ANC belongs to the people; it is their shield and spear.

Thus, Mr Letlalo, who had joined the ANC in 1917, told us Africans had not been allowed to walk on the pavements in Pretoria, with the consequence that African women and children were injured daily. So, one day, together with a few other men, they defied this municipal regulation and walked on the pavement. They were arrested. During the court hearing, they stated the plight of black people, especially of women and children. The regulation was rescinded. From that victory, they went on to break the railway regulation which made Africans travel in goods carriages instead of compartments. For that, too, they were arrested, but their campaign led to the railways introducing third class carriages, for Africans. These people govern by regulation. That is why Africans are always in trouble, because even when one thinks one is within the law, one ends up being caught up in the regulations by which these race laws are administered. It is a real nightmare for African people under apartheid. Right along the way, the ANC has fought one law after another.

But the longest, and most bitter, of the many battles the ANC has fought has been that against the Pass Laws. It is a fight that has gone on from generation to generation, that has left many landmarks engraved with the names of men and women alike. The story I want to tell here is the one about the contribution of the women to the anti-pass law campaigns of my time, since their story is very special, and because no story of the liberation struggle can be complete without highlighting their particular participation.

110

It was no surprise that in the first year of the operation of the Land Act (which should have been called the Land Grab Act because it reserved 87 per cent of the country for the white population) one of the first major confrontations was with the women, when the regime attempted to extend the Pass Laws. But the women would have none of it! For instance, at Vrededorp (City of Peace!) near Johannesburg, women demonstrators fought pitched battles with the police, who were mounted on horses. Women, as well as policemen and horses were injured in the battle.

In Sophiatown, during the Women's Anti-Pass Campaign of the late Fifties some of us had the opportunity to get living testimony from Mrs Mary Mqhweto, who had taken part in that 1913 campaign; known as Auntie Mary, she was obviously very old at that time, and living in the township. Her advice to us was: 'Unity begets bravery and strength'. It was from her that we learnt that the women of Johannesburg had co-ordinated their action with that of the women of Mangaung in the Orange Free State, who had been cheated by the chiefs into taking passes. But once they discovered the deception, they burnt their passes by the sackload in front of the local municipal offices. Because of this resistance, the regime retreated, shelved the attempt to impose passes on women. However, the women remained vigilant, and each time the regime made fresh attempts to impose passes — as they continued to do — the women were ready to protect themselves from this badge of slavery, the pass.

When I went to see my landlady in 1956, for the signing of the petition to Pretoria, because I knew that she would not be able to go — she was no longer young, and she suffered from arthritis — and when she saw my anxiety, she told me that she would call Mary Mqhweto so that she could give us tips about how the 1913 women's resistance had been successful. My landlady, Mrs Edith Senaoane, was a cousin of Mrs Mqhweto. It was not until 1953, when the Sophiatown branch was formed, that I found out that Mrs Senaoane as well as her sister, Matilda Kopo, were members of the ANC.

Auntie Mary told us that it would be a shame if women of our day, who were enlightened and educated, could not

111

defeat the regime, whereas her generation had been successful, although they had not gone to school. She still hated the
pass!

It goes without saying that the Pass Laws were one of the
main pillars of apartheid. Indeed, when the Nationalist
Party took power in 1948, one of the many harsh laws the
regime added to the Statute Book was to tighten the Pass
Laws on men and extend them to include the women. For
their part, the women knew exactly what they were faced
with; they knew they were faced with Afrikaner diehards
and villains of racial segregation, who would stop at nothing.
To these, the Africans have been seen as nothing else except
tools of labour. To extend the Pass Laws was to pull down
the wall which protected the women from the humiliation of
carrying these documents. To do so would be to dispel the
belief that womanhood and motherhood deserved respect
and honour in society, irrespective of race or colour.

Under the direction of the ANC, the Federation of South
African Women, which was formed in 1954, and the African
National Congress Women's League, called upon women
throughout the country to resist this callous move. Women,
in towns as well as in the rural areas, staged demonstrations against local chiefs, Native Commissioners, magistrates. In 1955, 2,000 women from the Transvaal went to the
Union Building with a petition to the then prime minister
Strijdom, who snubbed them, and to which the women
responded by organising a demonstration to the same place
by women from all over the country.

However, right at home, in Western Native Township
(WNT), there was a bit of a hitch. Ida Mtwana, who had
been President of the Federation as well as of the Women's
League before Lilian Ngoyi, had sort of drifted away from
womens' activities, and she had half of the WNT following
her lead. After we had discussed this snag at the Federation
Executive, Lilian proposed that, as I had worked with Ida
longer than anyone else had done, and that since we both
resided in the same region, I should go to tackle her to join
the march. I was a bit reluctant to see Ida, because there
had been reports that she was not satisfied about not being

112

consulted on some issues concerning the organisation. Anyway, the thought of the anticipated success of the march subdued the fear of my going to talk to her. And, thanks to Lilian's tactic, Ida agreed that we should sink our differences and that she would join the march.

On my way to Ida's house, I passed Kate Mxakato's and successfully persuaded her to accompany me. Kate lived in WNT — but she was not in Ida's new group. She was a militant woman and later became provincial secretary of the Women's League. We both convinced ourselves that seeing two people would make Ida see how we still believe her contribution valuable in the struggle.

I was very relieved when Ida agreed to join the march, and I there and then told her that I would be delivering leaflets and petitions to cover Western Native Township. With the help of the male comrades of the Congress Alliance thousands and thousands of leaflets were cyclostyled and distributed. These leaflets explained what the march was about, and called upon all women to organise their neighbours as well as all women on buses and in trains. The country was flooded with leaflets. It was accompanied by petitions, which were to be signed by women only, whether they were going to join the march or not. In these petitions there was an emphatic 'No!' to the proposal to extend passes to women, as well as a scathing attack on all racist laws. When all the copies were collected on 9 August 1956, there were over 100,000 signatures.

I do not know whether to claim that this was the busiest time for the women, because we seemed to be busy all of the time. It was just a year after we had been engaged in organising for the Congress of the People, and just before that there had been the campaign against the removal of Sophiatown, which kept us on our toes day in and day out, about which I wrote in an earlier chapter. But what made the organisation of the march difficult was that we had to go around carrying leaflets, and no one could be sure as to whether or not she would not be caught by the police. So we had to be on our guard all the time.

I remember that, two days before we went to Pretoria, I

thought that there might be some women we might have missed because Sophiatown was so overcrowded. So, coming home from work in the afternoon, I decided to go to organise in the street in the north of the township. I was carrying some leaflets and petitions in a little suitcase. At the corner of one street I met two women who were carrying their babies on their backs. As I was talking to them, explaining about the march, a black SB passed near us, in a rush. I did not know whether to drop the leaflets I was holding, because I was trying to tell the women that, since they had babies, they could just sign the petitions. But the SB man said to me: 'Oh, Mrs Resha, I thought you were carrying equipment in your case for delivering babies, but it seems that you use it for leaflets as well!' I took no notice of him, and he left us alone.

As the women were signing the petitions, the one said to the other: 'You know, we can go to Pretoria with our babies; our mothers used to go to the fields and come back, carrying a large *seroto* (large grass carrier) of mealies on their heads, with their babies on their backs'. 'Yes', replied the other, and then continued, 'In any case, when we are arrested for pass offences, we will either have to go to jail and take our babies with us, or be separated from them'. There and then they asked me to put their names on the list of those who would be going to Pretoria the next day.

In the morning, I met them at the bus rank, and we took the same bus to Pretoria. Those two women were now the ones preaching about the evils of the Pass Laws to the others. I was happy, but I was also amazed by their determination, and I saw what conviction could do to a person. In Pretoria, they were even more happy to see that there were many, many thousands of other women who had come with their babies, and that even women who were highly expectant had made the journey. Those are the women of South Africa; the women who are prepared to fight because they want health, happiness and security for their children.

This demonstration, which was well-organised beforehand, was planned for 9 August 1956, and Strijdom was notified, in advance, that he should be available to receive the

114

women. The regime panicked, as usual, and tried, unsuccessfully to disrupt the march by putting various obstacles in the way. Transport was cancelled in many areas. Women from Natal, the Cape Province and the Orange Free State paid large sums of money to book carriages to take them to Pretoria. Many women from the Transvaal went to Pretoria overnight to avoid the disruption of the transport.

I remember that I was, with several other women from our area, part of a bus group who went to Pretoria. Our bus was stopped at a police roadblock, and two white policemen, both young men, climbed aboard. As they came in, we started to sing a hymn. This made them look at us in great puzzlement — perhaps they thought we were going to a funeral. After a few minutes they allowed the bus driver to continue his journey. While we felt jubilant, we were not absolutely sure that we had passed our last roadblock.

A few days before the day of the demonstration the regime had announced a ban on all gatherings of more than three people. It became a real problem then to walk together in a group, since even walking was technically a breach of the law. So we each took different ways and streets, never stopping, through Pretoria, as if we were just pedestrians in a large city. Everyone knew where the Union Buildings were; noone could get lost. By ten o'clock, 20,000 women had assembled in the grounds of the venue, around the statue of Louis Botha (1862–1919) on horseback, impressive in his wide-brimmed hat, looking across the city. To many women from the Transvaal, who had visited these grounds, the statue was familiar. But to many others, who had come from other provinces, one could see the curiosity in their faces as they read the name on the statue of the man who had become the first Prime Minister of the white union of Boer and Briton in 1910.

From the bottom of the gardens to the building itself must be about half a mile; we had to climb hundreds of steps and terraces, each of which was filled with gardens of the loveliest flowers. Because of the vastness of the crowds who were assembling, many people had to trample over the flowers in order to get to the Amphitheatre. Some, including myself, had sore feet from going up these hundreds of steps with our shoes on. But it was like a real invasion when the women surged forward and ever upward towards the building. I don't think that at that stage anyone even thought of the ban upon a gathering of more than three; this was a multitude of angry and defiant women of all races from every walk of life — some were carrying babies on their backs. But each one of us held a petition denouncing the Pass Laws and all other racist laws. What was noticeable was the absence of uniformed police, while there were scores of Special Branch and many journalists.

Because of the volume of petitions to be presented (there were 100,000 in all) we needed a delegation of ten or eleven people to carry them all. But the representativeness of the delegation also had to be considered; for example, a representative from each racial group, and a representative from each province. Lilian Ngoyi and Helen Joseph, respectively President and Secretary of the Federation, were to lead the delegation to the Prime Minister's office. I was not part of the delegation. Many of the nurses who were present had been asked to keep a watchful eye on the crowd. Anything could have happened because of the strain of going up the steps and because of the scorching sun.

But, thanks God, there were no mishaps. Before we could settle down in the Amphitheatre, we were met with stink bombs. Everyone had to put her hand on her nose. What a welcome! Nevertheless, the delegation was determined to press on. By the time it went up, I could see clearly the anger on Lilian's face. The magic sweat she once talked about which she had during the Cape Town ship incident in 1954, was rolling down her temples. It was at this moment that the Union Buildings came to a standstill. When I cast my eyes up to this pompous building, with its two domes (signifying the union of the Boers and the British) the verandahs of the building were covered with hundreds of pink faces, giving the impression of hanging like linen on a drying fence. The workers inside had abandoned their desks to come to witness a spectacle that had never been seen since the formation of the Union — black women in occupation of the Amphitheatre: a no-go area for an African even as gardener or sweeper. The Amphitheatre, I had been told, is the holiest of places for the Boers — only their President or Prime Minister stands there when giving important announcements about war and peace.

The secretary to the Prime Minister told the delegation that his boss was unavailable. The women, in their anger, dumped the petition outside his office. Yes, the 'Lion of the North', as Strijdom was called, had lost his courage to face this army of angry women.

Lilian asked the crowd to observe a thirty-minute silence in protest. During this period not a cough, not a child's cry, was to be heard. It was like a calm lake whose waters were undisturbed by even a breeze. A thirty-minute silence is unprecedented in my experience. I could hardly believe my ears when I heard Lilian call for it. Yet, because of our anger, the time seemed to pass almost in a flash. Following that silence the women burst into a taunting revolutionary song, which had been composed by the Natal women at a previous conference: *'Heyi Strijdom! watint a bafazi, watint'-imbokotho uzokufa'* (Strijdom beware! Now that you have touched the women, you have struck a rock, and you will die). It was only one of several songs that were composed against him. For instance, in Sophiatown, they sang *'koloi ena haena mabili, sutha sutha uena Strydom. Haosa, suthe, etla uhata'* (This wagon has no wheels. Clear off, clear off, Strydom. If you don't, it will crush you!).

Before the day was wound up with *'Nkosi Sikilel' iAfrika'*, Lillian's voice echoed from the walls of the Union Buildings as she cried out: 'A ... frika!' The atmosphere seemed electrified by the power of her voice, and the crowd responded: *'Mayibuye!'* (May it Return!). By this time, many of the women, myself included, were weeping quietly. Yes, the women had done it! Women from the ghettoes of the locations, from the farms, from the villages, young and old, had dared to invade the very citadel of oppression in order to express their indignation and detestation for apartheid laws.

To see how heartless and thoughtless the leaders of the white regime could be, the following day they issued state-

117

ments complaining bitterly about the damage done to the flowers at the Union Buildings terraces and grounds, the cost of which they put at hundreds of pounds. They also complained of the litter that had been left behind. It was most thoughtless of a repressive regime to cry for flowers; it did not cross their minds what a sacrifice it had been for the women, who had left their sick, their old, their homes, their young, to travel, under difficult conditions, risking arrest, to get to Pretoria.

Although the leadership of the ANC were concerned about the risks involved, when the idea of the march first came up, it now declared the 9 August as 'South Africa Women's Day' in order to honour the gallantry of the women. That day has since that time been added to the calendar of the ANC struggle against apartheid, as one of the landmarks of our history.

* * *

Rebuffed in its frontal assault, but true to its nature of working by trickery and deceit, the regime through various means known to it alone, now directed the South African Nursing Council to demand 'identity numbers' from all nurses and student nurses. This directive was communicated to all hospitals, throughout the country, by the Nursing Council, from Pretoria.

Nurses were, on the whole, always regarded as conservative. And perhaps that was the reason why the regime chose them as the first to be issued with passes. However, in this the regime was to be mistaken. The nurses immediately called big meetings to discuss this demand for 'identity numbers', and they soon co-ordinated their activities with the Federation of South African Women.

During one of these meetings of the nurses, it was decided that one nurse should be chosen as a guinea pig to go to the pass office to ask for her 'identity number'. I was chosen to do this job.

The bureaucrats in the first two offices to which I went did not know what I was talking about; finally, they directed me to the highest official, whose name, too, was Strydom. He told me that I could have my 'identity number' only if I had a pass. So that was it — the regime was trying to cheat the nurses into carrying passes.

The Federation of South African Women immediately organised for a protest demonstration to the very big Baragwanath Hospital. A letter was sent to the authorities, asking them to receive a delegation of women. However, the night before the protest demonstration we heard that female doctors (they were all white; there were no black doctors at that time at Baragwanath) at the hospital had been told not to come to work the next day. Then, the morning of the demonstration, my husband, who had been out early, came back to tell me that the bus company had cancelled taking the women from our area to the hospital.

Our response was to book all taxis at the rank to take us; they took about eight people at a time. When we arrived at the hospital, Helen Joseph was already there with a few women, and with hundreds of policemen present. Helen told us that buses carrying women from the eastern areas had been stopped by police road blocks. We then went to Colonel Pienaar, who was in charge, and told him that if he let the women come to the demonstration we would send only six or seven women to meet the authorities. Strange enough, he agreed to lift the roadblocks; but he warned us that the women should remain on the opposite side of the road. Within a short space of time busloads of women joined us.

What the delegation saw when it went in to meet the authorities was unbelievable. Policemen were in evidence in all the hospital corridors; hosepipes were held in readiness; the casualty department, usually packed with patients, was completely empty. Finally, the police even went in with the delegation that went to meet the Superintendent, the Matron, and other officials.

Our delegation, of which I was a member, bitterly criticised what it regarded as war preparations at the hospital. Our statement pointed out that the 'identity number 'which the Nursing Council had asked them to demand from nurses, meant that nurses had to carry passes. The statement elaborated on the dangers of the pass, which would affect not

119

only nurses, but the whole administration at the hospitals or clinics. The hospital authorities told us that they did not make the laws, but said that they would pass our memorandum to the Nursing Council.

By the time the delegation came out, scores of nurses had forgone their tea time and had crossed the demarcation line to join the women to thank them for their protest. Within a few months the Nursing Council dropped their demand for 'identity numbers' from nurses.

* * *

There were endless protests and demonstrations in every province in the country to the authorities after the Pretoria march. Some went to Native Commissioners in Johannesburg, finally to city councillors. The protest to the city councillors, like the others, were prepared well in advance by the women from the West Rand and the East Rand. Unlike the Prime Minister, the councillors agreed to meet the delegations.

On the day of the protest there were hardly any police near the City Hall, except for the Special Branch detectives. The uniformed police were posted mostly at the outskirts of the city to stop the crowds of women from entering the city on their way to the City Hall. But the police were unable to stop between 2,000 and 3,000 women from entering the city centre, because, after their experiences of getting to Pretoria in 1956, the women had developed tricky ways of eluding the police, to such an extent that one newspaper reported: 'The women outwit the police!'

Yes indeed, the women had outwitted the police. By ten am a huge crowd of women were squatting silently outside the City Hall. Unlike at the Baragwanath protest, no police or Special Branch went in with the delegation to meet the city councillors. But the arrangements inside the meeting hall were enough to prove the attitude of these gentlemen.

I was part of this delegation of seven. We were seated near the door, on the east corner of the long table, facing the councillors on the west corner. The distance between us could easily have been between eight and ten metres. This made communication between them and us virtually inaudible. As a result, time was lost because some of them kept asking us to repeat what we had just said; we had to shout at the top of our voices. It was clear that this was a deliberate tactic on their part in order to waste time and to discourage us. And there is nothing as annoying as being asked to repeat what you have just said when the time fixed for the appointment is in your mind. We all complained bitterly about this when we left the hall, of course, among ourselves. Ruth Matseoane was carrying her baby, less than a year old, and the baby was restless. Of course the baby could not know that his mother carried him there to fight for his future.

We told the councillors that the women were against the extension of passes to them, and hammered it to them on the squalor of the locations. We told them about high rents and low wages, dark streets and crowded trains, and the plight of the African youth — of our children, who were turning into tsotsis because of arrests under the Pass Laws. These laws, we said, were the main cause of unemployment among African youth. Their reply was that the laws of the country had to be obeyed. They promised to pass our complaints to the government. Of course, nothing was done to remedy our complaints.

As we left, a whisper went out to all the women to leave in the same manner as they had come, and to assemble in Freedom Square, Sophiatown, for a rally. Thankfully, that day ended without incident.

Meanwhile, reports were coming in from other areas and provinces about womens' protests. In Pretoria, a huge crowd of women on their way to the a police station were dispersed with tear gas and baton charges. Many were injured. In Natal, women stopped men from patronising municipal beer halls; they chased and beat their men with sticks when they resisted. The women destroyed cattle dipping tanks and burnt beer halls. Mrs Luthuli, together with Mrs Dube and Dorothy Nyembe led a group of women to the Paramount Chief of Zululand to tell him that they were against passes for women.

Other prominent women in the campaign in Natal included Florence Mkhize; her aunt, Bertha Mkhize, the provincial president of the ANC Women's League; and Dr M. Chuene. Dorothy Nyembe was a prominent woman in Natal. During the late Sixties she was arrested and served fifteen years for alleged participation in ANC underground activities. Mrs Dube was the wife of Dr Dube, first President of the ANC, while Mrs Mkhize was one of the 156 charged during the Treason Trial. Dr Margaret Chuene studied medicine at the University of the Witwatersrand, and acted as locum in the surgery of Dr Conco when he was in Pretoria as one of the accused in the Treason Trial. She soon got embroiled in the Women's Anti-Pass Campaign, and was arrested, together with other women, in 1958. I had a picture, which I have lost, showing some of the women from Natal who were arrested at that time. In it Dr Chuene is seated next to a woman *dingaka* (traditional doctor). I remember us remarking how strange it was that these two women, who would not normally agree with each other, in their work, should work together in politics. Because of police persecution, Dr Chuene escaped into Swaziland, where she remained for several years. I am not certain of her whereabouts now.

In the Orange Free State, the leaders included Mrs Mohlakoana and Mrs Mafora. Here, women again burnt passes, as they had done in 1913. They had again been cheated by chiefs who said they would not be given permission to register their marriages and christen their children if they had no passes. There was a song composed for the women of the Free State: 'Liea chesoa koana Free State lipasa' (In the Free State passes are burnt). From the women of the Cape came the slogan, 'We do not want passes, even if they are trimmed with gold!' Many women were arrested all over the country. In Johannesburg, at one meeting, one old woman said, 'I don't know why the government says we must carry passes, because we have already got them. Yes, these passes are stamped even if a woman rebels by pretending that she has a headache or a toothache'. There was laughter, because everyone could read between the lines, as the Sesotho proverb tells us: *Lelefung hoa tseoa* (Of course, there is laughter, even in mourning.)

The anti-pass campaign by the women had reached new dimensions. In rallying the women to resist the Pass Laws, Lilian Ngoyi used to remind the women of an old African proverb: *Mangoana o tsoara thipa ka bohaleng* (The mother grabs the sharp edge of the knife to protect her child). This proverb is familiar to all Africans in South Africa. It originates from an old African myth.

The story of the bravery of a woman, expressed in the proverb, goes like this. Long ago, in some part of South Africa, there was a Black Mamba snake that lived in the tops of trees in the bush. It had killed several herdboys, who had passed through the bush, while tending their flocks, driving them to pastures. There was much wailing in the community each time one of the boys was struck and killed by the vicious snake. Because of the wailing of the women, men had gone out on two or three occasions, armed with sticks and assegais to hunt this killer snake. But, on each of these occasions the poor men got so frightened that they raced back home, even before reaching the spot where the snake was supposed to be.

One day, a woman who had lost both of her sons, decided that she would die rather than have the remaining boys of the village become victims to the snake. Early in the morning she cooked a large pot of porridge; she then filled a large clay watercarrier with this porridge. This waterpot had a large, u-shaped opening at the top. She put this waterpot on her head, which she balanced with a *khare* (a woven ring of grass or cloth) which also protected her form being burnt on the head. She then set out for the woods, timing her departure so that she was well ahead of the flocks following slowly behind, being driven by the herdboys.

The snake, as usual, struck at the passing figure. But this time its target was hot porridge. It fell into the waterpot, and drowned. The whole village came out to see the dead snake that had tormented them for so long. That is how the myth and the idiom came about because of the bravery of that woman.

That is why the tenacity of the Women's Anti-Pass

Campaign went on unabated from 1956 to 1960. It became what one could call a crusade throughout the length and breadth of the country. African women had already witnessed what the Pass Laws brought to their menfolk and to their families, and they saw themselves as having been directly affected. At the same time the people of Pondoland, Sekhukhuniland and Zeerust were revolting against the Bantu Authorities, a history brilliantly related by Govan Mbeki in his book *The Peasant's Revolt* (1964).

Once again, women played an important role in these struggles, and many were arrested and sent to prison, including a chieftainess, Malinoha, who was sentenced to death, although her sentence was later commuted to life imprisonment. Lilian Ngoyi had met her during her organising visits to Sekhukhuniland. She had a twelve-year-old daughter at the time she was sentenced to death.

* * *

The atmosphere in the country was so charged and full of resentment that it precipiated spontaneous actions in many areas. For instance, in Sophiatown, early one morning in 1958, two women came to my house and told me that women were assembling in Freedom Square for a protest march to the pass office in Market Street in the centre of the city. I was at that time chairwoman of the ANCWL in Sophiatown, with Kate Molale as secretary. I took no time to see what was happening, and — to my greatest surprise — I found the square already full of women.

We met briefly with Kate to see if we could persuade the protesters to hold off until we had reported to the branch executive, since the rule was that the auxilliary bodies of the ANC were to report all their activities to the 'mother' body — in this case, the branch executive — for guidance. But the mood of the women was beyond our estimation; they wanted to hear nothing of that. It was one of those times when the masses march ahead of the leaders instead of vice versa. Some women were suggesting the burning of the beer hall in Western Native Township. We stood firmly against that idea, supporting rather the march to the pass office, which, we pointed out, was in the programme of the ANC.

Once everybody had accepted that the 'rule of law' of the ANC was supreme, and that it had to be observed no matter how angry or how militant we were, we at once made arrangements to get to the pass office. Those not so young and the ones carrying babies were to take buses, while the rest were to walk to the city, a distance of between three and a half to four miles.

The time was about eight o'clock in the morning, yet the Special Branch were already on the scene in their cars. They drove slowly on the road while we walked on the pavement. Time and time again they pointed fingers at us, but we took no notice of them as we hurried in order to join the group who had left by buses. As we walked through the white residential areas of Westdene and Brixton, women domestic workers cheered us — some even joined us! We had passed the Bridgeman Maternity Hospital on the right, and the Radio South Africa Tower on the left, so that we were now facing Vrededorp, the scene of the 1913 encounter between women protesters and the police. The enthusiasm and excitement was growing as we were halfway to our destination.

However, at that very moment we noticed scores of police and vans blocking the road about 200 yards ahead of us. The spot where the police had placed their road blocks was a great disadvantage to us in that, on the left, was a fenced-in cemetery that stretched as far as Vrededorp, while there was another white residential area on the right. We stopped to plan how to get out of that bottleneck. We ruled out being dispersed by teargas because of the white residential area, and thought that it was likely that the police would baton-charge us, or just arrest us. Finally, as all traffic was by now at a standstill, we decided that we would not turn back if the 'disperse' order was given, but surge into the road and mix with the rest of the traffic. The aim was that everyone should then find her own way to the pass office.

When we were a few yards from them, the police, hailing us through a loudspeaker, ordered us to stop. Then Colonel Pienaar, holding a little stick under his armpit, came forward with a black policeman. The latter pointed at me, and said: 'This one!' I hardly knew what that was supposed to mean. The Colonel told us that our procession was illegal, because we did not have permission for it, and that we were blocking traffic. He then went on to say that he would give us two minutes to disperse. Then, suddenly, he handed the loudspeaker into my right hand and asked me to repeat to the women what he had just said to me.

My mind was still occupied with my identification by the black policeman, and also by the decision we had taken when we had spotted the police. However, thanks to the astonishing human brain,'click' went another wavelength. I looked down, shuffled my feet, and produced an artificial cough, as if to clear my voice. 'The Colonel is a miserable fool,' I said, inwardly, 'but what an opportunity to remind the women of our resolution,' said another voice within me. And there I went, speaking in a mixture of Xhosa and Sesotho. '*Makosikazi, amapoyisa athi asina mvume ya lo mqodi. Kodwa nonke niyazi apho siya khona. Lea tseba moo reeang teng phambile. Pele basali*' (Women, the police say we have no permit for this procession. But you all know where we are going to. Forward women). As I said the last word, I pushed the loudspeaker into the hand of the black policeman, and slipped under his arm into the road. An African in a car opened the back door, and I jumped in.

I did not know what orders the Colonel gave, but, as the traffic began to start moving, through the back window of the car I could see the police surging forward, trying to catch the women. Others had their batons out, as if beating up the women. It was a real pandemonium. But I soon lost sight of these events, because the cars started to move fast. There were no words spoken between me and the other occupants of the car and I hardly knew them. However, I hoped that other women might have escaped, like I had done.

I waited at the bus rank in town for a good fifteen minutes, but nobody came. So I walked to the pass office in Market Street, which was about 300 yards away from the bus rank, hoping to join the women who had left in buses earlier on from Sophiatown. When I got there, I found the

126

place had been sealed off by the police. I walked straight towards them, and tried to pass through. From where I stood I could see the backs of women in the yard, and also some policemen. One policeman pushed me back, saying 'Can't you see the place is sealed'. I took about four paces backwards. Then, deciding to be polite, I came forward again and said to them, 'Gentlemen, I am going with these women'.

'You can't get in; these people have been arrested,' said another.

'Well, arrest me then, because I am going with them,' I replied.

'*Mosali*' (woman) he said, 'can't you understand English? You get away from here if you don't want trouble.'

'I told you to arrest me, as you have arrested them,' I repeated, to which he replied, 'No! No! You F... off.'

I gave up, but I got a chill in my spine, and felt hot in the face. Tears just rolled out of my eyes from anger and disappointment. I turned my back away from them, and stood there, thinking, 'My God! How could this happen! My comrades are arrested, and I don't know what happened to the group which was intercepted on the way. And it seems that I am the only one who is out of trouble. What are the comrades going to think of me!'

I walked slowly to the ANC office, which was a few yards across the street, but there was nobody; it was still very early. I therefore decided to go back and take the bus to Sophiatown, thinking that perhaps I might see the remnants of the group I had marched with; but there was no sign of them.

I got off the bus at Toby Street, the first stop inside Sophiatown, and walked into Victoria Road. My street, Bertha Street, was the next one along. Before I reached Bertha Street, I met a man who worked for a burial society at the corner of Victoria Road and Bertha Street. He told me that all the typists had gone to the Newlands police station to demand the release of the women who had been arrested on their way to the pass office that morning. Without further question, I dashed to the police station.

At the police station I found another crowd of women; they

127

were being addressed by the same Colonel Pienaar. I arrived just as I heard him say 'And I am going to give you two minutes to disperse'. There then followed a police baton charge. As the police station was separated from Sophiatown by a main road, the police pursued us all the way into the township. Here we regrouped again. I told the women what had happened to the march in the morning, and that all the women who had gone to town in the buses had been arrested. Someone revived the idea of burning some of the beerhalls. Others thought that it would be better to go to our homes to organise food for those arrested and also to find out where small children were left uncared-for.

When I got home, the first thing was to have a cup of tea and bread, as I had left for Freedom Square in the morning without breakfast, thinking that I would come back swiftly. But, a few minutes later I heard the banging outside of car doors. Two policemen walked in. One was the policeman who had pointed me out on the march, and to whom I had handed the loudspeaker. Without even saying 'Good Afternoon', he stated, 'Mrs Resha, but why do you want to lose us our jobs? We have been looking for you all over. Come with us to the police station; the Colonel wants to speak to you.' My response was, 'Tell the Colonel he has a car; he can come and talk to me here'. We argued for some time, with me asking if they had come to arrest me. But they kept saying that the Colonel merely wanted to speak to me. I then suggested that I would come on foot, but they refused; they said that the Colonel was waiting for me, and that he was very busy. So I went into the kwela kwela (police van).

I left a note for my husband, to say that I had gone to the police station — the children were still at school. When I entered the charge office, the eyes of every policeman, white and black, were on me as if I had committed the highest crime. In a few minutes the black policeman came out with the Colonel. The latter looked at me with a flushed face, then nodded and said, 'Ja! this is the woman. Put her with the others'. To my statement, 'If you are arresting me, what is the charge?', the answer from the policeman at the desk was 'illegal procession'.

As I entered the huge cell, I found hundreds of women who had been picked up from the march. There were cheers and clapping as I entered. We then all sat down on the cement floor. The cell was stinking; it had an open toilet hole in the centre of the floor. The women told me that, when we had parted on the road, they had been surrounded and ordered into the vans. I then told them about the fate of the women who had left in the buses.

At six o'clock food started to come in from our friends. The women were really hungry; most of them had left very early, with only a cup of tea. By 7.45 pm my husband came, carrying my overcoat, in the pockets of which he had nicely stuck the first and late editions of the Johannebsurg *Star*. I returned the overcoat after taking the papers, telling him that my travelling rug was sufficient. We then started reading the papers. Everybody in the cell listened silently. Our demonstration was reported in the late edition. There was also a report on a similar demonstration by the women of Alexandra Township, reported to have been over a thousand strong, who had been packed into police vans, giving clenched fist salutes. These women had been arrested at the police station at Alexandra Township, where they had gone to protest and demand the release of the women arrested at Sophiatown. This demonstration was led by Florence Mophosho, and others.

Florence Mophosho lived in Alexandra Township. She was a self-made woman, who earned her living as a factory worker. And, like many other African women, she did bric-a-brac jobs in the townships to augment her wages in order to support her children and her mother. I had first met her at an ANCWL Conference at Germiston in 1953, at which conference the Transvaal Women's League had adopted Congress colours — green blouses, black skirts, gold chiffons. This uniform was later adopted by the Women's League nationally, as well as by the Federation of South African Women. Florence was a magic organiser, and she contributed immensely to the stability and prominence of her branch, which was one of the strongest in the Transvaal.

She had a lovely voice, and she composed many Freedom

Songs. For instance, after the arrest of Nelson Mandela, in 1962, she composed the song *'Mandela ke senatla'* (Mandela you are a giant! We stand by you, Mandela!). In the mid-Sixties she had to escape into exile, due to the harassment of the police. For several years she was the ANCWL representative on the Secretariat of the Women's International Democractic federation (WIDF), which had its headquarters in the then German Democratic Republic. Later, she was stationed at ANC headquarters in Tanzania, where she was production editor of the Women's Section Bulletin, *Voice of Women*. She later became a member of the ANC NEC in exile. Florence was a brave woman; she bore the pains of a long illness with great dignity, and died in 1986. The news of her death was reported at a meeting celebrating South Africa Women's Day, a day which, through her militancy and of others like herself, became an historic date in the calendar of the liberation struggle.

In our cell the women were in a jubilant mood; we sang freedom songs and made speeches until the early hours of the morning. Of course, some women were worried about the children, but morale was very high. The following day the ANC arranged for bail for all the women. Finally, we all appeared in the Johannesburg Magistrates court, where we were defended by the firm of Mandela & Tambo. The sentence was either one month imprisonment or £60 fine each. All the women (except one or two, whose husbands paid the fines because of problems of small children) went to prison.

My case was the last to be heard. I was charged with two offences: (a) leading an illegal procession; (b) escaping from custody. What! escaping from custody? I had told my solicitor, Mr Godfrey Pitje (who was articled to Mandela and Tambo) how I had been separated from the other women during the pandemonium created by the police while we were on our way to the city. And I had also told him the actual words I had used in the two languages when the Colonel asked me to repeat what he had said during our march. So my solicitor pinned down the black policeman who was the chief witness. He neither knew in what language I spoke (whether Xhosa or Sesotho), nor could he even remember the words I had said. So, in other words, his evidence was not credible. But a white policeman witness had heard me say 'forward, women!' Apparently he knew Sesotho very well, because all white children are brought up by black women, who speak our languages to them. At the Pretoria Hospital, I discovered many doctors knew Sepedi, though they wanted us to interpret for them. The second charge, that of escaping from custody was dropped.

On the first day of the hearing I had agreed that I did not need an interpreter. But, seeing the hostility of the prosecution, I suddenly told the magistrate that I wanted one. The case was not adjourned, but the magistrate sent for an interpreter. While I waited in the witness-box I had fears that the prosecutor might trick me with legal terms. Before he passed sentence, the magistrate spoke to me in a very polite tone, unlike the prosecutor. 'Mrs Resha', he said, 'I know you are a midwife, but I want to know what is your educational standard.' I told him, but I was suspicious about this polite question, because of the usual belief of whites in South Africa that the educated Africans were the ones misleading others. Finally, my sentence was the same as that passed on the other women.

Many women came to my case. On some days, among them was my old colleague, Albertina Sisulu. I was very pleased, because when you are about to be sent to prison, it is so encouraging to get that solidarity from friends and colleagues. My husband also attended because they had some adjournment from the Treason Trial that time.

By the time I went to prison to serve my sentence, all the Sophiatown women had been discharged. This was because their case was the first to be heard; they stayed in jail for two weeks and then the ANC paid the remaining fines in order to get them out. My case was heard a few days before the Alexandra women were sentenced, so when I came to jail, they had been there for three or four days. I think all this was done for the convenience of the courts or the number of inmates at the Fort, because all the women were sent there, and not to other prisons. So I ended up in the Fort, the Johannesburg prison, which is situated behind the General

Hospital where I used to work.

This was the first time I had gone to jail to serve a sentence, because, when I was first arrested in 1958 with Kate Molale and Violet Molwantwa, we were remand prisoners.

Nelson Mandela came to see us after the end of the first week. When he came again, at the end of the second week, he told us that the ANC had decided to pay the remaining fines so that we could be released. Indeed, we were all released after two weeks. Although it was dark outside, because it was a wintry day, we found quite a large crowd gathered outside the prison. Many were relatives; others were friends from the Movement. Above all, we were happy to be welcomed upon our release by some of the top leaders of the ANC, including Moses Kotane — 'Malome' (uncle), as he was called by everyone in the ANC.

The ANC Womens' League is not a separate organisation from the ANC: its programmes are guided by it. But women do take initiatives when directly affected by apartheid laws. In 1958 women were deeply involved in the work of solidarity and popularising the defence of the leaders charged with treason. This in itself was a national campaign; therefore, it had some influence on the decision to bail out the arrested women and also having their fines paid. As I wrote earlier, in some areas the actions of the women were spontaneous and taken without proper planning. The women themselves realised this, because leaving small children uncared for is a problem where there are no nannys.

My children were very happy when we got home with my husband. My eldest daughter, Nosipo, who was then nine years of age, was a bit showy, telling me how she had looked after her younger sister, Masechaba, who was six years of age. I got a bit stuck when they asked me if I would go to jail again. So, in order to calm them down, I said that they had seen people arrested every day, so that the whole thing depended upon the police. Anyway, I was happy with myself, because after the experience of those two weeks, my dread for jail seemed to have subsided. I felt the necessity and the correctness of our cause as an oppressed nation was worth more than temporary setbacks like imprisonment. Some of

132

the women told us that they had been arrested because they had been eating fish and chips in the street. Yes, many people have been arrested for this kind of nonsense, called drunk by the police. Yet there were no restaurants where Africans could have their lunches in the City, and they could not go twenty-three miles away to the locations, since most lunch times was one hour only.

* * *

South African prisons are never short of political prisoners. In 1958, after the women of Sophiatown and Alexandra township had been disciplined — as had been happening in many other parts of the country — another group of women from Soweto, among them Mrs Sisulu, Mrs Mandela, Mrs Nokwe and Mrs Molefe, were the next inmates; they had staged a big demonstration at the Orlando police station, against the pass laws. The cycle of detentions continues.

The freedom song which was composed for the women of the Orange Free State, when they burnt their passes, got additional words: 'Malibongwe igama la makhosikazi (Praise be to the Women). The women had now become the spearhead of the struggle; they had become a formidable force within the ANC. And, once again, the ANC saw fit to honour the women by issuing Awards of Merit to all the women across the country who had been imprisoned during the campaign. I have added my certificate to this book because it is, indeed, the most precious document I possess. Perhaps I value it so highly because none of us expected such an honour and because any professional certificate without freedom is nothing.

Although Robert and I shared many a secret, there are things that he never divulged to me. Especially matters discussed in the NEC. To prove my point here, the issuing of Certificates of Merit to the women protesters in 1958 was a decision of the NEC, of which Robert was a member. But I never knew anything about it until the day the awards were issued at our branch meeting. It really took all the women by

133

surprise when the chairman announced that the secretary was going to read the names of people who were to receive awards.

What was touching about the awards was the choice of words written in them. When you are in the struggle, you really never think that you are doing anything extraordinary, but simply that you are working side by side with your comrades-in-arms for the realisation of those ideals dear to you all — freedom, justice and equality for all South Africans. The issuing of the awards was therefore a great encouragement which picked up the morale of the women to redouble their efforts in the struggle. And (as I said earlier on) it proved that our menfolk recognised the importance of the participation in the struggle of the women. Precisely because African women suffer a double oppression — as a black person as well as a woman — their struggle is central.

Women were fighting against the Pass Laws because of instinctive self-protection from insecurity, degradation and humiliation, which was epitomised by these laws. And, from what they had experienced as mothers, wives and sweethearts of passbearers, they were fighting to protect their families from being plunged into disarray. Last, but not least, they were fighting to protect their children from being turned into the street— wandering, hungry orphans when both parents were picked up and locked up in jail or sold to white farmers for slave labour.

This Women's Anti-Pass Campaign engendered a highly-charged atmosphere among the African population right across the country, against all apartheid laws. At ANC branch, regional and provincial gatherings, there were systematic calls for men to get rid of their passes in order to link up with the campaign by the women. These demands led to the annual National Conference of the ANC in 1959, unanimously adopting a resolution to that effect. The date set by the conference was the 31 March 1960. On that day, men and women would stage mass demonstrations to local authorities, that is, pass offices, municipal offices, Native Commissioners, with passes packed in bags, and destroyed by burning them there.

The resolution further stipulated that every member of the ANC should organise at their places of work, in buses and on trains. The provinces and branches were to have fulltime organisers to travel to remote areas of the country, rural areas and farms to spread the gospel. There was certainly a mammoth job to do; but three months of brisk organising was quite reasonable. Because funds were essential to the campaign, women organised parties, raffles and stokvels. Some of the organisers abandoned their jobs to work fulltime on the campaign; so they had to get allowances to keep their home fires burning. The ANC was to make the biggest onslaught against the Pass Laws.

Then, ten days before the ANC Anti-Pass Campaign was due to begin on 31 March, the PAC announced that it was launching its own Anti-Pass Campaign on 21 March. This time, an invitation was extended to the ANC, who turned it down: the two campaigns were different; the ANC had had the Defiance Campaign in 1952.

Despite the short-circuiting of this campaign because of the Sharpeville massacre, which I mentioned earlier, the ANC once again displayed its maturity and faced its responsibility by viewing the situation as a national tragedy. Five days after the massacre Chief Luthuli, President of the ANC, after deliberating with his executive, called for a Day of Mourning and Prayer for the victims and their relatives. He further asked people to stay at home as a protest against the killing and maiming of unarmed men, women, and children by the racist regime.

Consequently, on 26 March, Chief as Volunteer-in-chief publicly burnt his pass, and directed all other men to do the same. For these actions, Chief had three charges laid against him: (a) burning his pass; (b) disobeying a law by way of protest; (c) inciting others to do the same. The case eventually came before the court in June, but with repeated adjournments, it dragged on until the ending of the State of Emergency at the end of August. Chief was finally found guilty on the first two counts. For burning his pass he was sentenced to six months imprisonment without the option of a fine, suspended for three years because of his health. For

135

disobeying a law by way of protest he was sentenced to one year in prison or a fine of £100. The fine was paid by friends.

On 28 March, as the campaign of pass-burning spread like wild-fire across the whole country, the regime specially passed the Unlawful Organisations Act, under whose provisions both the ANC and the PAC were banned. In terms of this Act, the maximum penalties for 'intimidation', laid down in the Riotous Assemblies Act for people who went on strike, or who boycotted, were increased to five years in prison, or ten lashes, or a combination of any two of these. The regime also declared a 'State of Emergency (which lasted until the end of August of that year), under which thousands of people of all races were detained, and newspapers banned.

The ANC had been banned in some areas before, but, never since its foundation in 1912, had it been pronounced an illegal organisation. Despite the fact that, since its inception, its leaders had been banned, banished, imprisoned, and were now facing the highest charge in the land, it was becoming stronger and stronger. It was the genuine voice of the dispossessed, voteless black masses, who were being denied fundamental human rights in their motherland. So, in reply to this callous move by the regime, the ANC announced that it would continue the struggle underground, and that the will of the people would not be dampened by what was clearly an act of desperation by the regime.

The banning of the ANC in 1960 came as no surprise to the membership in general. The leadership had anticipated this move for some time, because of their analysis of speeches by ministers here and there. It was because of these statements that the ANC had ordered the branches to master the 'M Plan', that is, mass organisation from house to house, street by street, and the formation of an elaborate system of cells which would be able to function, undetected, in case the organisation had to go underground. That was from the early Fifties. When the ban came, the cells were streamlined, and reduced to a maximum of seven people in each one. The new instructions to the cells were (a) that they knew only what they were supposed to know; (b) to keep time very strictly; (c) members of a cell to observe strict discipline. As a result, members of the same branch did not know who was in which cell, a design also intended at eliminating informers.

Still, the money-dangling regime did manage to buy informers to infiltrate the cells. The infiltration became so serious that there was talk that it reached the High Command, hence the Rivonia arrests. In his defence speech at that trial, Nelson Mandela restated the assertions in the underground document the ANC had issued after the ban:

> The ANC has decided not to obey the decree. The African people are not part of the government and did not make the laws by which they were governed. We believe in the words of the Universal Declaration of Human Rights that "the will of the people shall be the basis of authority of the government, and for us to accept the banning was equivalent to accepting the silencing of the Africans for all time. The ANC refuses to dissolve, but instead goes underground".

With real, effective opposition put out of action, the regime unleashed a reign of terror against its opponents. The use of spies and informers reached such levels that those who committed this treachery went about as if they were doing a prestigious job. Leaders of liberation movements were incarcerated in prisons, without trial. Some were tortured and killed. Others were put under house arrest, or served with perpetual banning orders. Because of the crippling effects of these measures, many leaders were forced to go into voluntary exile to continue the struggle.

Perhaps at the time when the regime persecuted the black people, the white voters saw it as a sign of strength of government. They did not realise that oppression of one section of the population could not be insulated from affecting the rest; it was injury to all South Africans. Indeed, within a very short time the whites were to taste the fruit of their own folly.

Thereafter, the regime issued a decree to the effect that all white employers, be it in industry, on the farms, or in private houses, would face a fine or imprisonment if they hired or kept Africans without a pass. This was, of course, an ingenious way of forcing African women into carrying passes. There was, clearly, terror and panic among the whites after this decree was passed. This was particularly discernible within the ranks of white women householders, the majority of whom kept up to six domestic workers. There were no contracts signed between the parties, and salaries depended upon what employers chose to pay. In all, salaries of domestic workers amounted to tips. But the work was of such a nature that each white family enjoyed a comfortable life from cradle to grave, just as it had been during the times of slavery.

In order to beat this ultimatum and the threat to their way of life, the 'Madams' (as white women insisted on being called) loaded their workers into their posh cars and drove them to the nearest pass offices to see that they took their passes. The domestic workers were very bitter, because no consent was sought from them by their employers; they related how they were abused and insulted by pass office officials, how they were herded in like cattle into a dipping tank, their headcovers ripped off for one-minute photographs. Many had hardly had time to comb their hair, since they had to leave their homes at five in the morning to be on time to prepare breakfast for their madams. Of course, the regime knew the vulnerability of domestic workers, so it used their employers as a springboard to introduce passes to women by the back door. White women were the ones to pull the noose to strangle members of their own sex, who, except for their skin colour, shared so much in common with them.

* * *

The women's campaign depended very heavily on the elaborate engagement of couriers. Young women very effectively constituted a network which criss-crossed the country from the cities to the rural areas and from province to province: women like Tozi Mqota, Kate Molale, Karabo Sello and many others carried out this task brilliantly at great

138

personal risk.

Before I pass on to the next chapter, I think it is proper to mention one more apartheid law which has affected a large number of African workers, the nurses. I refer to the 1957 Nursing Act. Under the original, 1944 Nursing Act, the names of all State Registered Nurses and Midwives appeared on the same register, alphabetically. They also all automatically enjoyed membership of SANA, The South African Nursing Association.

As nurses were not allowed to join trades unions, SANA was supposed to be the body looking after the interests of its members — working conditions; salaries; protection of all aspects of their work. Black and white nurses all paid the same amount as annual subscriptions to SANA for its work. But, under apartheid, there was no protection or guarding of the interests of the black nurses. Salaries were decided according to the colour of the skin. African nurses were at the bottom of the scale, with Coloureds and Indians next to bottom, with that of whites at the top. There were other forms of discrimination. For instance, African nurses were not allowed maternity leave — when they were expecting a baby, they had to resign, then reapply when they were ready to start work again. But even then, on most occassions, they did not get their job back. And when they did, their salary scale was dropped to that of beginners' salary. Black nurses were not paid for working unsocial hours; they could not give instructions to any white person, including orderlies and ambulance drivers. But, to see the hypocrisy of the whites in South Africa, white medical students agreed to be instructed by black midwives in places like the Pretoria Maternity Hospital (Non-European Section).

Black nurses got discouraged with the SANA for not looking after their interests. However, their subscriptions continued to fatten the coffers of the Association. Requests to act on their behalf led to the doors being slammed in their faces. All this came to a head because of the decision of the regime to repeal the 1944 Nursing Act, and to replace it with a new one, by which apartheid in the nursing profession would be institutionalised. Under this new Act, there were to be sepa-

139

rate registers, one for each racial group, with a separate Association for each group as well: a Bantu Nursing Association; a Coloured Nursing Association; an Indian Nursing Association. Only whites were to remain members of the 'South African' Nursing Association, which was affiliated to the International Council of Nurses, which has its headquarters in Geneva, and which recognised the South African Nursing Association, although it had become, in effect, a racist organisation representing white nurses only. But, before the Bill was discussed in the white parliament, it was rumoured that some white matrons and heads of hospitals had been summoned to Cape Town to give evidence to a Select Committee to show that black nurses were not fit to be members of the Nursing Council and of the Nursing Association, because they were inferior, whatever that was supposed to mean.

The new Act also required a higher standard of education for black nurses, that is, candidates were required to hold either a matriculation certificate, or be a graduate. This new requirement was clearly to reduce the numbers of black women taking up nursing. (There were very few black male nurses at the time.) In the past, black pupils could enter nursing for State Registration after acquiring a Junior Certificate or a Native Primary Lower Certificate. But, with Bantu Education having being enforced from 1954, it meant that the numbers of qualified candidates would go even lower. Meanwhile, health services were inadequate for Africans (and even non-existent in some areas).

The Act also stated that it was an offence to place a black nurse in charge of a white one; to do so was punishable by a fine of £200. Finally, under the Act, the Nursing Council had the power to introduce any discrimination it saw fit — like different syllabuses, different examinations, certificates, uniforms, etc. It was only after protests and demonstrations and condemnations by non-white nurses all over the country that assurances were given that syllabuses, examinations and certificates would continue to be the same for nurses of all racial groups. However, as I pointed out, the numbers would be greatly reduced because of Bantu Education.

During this debate on the Bill, there were elections for the SANA branch of the West Rand, of which I was a member. Black nurses, who were usually few in number at these election meetings, decided that, because of the reasons stated above, to participate fully in that meeting. Their numbers overwhelmed the white members present, many of whom had stayed away, perhaps out of complacency, as they knew that they controlled the branch. The results were devastating for the white nurses: although a white nurse was re-elected as chairman, three-quarters of the new executive were black. The panic that struck the white nurses was such that one would think that the blacks had taken all power and the country as well. This reaction really astonished the blacks, because the whites had always controlled the branch. According to our reckoning, the Bill became law even faster, because of this event, so that no other group of white nurses should ever go through what had happened to the white nurses on the West Rand. The Act was passed.

Because the Act had become law much sooner than we had expected, there were no meetings of the West Rand branch. Instead, black nurses formed a non-racial organisation, because they had now been thrown out of the SANA. The last time we saw the Chairman of SANA was the day black nurses went to demonstate at the City Hall; she came to stop us because, she said, we would be arrested, as we had not sought permission to go on a protest march. We ignored her appeals, and she found herself marching with us to the City, where we read the Florence Nightingale Pledge. The day ended without incidents.

So, black nurses continued to carry on their struggle even after the passing of the Act. In the Transvaal, black nurses formed the Rand Nurses Professional Club. From there we contacted nurses and midwives in other parts of the country, and it was out of these actions that we formed the Federation of South African Nurses and Midwives in 1958 in Johannesburg. In the following year we held a conference in Cape Town, where we took a decision to have nothing to do with segregated associations. We held another conference in Johannesburg in 1961. Only one white person, Iris

141

Goldstein, joined our Federation. Nurses demonstrated in all the Provinces. Nurses from Pretoria, the West and East Rand, held a demonstration at the Johannesburg City Hall; in Cape Town, black nurses, led by Mrs Blanche La Guma demonstrated in the streets of the City. They carried placards which said that disease knows no colour. and that nursing is care for the sick and the suffering. In Durban Mrs Ignitia Manyoni was a diligent member of the Federation and so was Mrs Bovungana in East London and many others.

Our Federation became really strong, and we were very proud of it. However, by 1961, the cracks began to show in its ranks. A few senior nurses, who were showered with posts of 'Bantu Matrons', were secretly summoned to Pretoria by the Nursing Council, and asked to accept the segregated Nursing Council and Nursing Associations. This they did, and by the late Sixties the Federation was dead because like all apartheid laws, the 1957 Nursing Act was rammed down our throats. However, the Federation had existed for five years which was remarkable considering the regime's onslaught. On the executive of the Rand Nurses Professsional Club were Gladys Kala, Vivian Pheteni, Mrs Sisulu, Mrs Massina, Mrs Ncapayi, Constance Mbekeni, Betty Nyama, Iris Goldstein, Mary Morare, and myself. Some were also on the executive of the Federation.

The Fifties was the decade in which the womens' consciousness as well as their conscientious participation in the liberation struggle reached their highest peak. It was a decade of great sacrifices by women of all social strata in many ways, and if South Africa had then been governed by civilised and democratic leaders, there would have been a change for the better. Many women were awakened into politics by the very extremism of the Nationalist government; the majority of these women had never been inside a jail before, and many, like myself, were terrified of the jail.

During the campaign, a freedom song was composed; it went: 'Hey Verwoerd! Vulitirongo tina sizongena ama-Volontiya' (Hey Verwoerd! Open the jail; we volunteers will go in).

142

8

■

On The Way To Soweto

The Government Gazette of 1953 or 1955 published the names of all African men whose Exemption Certificates had been cancelled. My husband's name appeared among these. After that, Robert stopped bothering to apply for the green Reference Book, which was intended as a replacement for the Exemption Certificate.

The difference between the brown Reference Book, which the majority of African men carried, and the green one (the so-called 'Exemption') was only in the cover, and, in contrast with the name applied to them, their effect was to tighten the screws of the Pass Laws and extend them to women. While the first part of the law spoke of the 'Abolition' of Passes, the second part was about the consolidation and co-ordination of these documents. So, it was just another Machiavellian way of insulting the intelligence of Africans. One need only ask, 'Which documents need to be consolidated if passes were to be abolished!' In any case, how could a policeman tell which African man was 'exempt' from carrying a pass? You still had to carry the green one to show the policeman that you were 'exempt'.

I fully supported my husband in his decision not to apply

144

for the pass. He had been arrested several times, and paid fines, for not producing it on demand. But, life had to go on like that because, after all, to have a pass or not to have one did not make any difference; the real motive of the regime was to make Africans aliens in their own land and to have complete control of their lives. However, the thought of Robert being arrested, and sold to the farms, never totally escaped my mind. The idea of a happy, enviable life was, for an African, as remote as being in a sputnik. Each time Robert was arrested I prayed that the worst should not happen.

By 1959 Sophiatown had become a heap of rubble, and sanitary facilities had diminished to a level beyond human tolerance. Terror of police raids, arrests, homelessness, had reached their summit. Then it became our turn. Robert had gone to Pretoria as usual to attend the trial; I left for work about one hour later. When we returned that evening, we found the children, as well as our household goods, on the pavement. The Resettlement Board demolishers had arrived shortly after our departure, and had commenced the demolition of our house without having given us any notice of their intentions.

We thought that it was vindictiveness of the Resettlement Board that made the demolishers come at that time. This was the second time that our house had been demolished. When they had come the first time, without having given us prior notice to vacate, we had managed to persuade the demolishers to allow us to take out our belongings, before they proceeded to remove the roof. Before sunset that day we moved into another house — one which we had found standing empty, presumably because the previous occupants had found accommodation elsewhere. Other people, too, had squatted in partly- demolished houses, or even in the streets, since it was not easy to move from place to place with furniture. Although the SB knew where we had gone, we managed to stay in this new house for about four and a half months. I recall that a policeman had said to Robert the day they broke into our kitchen that, if he (Robert) moved, then the people would move. On this second occasion, our house

145

was the only one to be demolished that day.

What struck me, when I was about 200 yards away, was the sight of a group of people in front of our house. As I looked closer, I saw that the tiles of the roof were gone. Then, when the children saw me as I came nearer, they ran to meet me; they started telling me of their plight in the excited way of frightened children. They said that it was just after having had their breakfast that there had been a knock on the roof, and that a tile had plunged on to the ground. Then a man had come to the door; he told them to take out all the furniture. It was clear that the demolishers had started their job even without first checking to see if the place was empty. Fortunately, my sister was with the children. She poured buckets of cold water on the stove, which was red-hot from the burning coal. The neighbours had all come, rushing to help; they told me that they found moving the furniture out, and keeping it safe, was difficult, because the demolishers dropped one tile after another, without any care.

When I got to the house I found Robert already there. He had heard the story from a colleague in the city, when he had come back from the Treason Trial in Pretoria, so he had rushed home even before going to his office. Anyway, he told me, he had already got an offer from an Indian friend that we could move into his empty shop for that evening. Meantime, people had been very helpful to my sister and our children; many remained with us until we could hire a lorry to move us to the shop. Although the shop was no longer open for trading, there were still bottles of sweets and other items on the shelves. The space was too small for our household goods, so there was no sense in unpacking; we just piled everything into the shop the best we could, and bought ourselves a meal of fish and chips as we had no cooking facilities. Friends also brought us food and drinks. We stayed in the shop for two days, surrounded by bundles wrapped in sheets, some of which had been ripped down the middle by the men who lifted the bundles into the lorry. Beds were left leaning against the counters, while chairs and other things were piled on top of tables. During the night, my sister and

146

the children crammed together on the sofa to get some sleep, while Robert and I stretched out a divan for seating and for sleeping.

The following day I went to work, but I also started looking around for another place. With the help of friends, we next moved into an unused garage in Meyer Street. It was very dusty, but spacious enough for our belongings. I was worried sick for the health of my children. The lady who told me about the garage, and who gave me the key, had earlier stored her sister's furniture there. So, we hired the lorry again, to move to the garage. It was only after we got there that we unpacked some of the things. The first item we fixed was the stove because, fortunately, there was a round hole in the wall for the chimney; in the shop we had been limited to the use of a primus stove. As I unpacked I found that some of my crockery had been broken: glasses, plates, cups were in pieces — I think that this must have happened during the rush when our possessions were being taken from our demolished house. Father Blake from St. Cyprian's came to see us here; we told him that we were trying to get a place in Soweto.

But our next problem was that Robert had no pass, and without that document we could not apply to any municipal location for a house. So, once again, the document of slavery — which in the past had barred the dead from being buried, stopped people from being married, babies from being christened — obstructed our path. So Robert had to apply for a pass: not from choice, but as a necessity.

To apply for a pass, the applicant has to have a form filled in. Clerks at the pass office ask the questions of the applicant, and even if the applicant can write, it is they who fill in the form. Apart from obvious details like name, address, marital status, and place of work, the applicant is also asked where he, his father, and his grandfather had been born: this is done in order to connect the applicant with some 'Reserve' or 'Bantustan'. Next, the applicant's photograph is taken, and placed on the first page of the booklet. Then, the applicant's fingerprints are taken and applied to the page; copies are sent to Pretoria. It would usually take about two weeks for the pass to be issued, if one were known by the clerks. Unfortunate ones were told 'Come to-morrow', until their permits have expired, and the next thing would be arrest and farm labour. School leavers used to suffer most from this process. Some clerks were known for taking bribes for pushing names through, while others actually helped applicants by filling in false information in order to save people from being arrested, or endorsed out of the city.

Without a home, we were now hostages of the Pass Laws. Could we be sure that after getting it, the ransom would be considered paid ? Alas, no! Shock awaited us at the next corner. When Robert arrived with his pass one evening, he had nothing to be happy about, because the document bore on one page a red stamp, which said, 'Endorsed Out of Johannesburg'. That was in contradiction of the banning order which had been served on Robert a few months earlier in 1959, after he had addressed a mass meeting at Currie's Fountain, near Durban. That banning order had specifically confined him to the magisterial area of Johannesburg. The police had actually sought him out in the crowd in order to serve the banning order on him immediately after he had spoken! What bureaucratic confusion was here!

The meeting that Robert had addressed at Currie's Fountain had been for the launching of the boycott of Nationalist goods. The ANC had a list of firms — especially cigarette manufacturers — with close ties to the Nationalist Party, against which it mounted a nation-wide campaign. The meeting was described in the daily papers and by ANC leaders as the largest ever to have been held and addressed by an ANC leader (the crowd was estimated at 60,000). Robert then disappeared into the crowd, chased by the SB, who finally caught up with him, served him with a banning order and told him to get back to Johannesburg immediately, on pain of being arrested for being in the wrong area illegally. That was on the Saturday. At mid-morning on Sunday, Peter Ntite entered my place, looking a bit cowed, so I asked him why he was pulling his face. When he said, 'Sit down, Sis Maggie', I started to panic. But, after he had assured me that Robert was all right, he told me about the banning order. Peter had been told to come to tell me that Robert was on his way back, and that I should not worry; he was safe.

During this time the regime's intention was to cripple the ANC by banning as many of its leaders as it could. Within a few weeks, four ANC leaders — Chief Luthuli, Oliver Tambo, Duma Nokwe and my husband — were banned, while others like Moses Kotane, J. B. Marks, Govan Mbeki, Walter Sisulu and Nelson Mandela were under perpetual bans. Sometimes, if the regime did not renew the ban immediately, the leaders would at once address public meetings. Nelson Mandela was ordered to resign from the ANC, while others were 'named' communists even if they were not members of that organisation.

Then, a few months later, the Resettlement Board office in Sophiatown added their own red stamp, 'Endorsed Out of Sophiatown'. Really, this was the limit! Exactly where were we supposed to live? We knew that the answer was supposed to be 'Homeland' ruins, which Robert had left at the age of sixteen. This was the true face of the Pass Laws. As I said earlier, to have it or not to have it made no difference; we were now faced with the choice, either of going to the 'homelands' together, or be separated.

On examining the situation together closely, we came to the conclusion that the endorsement out of Sophiatown would enable us to get a house in another location, but that the endorsement out of Johannesburg would bar us from settling in any location under the jurisdiction of that city. So, we decided that, as I had no pass, I should go to the municipal offices to look for a house. Someone had tipped us off that some clerks in the municipal offices sometimes bent the rules in favour of women when they see they will be able to pay the rent. We knew that the officials would not ask me to bring my husband's pass, but that, if they did, I should say that the pass was with my husband in Pretoria, and that he could be arrested if he gave it to me, even for a day. At least, that was how the law then operated. Men had been arrested while working in their gardens, having left their passes in their jackets inside their houses.

At the Mofolo office, which was the first one that I visited,

149

the clerk gave me the names of two or three people who were selling their houses, as well as the contacts I could see in order to view these places. As my husband was a Xhosa, the house we could buy, on a ninety-nine year lease, had to be in either Mofolo South or Mofolo North. Mofolo Central was for Sesotho-speaking people. These ethnic residential boundaries were applied very strictly in these new locations, unlike in older locations, like Orlando, which had been built before the Nationalist regime had come to power.

After I had chosen a house, the clerk told me that I should make an appointment to meet with the owner at the housing department. He told me that all final transactions, as well as the money we had to pay, were made there. The money we had to pay the owner was calculated by the Council; it included the monthly rent, and came to £108. Furthermore, the clerk reminded me that my husband should present his pass to the authorities there, otherwise no transaction could be concluded. Fortunately, there was to be a two-week adjournment of the Treason Trial, and we made an arrangement with the owner of the house to meet at the housing office.

My husband and I were both very tense on our way to the meeting; we had already spent three weeks living in the garage home, and the police had already been there once, during permit raids, to warn us to move. As we approached, Robert said softly, 'I pray God that this white man (the housing officer) is reasonable, otherwise either he or I will go out through the third floor window'.

When we arrived at the housing office, we found out that the housing officer's name was Mr Carr; Robert said that he knew him from the time when he had been Superintendent at Western Native Township. I now got really worried, because I knew that Robert would do what he had said. But what then? He would be arrested, and charged with assault, and it would not get us the house. On top of that, he was already on trial for treason. So I said, 'Darling; let us first move out of the garage, and we continue the struggle after we have a shelter for our heads'. The 'Out of Johannesburg' endorsement on his pass was tearing me to pieces, since I knew of several people who had been banished to remote areas, where they could not earn a living, where they knew nobody, and where they were completely ruined in every respect.

When we arrived, we found lots of people in the queue in the first clerk's office; so we joined it. When our turn came the clerk, who knew Robert because they had played rugby together, greeted him as an old mate. 'Hello Robbie', he said, 'what can I do for you?' Robert, speaking in his polished, deep Xhosa (it is called 'Xhosa A'), replied: 'Mfondini (mate) my family is literally in the street. Can we still get the house we were offered by the Municipality in 1951, but which we declined?' The clerk went to get the file. When he returned, he confirmed that we had been allocated a house number in 1951, but that our name had been removed when we had declined the offer. But, he added, we could join the waiting list again, although to get another offer would take many years.

It was now that Robert told him that we wanted to buy a house, and that the owner had come with us as the Mofolo office had directed. She was a widow, who was going back to Natal, according to the story that our contact had told us; we really only saw her, for the first time, at the Housing Office. The clerk replied that, in that case, we need not have to join the waiting-list. He then started to prepare the forms for the transaction.

At this stage I moved backwards, and sat myself down on one of the benches. But, while they were talking, my head moved like that of a puppet, from one to the other, as I watched them. I heard the clerk ask Robert for his pass number. This was the crucial moment. After copying the number, he gave the pass back to him. I was amazed at how smoothly it went. But the smoothness was due to the fact that the clerk never looked at any other page, except the one that carried the number of the pass and Robert's photograph. After everything had been finalised, he took the forms into the housing officer's room next door, for his signature. After that, he gave a duplicate of the transaction to us to take to the Mofolo office in order to get the keys. And that was that; we had succeeded — miraculously.

Although the Treason Trial was still adjourned, I went to the office on my own to get the keys. The Superintendent gave me the keys, but he said that I should tell my husband to come to the office with his pass as soon as he could, so that we could get the receipt. Think of it — even to get a receipt for what you have paid for, you must produce a pass! Are not these some of the things which make the whites fear to share power with us, because they think that we shall treat them in the same way as they are treating us? Yet they are mistaken: Africans are too civilised to correct wrongs with wrongs. Apartheid is one word which will be banished in a new South Africa.

It was on a Friday that I went to the office; the Superintendent said that we could commence occupation only on the Monday. Although I told him that our situation was desperate, he was adamant about his Monday, although he never gave me the reasons. It was one of those red-tapes which the location superintendents displayed to remind people of their authority. But we just ignored this bureaucratic stunt; we moved into the house on Sunday 29 November 1959, and Robert never took his pass to the office, because, he said, he would not go around with a policeman in his pocket.

Our house was one of those called 'Italian houses'. They are called that because they were built by Italian constructors; they looked different from other houses in that they were made out of cement slabs instead of bricks. The outside doors (front and back) were made out of steel, specially made so that they could make the most noise when the police came and either knocked hard, but more usually kicked at them. The roof, ceilings and floors were also made out of cement, while the doors inside the house were just open holes, without frames. The houses each contained two bedrooms and a kitchen, but no bathroom. It was just another pigeon-hole We had to get a carpenter to fix doors for us. Because there was no electricity in Soweto, we used a paraffin-run fridge and a battery-run radio. Because there was no bathroom, we could not fix our enamel bath we had brought from

152

Sophiatown, and had to make do with a sponge instead of a full bath. Still, after some time I bought a big tin bath which we used for washing clothes and also as a bath; it was big enough for an adult to sit in. Water had to be warmed on the stove in a large four-gallon paraffin tin; it was a boring business, so we mostly had baths in the evening.

Toilets, with doors which had two-feet openings top and bottom, were outside. When one was in these, anyone at the gate could see the feet of the person in occupation. The toilets were specially made like that so that the police could see someone hiding when they came on raids. The bucket system of sanitation was still in use; it was terrible. Flies were all over the place, because the bucket collectors left them in the street after emptying their contents into their little wagon. Each household had to collect his or her bucket from the street, and wash it before more flies covered it. Unlike our Sophiatown, this was a real slum — created and built by the regime. The streets were dusty and full of holes, which collected rainwater, so that there were swamps right in front of the houses.

The area where we stayed was called 'Crossroads', because it was an important junction for road traffic. This meant that transport was very convenient. There were also two shops and a garage on the main road behind our house. In fact, I knew one of the shopkeepers, Mr Nkosi. I had been his wife's midwife when I was still in Sophiatown. The other shopkeeper, Mr Kazamula, was a very likeable man, who had two wives. Immediately we came to Mofolo, he engaged me to deliver his junior wife; I had put a plaque with my name on it, stating that I was a midwife, on the wall of the house. That attracted a lot of people, but I am not sure that did not also attract the SB. Mr Kazamula also received my telephone messages; he was very happy to help with that — he would send one of his workers to cycle to our place, and I would then run to the phone, since the place was only about two minutes' walk away. Although I had applied for a telephone immediately we had come to Soweto, I was told that there were none yet in our area. So I had to depend on messages from Mr Kazamula's shop.

153

Whenever I saw him in the shop, Mr Kazamula would always discuss with me what he had read in the newspapers about the Treason Trial. So, although we lost many friends from Sophiatown, we soon made new ones at our new home. But we kept up contacts with others who had been moved. For instance, Mr and Mrs Makhoti had moved from Sophiatown before we did; they were in Mofolo Central, which was an area reserved for the Basotho group, and from which we, who were in the Nguni section, were separated by a street. But we were only five minutes walk away from each other. Another former inhabitant of Sophiatown, who was originally from Nyasaland, and who had lived in Toby Street, also, lived in our area. Perhaps he had been classified as Nguni!

A few weeks after we moved in, Nelson and Winnie Mandela came to visit us in our new place. Their car got stuck in the mud, and Nelson had to take over the wheel from Winnie, who had been driving, in order to get it out. It was a short visit, one of the many unannounced visits Nelson frequently made to Robert, and vice versa. On this occasion, Robert was not at home, so they left after Nelson had succeeded in taking the car out of the mud, while Winnie was in the kitchen with me, where I had been busy making peach jam. Winnie was quite amused at her husband as he struggled with the steering wheel as the car's tyres gyrated in the mud.

In December 1959, when we had spent one month in Mofolo, there was an annual meeting of the Women's League at which I was elected chair. It was a very big branch which included Mofolo South and North, and Mofolo Central. There were active women like Mrs Loabile, the former chairperson, and Mrs Dlamini, who was from Sophiatown and with whom I had shared a cell in 1958 at Newlands police station.

Anyway, as soon as we were settled, I started to revive my midwifery with the help of doctors in private practice. By this time we were really broke. Father Black had advised us about a good Anglican boarding school in Lesotho, and it was here that our children went in January 1960. I was now also able to recruit another midwife as a partner, so that she

154

could take over my cases when I went to jail for four months, as I will describe in the next chapter. I could now say that life was becoming a bit settled, according to South African standards. But still, to be uprooted from your home against your will is very traumatic. And to be forced to be where we ended up because of race group policy was further disturbing. Yet the white tribes choose where they want to live; they have no idea of what it feels like for people to be moving up and down, with bundles of belongings on their heads, or what sort of life that is for children.

* * *

On the morning of 2 May 1960 I suddenly woke up before dawn. After I had rubbed my feet together to feel if they were warm, I could find no apparent reason for my sleeplessness and abrupt awakening. I half opened my eyes to see if there was light outside, but the room was still dark. So I turned over, with my face away from the window. Perhaps I was sleeping on my arm, I thought, to myself. Then I had another thought — I might as well look at the time. I reached for the torch on the floor and shone it at the clock. Indeed, it was after four in the morning. I tried to sleep again, but the sleep timer in my brain was on the zero mark.

As I lay in bed, I started to ponder about the political climate in the country, which was under a State of Emergency, with thousands of people (my husband among them) in detention. The regime, caught with its pants down after the response of the people to the massacre at Sharpeville, had banned the ANC and the PAC. It had detained thousands of people, both black and white, although many activists managed to escape into neighbouring countries before they were caught in the net.

The morning of the declaration of the State of Emergency, my husband, like the other Treason Trialists, had boarded the bus that took them to the court in Pretoria. There they were all arrested as soon as the bus arrived outside the court-room. It was when I read this in the first editions of the evening papers that I realised the seriousness of the sit-

155

uation. Furthermore, our dear ANC, the only weapon Africans possessed to fight against injustice, had been snatched from our hands by the stroke of a pen, and in three days' time I was going to jail to serve a four-month sentence, stemming out of the incitement case of 1958. I felt angry, indignant, thoroughly frustrated. Then, as tension mounted in my body, I felt that I had to do something. Then, an idea came into my head. That something was to destroy my husband's pass, because the pass was the root of our troubles in our country. For some moments I debated with myself about the best way to set about doing what I had decided upon. So, at about six o'clock, I got up and went to the kitchen to make the coal fire, knowing that it would be ready in about an hour's time.

When the fire was ready, I took out my husband's pass from where I had hidden it, and pushed it into the red-hot coal fire. As it started to burn, I called my sister to witness 'the destruction of the evil', as I put it. She unreservedly agreed with me in the action I had taken; we both expressed resentment for the document, which was forced on people without freedom of choice. Robert had been detained before he had had the chance to destroy his pass. The strategy was that some of the leaders would destroy their documents in the presence of the Press, in order to keep up the momentum and to encourage others to follow Chief Luthuli's call to burn their passes. Meanwhile, as the Emergency Regulations forbade that the names of people detained be released, it was obvious that when Robert did not return from Pretoria that he was among the detained. But where?

As we watched the fire consuming the last bits of Robert's pass, I recalled how, in the first few days after the detentions, relatives had set about searching for their missing kin. I recalled that, together with a couple of women from my area, whose husbands had also been taken, we had gone to the Fort to enquire about their whereabouts. I had gone with Mrs Doreen Motsabi, from White City, Jabavu, whose husband John Motsabi was a senior member of the ANC, and who had been banned for a long time; we had been given a lift by David Mankazana, who was a member of the Jabavu

156

branch of the ANC. Whilst we were there, someone had come in to enquire about a relative. We heard a policeman shout, 'Mr Basner is not here!' Oh!, I thought, so Basner, the advocate is amongst those detained? We whispered to ourselves; we had read between the lines. But the policeman's face became expressionless when he realised our curiosity, because he had unwittingly revealed the name of a detainee, thus violating the terms of the regulations. He told us that the people for whom we were looking were not there.

So we dashed to Pretoria, where we found large crowds of people outside the prison, also looking for missing relatives. Mrs Luthuli and her daughter were amongst the crowd. One or two people had, in the meantime, instructed their solicitors to apply for Habeas Corpus on behalf of their relatives. It was only after midday that we were allowed into the prison yard, from where we could see our relatives, at a distance of about twelve yards, and separated from them by a wire mesh. However, the sight of them, even that far away, relieved our anxiety and agony — we had seen them, alive. I saw only Robert and Walter Sisulu on that day; the next visits I made were to the Synagogue, where the Treason Trial was held, after the hearings resumed.

But, for the ANC to be outlawed for the first time, put a great strain upon those members who were outside jail; we were afraid to talk to each other if we were more than three, as that number, seen together, was defined by the regulations as a 'gathering', and all 'gatherings' were illegal. People were also beginning to be suspicious of each other; we were always now afraid of informers and of spies. At my house, two or three individuals, not known to me, came at different times with suggestions that we should go and blow up government premises. I did not know these chaps from Adam.

When I questioned them about how they knew my residence in Soweto, which were built so uniformly that it was difficult sometimes for even their owners to find their houses, their answers were unconvincing. I immediately suspected that they were agents provocateurs, and so dismissed them with the contempt they deserved. I told them that my organisation was banned, and that I wanted to hear nothing from them. No meetings were held in my area during April and the beginning of May; when we met, we mostly talked about the Emergency — the atmosphere was very tense because the SB were racing up and down the country, trying to see if people were observing the regulations.

I cannot recall the date on which it was announced that the Treason Trial was to continue, despite the Emergency. Soon after that, we were told that we could visit our relatives at the court. I was really delighted about this, because it would enable me to pay my husband a few visits before I went in to serve my sentence. The detainees, meanwhile, needed food, as well as a change of clothes, and this was allowed.

Although the State of Emergency was in its second month at the time I burnt Robert's pass, there was no hint about when it would be lifted. The regime used that time to terrorise the people, with the help of the army and the police. It unleashed a stream of propaganda through the media, to the effect that the people should not be deceived by the ANC into destroying their passes, because many people among the detainees had held on to their passes. So, thousands of people who had destroyed their passes were arrested. My brother, who was one of those arrested for destroying his pass, was sold to a farmer near Pretoria, to work at a quarry; he escaped after two weeks, with three others. The morning he arrived back at our house, his suit and shirt looked as if they had been dipped in red mud. He immediately escaped into a neighbouring country.

My brother, who had obtained his Junior Certificate with a First Class examination pass, had originally come to Johannesburg as a migrant worker to look for work, with the intention of earning money to continue with his studies, but had deserted from the mine after three weeks. We had helped him, financially, while he studied at the Ohlange Institute in Durban, but, because of our own financial situation in the Fifties, he thought that he should try to get a job in order to relieve us of our burden. The problem was that his pass would not allow him to seek work in Johannesburg, since he was not from that city; his pass had been issued in Durban, and was for a student. So, he never carried his pass

158

with him while he was in Johannesburg.

Meantime, for about a month he worked for an ANC comrade who promised that he would be able to fix documents for him to be able to reside and work in the city. Unfortunately, this man was detained under the State of Emergency before he could help my brother (later, after his release, he too left the country because of harassment). Then, when my brother was arrested after burning his pass, my brother claimed that he did not need to have it since he was still a student. He then made a new application for a pass, but when he returned two weeks later to collect it, he was told that his fingerprints showed that he had been issued with a pass in Durban. This is how a pass incriminates its bearer. Robert was correct when he said that he could not go about with a policeman in his pocket.

When my brother did not come back from the pass office, we suspected that he had been arrested, but we did not know where to look for him. But one ANC comrade persisted in his searches; it was he who found out that my brother had been sent to the quarries in Pretoria, from where, as I mentioned earlier, he managed to escape.

What was haunting me most now about going to prison was that the children were coming home for their holidays in June. And, by the look of it, they would find neither of their parents at home. All parents strive to give health, happiness and love to their children, but that ideal is often a pipedream for black parents. Apartheid laws destroy the very fabric of what society calls family life. An eagle's nest on top of a precipice is more of a home, and more secure, than a black woman's home.

Thinking about prison also made me recall that, a few days before we were arrested in 1958, an African Special Branch man had dashed through the kitchen of our house, where we had been sitting. As he passed through from the front, through to the back door, he uttered the words, 'There are going to be arrests'. Then he slipped out.

His coming in and going out was so sudden that there was a momentary confusion in the house as to what the chap was up to. I stood up and tried to follow him, with the intention

159

of rebuking him for his rudeness in dashing in and out without knocking, but by the time I got to the door the police van had already roared away. However, we had got the message that there were to be arrests. The question was, who? As Robert was one of the 156 accused of high treason, we thought that perhaps there was going to be another round-up of other leaders around the country. Hardly did it click in my mind, or in that of Robert, that the man was talking about my own impending arrest. I think that we had become complacent; we thought that the regime had finished with us. But even if we had known differently, there was nothing that we could have done about it.

Three days later the Special Branch walked in. One was white, the other two were Africans. My sister had opened the door for them, then knocked on our door to say that the SB wanted to see me. 'What for?' I asked my sister. A man's voice behind her said, 'Mrs Resha, we have a warrant for your arrest for incitement'. As he said these words, he was already in the bedroom. As I quickly put on my gown, he handed the warrant to me to read. To tell the truth, I was shaken. I never expected this; it was the very first time in my life that I had been arrested. My husband just sat up in bed behind me; he did not say a word. The Special Branch man perhaps saw my predicament. The warrant was long, full of legal terms, like 'arrest under section so-and-so'. So the SB man came to my rescue. He told me that my arrest was in connection with the meeting I had addressed for the 'Stay-at-Home' campaign a few months earlier.

This campaign was in response to the whites-only elections of that year. The campaign was not launched on a large scale, like either the Congress of the People, or the Defiance Campaign. However, a meeting, organised by SACTU, was held in Johannesburg. That meeting called for a 'Stay-at-Home' and for a minimum wage of £1 per day for black workers. The campaign was therefore a joint effort on behalf of the ANC and the South African Congress of Trade Unions (SACTU). Still, despite the fact that the campaign was low-key, the white Press, together with the politicians of both white parties, condemned the campaign in quite hysterical terms. As a result, on the eve of the 'Stay-at-Home', the regime's Minister of Justice banned gatherings of more than nine people, and this over-reaction on the part of the white Press and politicians instilled much anger and frustration into the black masses.

In Sophiatown, by six o'clock as people were arriving home from work, they were greeted by ANC volunteers driving in an open lorry to which loudspeakers were fixed, calling them to attend a mass meeting at Freedom Square before midnight — the time from which the banning of gatherings would operate. The atmosphere in the township became very tense as people hurried over their suppers in order to get to the meeting on time. By 9.30, the Square was overflowing with people. Then the SB arrived, accompanied by truckloads of armed police. The trucks were parked at the edge of the Square, so as to block the entrance to Victoria Road, with their lights kept on.

The branch executive had chosen three women and three Youth Leaguers to speak. Each speaker was told to be as brief as possible in order that the meeting should be over before midnight. Violet, the treasurer of the Women's League, was the first speaker; she was to be followed by Kate, the secretary of the League, and myself. I was at that time chair of the Women's League. I can recall only the name of Patrick Letlalo as one of the Youth Leaguers who spoke. Because of my lack of height it was only when I climbed on to the platform that I noticed the police trucks and the police cars; the square itself was a bit dark because the few street lights could only give light to the areas near the edge, although these were aided by lights from neighbouring houses.

I remember that the first words I said were : 'De Villiers Graaff, leader of the United Party, says in the Press that we should not go on strike; yet our children are dying of malnutrition. I say we must stay at home tomorrow and pray because we are starving. We want a minimum wage of £1 per day'.

The meeting ended before midnight. The show of force by the police was useless. We were happy that their intimidation did not deter people from hearing the last word from the

161

ANC and SACTU. As I said earlier, the strike was a complete success in Sophiatown, despite the fact that the regime had sent Saracens and armed police into the township.

This was the background to my arrest, and why there now were SB men in my house. I gave the warrant back to the SB man, who then stepped back into the sitting room to give me time to get dressed. The only thing I could ask my husband was that he should ask our friend, Mrs Violet Matlou (wife of our political comrade, Joe) to take over my midwifery cases. As I left, the children and my sister, were standing between the kitchen door and the passage, so I just said 'good-bye', without embracing them. As I stepped out, Robert said that I should not worry, that I would be defended. However, the children were obviously confused — their father had been arrested a few years before; now it was the turn of their mother. They looked upset, but as both Robert and my sister were present, they were quickly made to understand that I would be coming back.

When we got to the police station at Marshall Square, I found Kate Molale and Violet Molwantwa already there. Here we were formally charged with incitement. After our particulars were taken, we went through an elaborate process of having our fingerprints, as well as our palm-prints, taken. For each of the three of us this was a first experience. Personally, I thought that the taking of fingerprints was humiliating, although the young policeman who instructed us seemed to do his task with great enjoyment; he took his time, and there seemed to be many papers on which our fingerprints had to be placed.

We were put in a cell, which was very cold, and which had no heating. We sat on benches for the whole day, without being given either food or water. From time to time other female prisoners arrested for other crimes were sent in to be with us — at one stage there must have been about a dozen of us in the one cell. The white SB man kept coming into the cell to tell us about the seriousness of the charge that we were facing. He reminded us about Steven Segale, at that time the President of the ANC Youth League in the Transvaal, who had earlier been sentenced to one year in

162

prison on the same charge. His behaviour became very nauseating to us; it was clear that he was terrorising us, whereas we had already resigned ourselves to our fate.

Later, about four o'clock, we were driven to the Fort, where we were made to take off our shoes and carry them to the quarters for awaiting-trial prisoners. Here we found quite a large number of women — there may have been thirty in all, awaiting trial. Some wore men's socks, because no one was allowed to wear shoes. We spent the night in the Fort, but were bailed the next day by the ANC. Our defence lawyer was Harold Wolpe, who at the time of the Rivonia arrests made a daring escape into Botswana. During the hearing, which lasted for three months, the court went to Freedom Square in Sophiatown, where we had addressed the meeting. The court went there because the Magistrate apparently wanted to see how far away from the Special Branch man who took notes at the meeting; he also wanted to see how much light could have been reflected on the platform for the SB man to be able to identify us. Some of the evidence by the State witnesses had been written down inaccurately, because the meeting had been at night. At that time, the majority of black SB men did not take notes in shorthand. So the SB men were known for putting pieces of speeches together so that it did not make sense. This also happened with the evidence of some SB at the Treason Trial.

The magistrate who presided over our case was most vindictive, to say the least. In summing up the case, before passing sentence, he called us 'irresponsible inciters', then went on to say that 'if this thing of yours had succeeded, I would not be sitting in this chair today'. He then went on to pass a sentence of one year in prison, as well as a fine of £50. The defence lawyer immediately launched an appeal. That appeal was heard in 1959, and the sentences were reduced to four months imprisonment and a fine of £25.

9

■

Labelled a Prostitute

The date set for us — Kate Molale, Violet Molwantwa and myself — to start serving our sentences was the 5 May 1960. As planned we assembled at the restaurant of Mr Moretsele (or 'Retsi', as he was commonly known) the popular and much-loved leader and President of the ANC in the Transvaal. A lady in the restaurant handed me a box, which, when I opened it, I found contained cream cakes. The box had been left at the restaurant by Robert's cousin Dorcas Nongxa, for my birthday, which was on that day. What a birthday I had, going to jail! Anyway, we had something to cheer ourselves with.

From Retsi's restaurant we walked to the Magistrate's Court, which was about 500–600 yards away. A policeman there directed us to the Clerk's office, where, after our names were checked, another policeman led us to the basement. This was a spacious room, in which there were many benches, which, by the time we got there, were already dotted with many women who had been sentenced for one thing and another; they were all waiting to be moved to the Fort. The atmosphere was very sombre; there were two policemen watching over us. It was so quiet that you could think that there were no people in that room. Presumably each one of us were thinking of the horror-talked-of-place, 'Number Four', as Africans call the Fort.

At four o'clock, we left for the Fort. More than 20 of us, men and women, were packed in a police van covered with wire mesh at the back. Most of the women sat down on benches at the sides of the van; the rest of us were standing. The men smoked; it was stuffy and terrible inside the van. One boy, a *tsotsi* who stayed in the same street as myself, came and stood next to me, and asked why I was arrested. I just said that it was Congress (as the ANC was usually called). I also asked him why he was arrested; he replied: '*Die f... pass*'.

On the way to the Fort, the police van had to stop at a traffic light. The boy next to me peeped out through the wire mesh. Waving his hand, he said: '*Jy, jy, die dag sal kom*'. (You, you, the day will come). I also peeped out, and saw that the car that had stopped behind the van had a white couple with a child in it. This made me look at the chap again, and ask: 'Why did you say that ?' His reply was; 'Sister, one day we shall kill these Boers. *Ons sukkel hier so*'. (We struggle so much here).

When we arrived at the Fort, all the women got off, after which the van continued round the corner, to the section for male prisoners. As we entered the prison door, the white wardress repeatedly shouted the same order: 'All shoes off!'. We were made to stand in line, for our particulars to be taken. Two women in front of me said that they had been sentenced for possessing *dagga*. When our turn came, the three of us said 'Incitement!' Someone behind us said, 'Drunken noise', whilst others said 'trespass' or for selling *mqombothi* (beer).

After the parade, the matron decided to give us a bit of a lecture. She was a tall, hefty woman in her mid-fifties, with a hunched back, a small waistline, and a flat backside. I was particularly struck by her mouth, which was exceptionally large, and by her cacophonous voice. She and another middle-aged wardress were so feared and hated that they were referred to as either escaped prisoners from World War Two, or as former guards of the concentration camps. She wore the same uniform as worn by others, except that she had some badges and epaulettes to distinguish her grade. She pointed to Kate, Violet and me, then said: 'These three have been arrested for rubbish, because they will never get the thing they are fighting for'. She then pointed to those arrested for drug offences and said: 'These, at least, were trying to make a living'. What an amazing statement! After the lecture we went into the changing room, accompanied by a black wardress.

There were four black wardresses, who worked in shifts — that is, two in the morning and two in the evening, the same as for the white ones. These black wardresses neither spoke roughly to the three of us, nor did they swear at us. One could see that they were restrained. The people who ran the show were the matron and the white wardresses. I observed that the long-term prisoners were greater bullies than the black wardresses. I recall that, one Sunday, while we were having a church service in the big hall, a long-term prisoner came in to call for someone. Because the person called did not stand up sufficiently quickly, a four-letter word was hurled at her by the prisoner. I was shocked, because I had never before heard anyone swear in a church.

Black wardresses are addressed *Abavakachi*, whereas white ones are called *Nonna*. As the order, 'March', was given, my heart started to pound very fast in my chest; I felt hot in the face. Unlike 1958, this time I had decided to smuggle a few aspirins hidden in my bosom and a few antibiotics into the prison. I had studied the procedures very carefully that last time, and realised then that I stood a small chance of smuggling something in. The reason for this was that, in 1958, one woman groaned for the whole night with pain in her chest, but she could not get help between the time the cells were locked at eight o'clock in the evening, and the next time we heard the keys rattle at seven in the morning.

I had wrapped the tablets in a little piece of plastic, then placed them under my breasts. Before we handed our clothes and shoes in, to be kept, we were made to go through the 'Tauza Dance', carrying our kits. This 'dance' is very disgust-

166

ing. One has to strip naked, then put one's hands on the floor and jump over one's legs in order to expose one's private parts. This is all done in public and is the worst humiliation I've ever experienced. As I undressed, I slipped the tablets into one of my shoes. Then, after I had done the dance, I put on my prison attire. This was made out of a rust-coloured brown cotton material, sewn into the shape of overalls, with long belts that were tied around the waist. All prisoners also had to wear red doeks on their heads. The combination of these two colours on 300 people was a most depressing sight.

It was at this stage that I transferred the tablets from my shoe back to my breasts. That time the *Nonna* and the *Mvakachi* were busy scrutinising the next prisoner's private parts; they could not see what the people who were already dressed were doing. My breasts served as my medicine cupboard for the whole period that I was in prison. However, I never got ill, so I did not have to use my medical provisions.

After everybody had handed in their kits, we were marched again, in line, to the next room, which led to the cells. Another order came: 'Stop!' We all stopped, facing the East. The orders that followed were given so harshly and monotonously that I soon forgot about the tablets. Then, 'There's Maggie! Hello Maggie! What are you doing here?' came from an open window, a few yards away from us. I was so surprised when I heard my name shouted like that in prison that I immediately raised my eyes to the window. The only two people my eyes could catch were those of Violet Weinberg and Betty du Toit; the others I could not see, because I was afraid that the *Nonna* was watching who would respond to the greeting. However, I tried to raise three fingers to tell them that there were three of us there. We were immediately told to march in. I was happy to have seen our white comrades from the Congress of Democrats who were being detained under the State of Emergency. I thought that I would see them again, or would send one of the long-term prisoners to them, because such prisoners worked in these areas where whites were kept. But, when I asked about them the following day, I was told that they had left. 'Where could they have been taken to?' the three of us asked ourselves. We did not get the answer until after our discharge, when we learnt that they had been transferred to the Pretoria prison.

We were now made to pass through the main hall (which had been used as a sleeping area for women protesters in 1958) and into the main courtyard, which was surrounded by a high wall, made out of red bricks. This courtyard was where the prisoners had their meals, if the weather was good. It was made of gravel, and prisoners had to sit on the gravel, without any protection.

After supper, which consisted of porridge, we were sent to our cells. Fortunately, we were not separated from each other. The cells were small — about 5 metres by 3. Although the walls and the ceilings of the cells were made out of thick steel, there were numerous gaps, by which means it was easy to communicate with someone in a cell about 25 yards away from the one you are in. Those whose cells were near the outside wall would make a ladder by climbing on top of each others' shoulders to peep outside through the small barred holes; they would shout out: 'Oh! *Kumnadi Pandle!*' (Oh! It is nice outside!)

Some of the women would relate about how they had plotted to go and steal at a certain place, and how they had been arrested. I remember that a lady from Benoni, whose husband was a preacher, told us how the police walked into her house seconds after she had bought goods, knowing that they had been stolen.

Those women who had white boyfriends related how they got to their hide-outs to meet without being seen by the police. When we talked about Congress, they all agreed that Congress was right in its fight, but then said immediately that they had problems which would not be solved by going to a meeting. Still, two long-term prisoners remembered me from 1958. They were very kind to me, and gave me extra blankets. They also related to others how the 'Congress Women' helped to solve the problem of the exchanging of sanitary pads. These were pieces of cloth, which after being washed were passed from woman to woman according to the time of her monthly periods. Following our revolt, we were supplied with disposable pads, even though these were cheap and difficult to keep in place, because we were not allowed underwear.

Because we had many blankets, we spread some of these on the sisal mats, which were so roughly made that they left marks on one's skin. Because we were not given any pillows, we slept together so that we could make pillows with the extra blankets. The lights were kept on for the whole night, which was a bit uncomfortable for the first few nights. The blankets were the brown coarse ones, usually used for race-horses at the stables. No nighties were given to us, so we wore the same overalls day and night, until changing day came, which was only when a visitor like the Inspector was coming.

In the morning we again had porridge, but some women who had kept some grains of mealies from lunch time now ate those, because the porridge was so bad. The women used to keep the mealie grains, wrapped in pieces of cloth, in their breasts, for the whole day. 'Coloured' prisoners were a bit better off — they were given two slices of brown bread, with black coffee, for breakfast and supper, and a little beans and rice at lunch time. Once or twice a week we had pumpkin or cabbage full of sand and not well washed. Once a week we had meat. But the majority of us did not take it because it consisted of pieces of boiled pork fat, and those who ate it had diarrhoea at night. Many prisoners pretended that they had loose bowels, so the following day they were given magnesium sulphate (Epsom salts) to drink. It was very strong, and each one was to take one pint. The result was that there was more diarrhoea that night, and the place stank because the toilet buckets were in the cells, kept near our bucket of drinking water.

Each morning, after breakfast, was time for laundry. We did heaps and heaps of washing: our uniforms, as well as that of the male prisoners. Those for the men were made out of canvas, and very difficult to wash. Worst of all, some of these uniforms of the men were full of blood and pieces of dead skin and pus on the area of the buttocks. We were told these had been worn by prisoners who had had lashes on

169

their buttocks as part of their sentence. Before that was explained to us, I had been puzzled about why these uniforms had blood and pieces of skin in them. These blood-stained clothes were always sorted out and put aside to be washed by women who were punished for one thing or the other. Noone could escape punishment in prison, because it seemed that prisoners were wrong all the time. The swearing at, and beating of prisoners, by the white wardresses was a daily thing. Other prisoners cleaned the cells and washed the dishes; but the majority did the laundry. White prisoners, we were told, did no work while in prison.

The reason why there was so much dirty linen, we heard, was because others prisons, like Leeukop and Modder B in Benoni, sent their dirty linen to the Fort. In other countries, prisoners are taught skills to help them in the future, but in South Africa a black prisoner is a slave of the government. Women ended up doing hard labour, although that was not specified when we were sentenced. Daily there were reports that in a certain section someone had been sent to solitary confinement for the small breakings of the rules, like being caught smoking a cigarette. There seemed to be easy smuggling of cigarettes between the male and female prisoners, which happened when the male prisoners brought food from their section, where it was cooked. How it was done I don't know, but I also heard that shopping could be done by sending money to the male section.

The period when lunch was served was another tense moment. The meals were served in steel bowls, while the spoons were made out of aluminium. These did not always go round, and in that case we had to eat with our fingers. The long-term prisoners who served the meals were frequently told by the watching wardress to be quick. If you missed to catch your bowl quickly, it was thrown to the ground, with the result that the food was spilled.

I can recall that, from the time I had been a teenager, I had dreaded the idea of going to jail, particularly because of the stories we had heard about the treatment inflicted on prisoners. Without question, the most hated and criticised thing about prison was the diet, which was said to be badly prepared and almost inedible. However, to hear is a different thing from practical experience. Nevertheless, I was still shocked and horrified to see what people were given to eat. It was not because my nursing training had included studies about balanced diets, but because of what I now saw I came to the conclusion that prison food was a form of punishment and torture. It is a policy that continues to this day, and it is therefore not surprising that Caesarina Makhoere, who spent six years in prison, calls the diet 'pigs' food' in her book *No Child's Play* (Women's Press, 1988). It was exactly what we called the food in 1958! It was so bad that, merely by looking at it, one became nauseated. Yet the regime has no shame in asserting that it is scientifically prepared.

For breakfast, we were given mealie (maize) meal porridge. It was always oversalted, and bitter to the taste, as if it had been made from rotten maize. Then, for lunch, we had grains of maize — again heavily over-cooked, but at least edible. But how much nutrition is there in such a diet every day? Lastly, for supper we had another helping of the same bitter porridge that was given at breakfast, but with this difference that, once or twice a week it came with rotten cabbage full of sand — inedible. Once a week rotten boiled squash (a kind of gourd) was added, but that too, was always rotten. What was galling was that, right in front of our eyes, slices of brown bread, together with tea or coffee, were being sent to the 'Coloured' prisoners. We were not given these, because we were black, and therefore not entitled to such items.

Throughout our stay in prison, we never had any of these foods, nor were we given sugar, milk, fruit, fish, cheese, butter or eggs, which we saw formed part of the everyday diet of the white prisoners — no matter what crime they had committed. No wonder, therefore, that the thing I'll never forget about life in prison is the diet. It is disgusting that people who know about calories, vitamins, and what is essential for the human body should prescribe such a diet for other human beings — until, of course, one realises that they do it deliberately as part of their overall policies.

At one o'clock the prisoners were locked in their cells so

171

that the wardresses could go for their lunch. When they came back, we would be sent to the big courtyard to collect gravel stones into plastic buckets. We had to go on our hands and knees to collect the gravel, and it really hurt the knees. We were not allowed to protect our knees with our uniforms when kneeling down. But, time and again, when the wardresses were far away, we protected our knees. We all suspected that the gravel stones we collected were not thrown away, but collected by the wardresses, who simply scattered them overnight in the same courtyard for us to collect the next day. It was a form of punishment because there was no laundry to be done in the afternoon, so we had to be made to do something drastic to remind us that we were in prison. At least, that is what everybody thought it was.

One day, when a wardress caught me protecting my knees, she reported me to the matron. I thought the matron was going to whip me. We had seen her whip a 'Coloured' prisoner with a light cane on the buttocks and shoulders because she had not addressed one of the wardresses by the title, *Nonna*. The 'Coloured' girl had also sworn at her during this punishment, and that offence made matters worse for her, because she was immediately bundled away into solitary confinement and we did not see her again until after we had left the prison. Punishment was done in public, perhaps to teach the rest of the prisoners not to repeat what she had done.

When the matron heard of my crime, she roared at the top of her voice: 'You Tickie Line! You will wash eight bloody trousers tomorrow morning and finish them before twelve mid-day!' That was it! What I had feared was physical punishment, but that was nothing compared to being called 'Tickie Line', which was a synonym for the cheapest of prostitutes. Although I was very angry, I was powerless to do anything about the label 'prostitute'. I have no idea where the phrase 'Tickie Line' originates from, but its meaning has always been associated with that of the cheapest of prostitutes. In our language, the term *Nongongo* (two shillings and sixpence) is applied to a woman who gets money by selling her body. Since the 'tickie' in old South African currency was three pence, or one-tenth of two shillings and sixpence, you can see how terrible the insult was.

Back in our cell, we discused my punishment and insult. Life was miserable for us! When I had finished the washing, my hands were red and the skin had broken open around my thumbs. I was now very worried about infection because it was obvious that the prisoners who had worn the clothes had open wounds, which had not been protected by bandages.

Because of my familiarity with wounds, I just wondered how these men managed to sit on their buttocks, for it was obvious that they must have had deep cuts that had turned septic. The episode also proved the widespread belief in the townships that people who had been flogged retained permanent scars on their bodies. I wondered how many white lawbreakers had undergone a similar mutilation. Anyway, on the second day I noticed that the broken skin on my thumb was dry and that the nail was growing; so I had no need for my antibiotics. Since I had only about 35 tablets, I wanted to keep them in case of emergencies for myself and my comrades.

One afternoon during the second week, we were told to have a bath instead of collecting gravel from the courtyard. We were also given clean uniforms. All this was in preparation for the Prison Inspector in the morning. Even that so-called bath was no bath at all. A piece of black, soapy paste was thrown at each prisoner, after which the wardresses scooped cold water from cement containers and flashed it on us. We could not get rid of the paste with the flash of water and our skin remained itchy. The other prisoners had made it known to us that the purpose of the Inspector's visit was to find out if we had any complaints. Nobody seemed to be interested in reporting to him, but Kate, Violet and myself saw this as a good chance to state our complaints, which were numerous.

At 10.30 a.m. we all stood at attention outside, in rows, waiting for the Inspector. He appeared with the matron, walking slowly, like a Head of State inspecting an Army parade. Personally, I never heard him ask if we had any complaints, as he was moving all the time — a strange visit, as the man never looked at us. Perhaps if he had stood still, even for a few seconds, we could have broken the pact of silence. I really felt insulted by this mockery.

After the Inspector had gone, we all went back to our usual washing. A few yards from the place where we did that were about fifteen to twenty prisoners who washed special laundry, which came in by the dozen, in suitcases with the names of the owner marked on in in huge black letters. Every day, these women would sit down near the lines where they had hung their washing, waiting for it to dry in order to put it back into the suitcases. Because this special laundry consisted of men's shirts, underwear, and the like, I got curious that day, and went to the women to see whose laundry it was that they were doing. One woman told me that it belonged to the 'big shorts' of the city. Another woman, who had been listening to our talk, showed me the label on the suitcase next to her, and boastingly said: 'See, I am washing for the Chief Magistrate!'

The name on the case was 'Mr Silk'. I argued that there were many Mr Silk's, but she insisted that the wardress who had given the suitcase to her had told her not to lose even one item because the contents belonged to 'Mr Silk, the Chief Magistrate'. Well, I knew that the Chief Magistrate of Johannesburg was a Mr Silk, but I was amazed. What came into my mind was 'so these white magistrates were filling the prisons by sentencing women for petty crimes, like drunken noise, to make sure that they got free prison labour'.

We were now on our third week in prison, and the only time we had some peace of mind was during the night, and between one and two o'clock in the afternoon As I said, we were always locked up in our cells as the wardresses went for lunch. This one hour seemed like a week away from the swearing and the insults one heard each hour of the day from the wardresses and from some of the long-term prisoners. The daily language was so foul that I felt sick of the place.

In the third week there were whispers and rumours that prisoners who were serving six months or less would benefit from an amnesty in honour of the white Republic Day, which fell on 31 May. Most prisoners who were serving less than six months were already celebrating their release, but to us it was a time of great anxiety and tension. We all dismissed the idea of political prisoners benefiting from the amnesty, especially since the State of Emergency was still in force.With my religious upbringing at St James' Mission, where I was born, I asked my friends that we should pray to ask God to be with us so that we be included in the amnesty. Although she was also an Anglican, and although she had a brother who was a priest, Kate just said: 'the same God should not have allowed us to be here in the first place!'

Kate Molale was one of the first women I got to know in the ANC; we worked together for many, many years. In fact, apart from Ida Mtwana, who was our elder, and Mrs Kraai, who became the first chairman of the Women's League in Sophiatown, Kate was the first young woman who gave me the guts to stand up at a meeting and make a speech. I used to see her casually at the ANC Youth League meeting in Western Native Township before the branch was established in Sophiatown. At that time she herself did not make speeches at meetings. She was a very tiny, frail-looking person. When we used to speak about her with Robert, we called her 'the little girl'. At the time of the formation of the ANC Women's League Sophiatown section, Mrs Kraai, who was a formidable and militant middle-aged woman who spoke Southern Sesotho, became the first chair, Kate was made treasurer and I became the secretary. Later, when I became chair, Kate became secretary and Mrs Kraai became part of the Women's League Executive.

I knew Kate when she was in a fighting mood; I also knew her when she was happy. Her first speech at the branch meeting in 1953 took everybody by surprise — not only was she a very tiny person, but she was then still very young; that she should speak so well was rather unexpected. She never wavered in her convictions, and she became a great activist, and her devotion and courage inspired many other young women to join the ranks of the ANC. Her mother was one of the many Sophiatown women who worked in the white affluent suburbs of Johannesburg, from which work she was able to educate both Kate and her brother Mike up to secondary school standard. Mike later got help from the missionaries and he became a priest in the Anglican Church. Kate helped her mother with the laundry, which she had to bring home from the white suburbs to wash and iron. Kate also baked fat cakes, which her mother sold at a street corner stall. Theirs was a tough life of living from hand to mouth, but the smiling Kate was always there, together with other volunteers to distribute leaflets in the townships and to go from house to house, organising people to join the ANC. Kate participated in all the campaigns about which I write in these chapters. She was one of those who did a full-time job, organising during the Anti-Pass Campaign, travelling especially to the farms and the rural areas. Later, in exile, she was on the Secretariat of the Womens International Democratic Federation (WIDF), replacing Florence Mophosho. Kate died in Dar-es-Salaam a few years ago, following a car accident.

I decided to pray privately. The tension was so high by then that, when we sat down in the yard for lunch on the following days, I could hear the traffic and noises in the streets even more than usual. When birds passed in the sky, I just envied them and continued to look at them until they disappeared from the space. I could think of my friends, who were working just across the street at the General Hospital, where I had worked as a nurse before I specialised in midwifery. I imagined what they were doing at given times: arriving at work, going for tea or for lunch, wearing their clean, white uniforms. And the more I put this in my mind, the more I hated the ugly uniform we had on, and the red scarves on our heads. It was so depressing; I felt as if I were in a lunatic asylum.

On the night of 29 May I had a dream. Now, I am, in fact, a person who has always entertained my dreams — up till then. But now I was even more depressed. In my dream, I saw a man dressed in red clothes carrying a bunch of keys; he opened all the gates and doors for us and told us to go. I never told my friends about it, because some of my dreams

176

come true, but others the opposite. My husband used to listen to me telling about my dreams; but, later, he tried to discourage me.

The morning of the 31, after breakfast, we were told to sit where we were on the courtyard, and not to go to our work, as usual. The senior wardress came out to us, carrying about three lists of papers. Everyone was now certain that the talk about amnesty was no longer a rumour, but a reality. As she started calling the names of those to be released, we all listened attentively for ours. Mine was called first, before that of my two friends. As the wardress called it, I jumped up spontaneously and said 'Afrika!'; my right hand was clenched and raised in an 'Afrika' salute. Kate and Violet had their names called next. They, too, stood up and raised their hands, crying 'Afrika!'

When we were dressed in our crushed clothes, the door was opened for us to leave. As we came out, some of the women started to run. We also took to our heels until we were about 100–200 yards away from the prison. Then we stopped and started to laugh. The thing was that the running seemed to have been spontaneous. After we had stopped one woman said that she had run because she had thought that we could be called back. I was really feeling very disorientated when we came out, as if I was coming into a new world, one that I had not seen before. The picture of women wearing read scarves on their heads seemed to be imprinted on my mind, and the swear words and control orders every day were difficult to get out of my mind.

As we had no money for bus fares, we passed by the Treason Trial Fund office to ask for fares. The lady who saw us there was amazed to see us so shabbily dressed, in our crushed clothes. After getting our fares, we parted, and went to our homes. My sister had not expected me; we had come out after twenty-six days instead of four months. Yet it was twenty-six days that I will never forget.

Within a few days friends started to come to congratulate us. Father Blake also came; he told me that he had done everything he could to contact the school where our children were, and that they were all right; they were coming home

177

for the June holidays, so it was better at least they could see
one parent.

On the second day of my freedom I dashed to Pretoria to
see my husband at the Old Synagogue, where the Treason
Trial was still in progress. Everyone there were delighted;
they had not expected us to be released under the terms of
the amnesty. Robert told me that he had not forgotten my
birthday; he had written '5th of May' in big letters on the
prison wall in order to remind himself. But I was amused,
because all those who were with him in the same prison cell
were continuing to congratulate me for a birthday which had
long since passed.

I had a week's rest before I started my work; I did not pay
the £25 fine (which was part of the sentence imposed after
the appeal) because there was no deadline put for it to be
paid; I thought that I would be sent a reminder, or a final
warning. Secondly, we just did not have the money; the
Sophiatown removal had ruined us like it had done all the
other former residents of the township. However, I did not
expect to be arrested for not paying. But, unfortunately for
me, a warrant of arrest for non-payment had been issued.
Twice, when I had come back from work, my sister Mpati
had told me that uniformed police had been looking for me.
Because they did not leave a message I never bothered about
it, since police visits had become part of our lives in the
townships. However, they had mentioned that they had
wanted me, not my husband. In the meantime, because I
had no money, I had applied for aid from the Treason Trial
Fund. We had not applied for it when the trial started in
1956, because Robert had kept on with his job as a part-time
reporter, and because my practice was doing well in
Sophiatown. But now I signed for the food voucher and for
money for rent; it was £11 per month for each family.

The Fund carried on for some time after the trial had
ended, then it was wound up. We were asked to state how
many bills we paid per month as well as what monies we
still owed, so that some of these could be halved. So, after I
had given all my answers to these questions, I was given £76
to tidy up my bills. That helped me a great deal, because

Robert was by now already abroad, and I was struggling with the fees for the school in Lesotho, as well as running the car. The Fund was a real help to the accused and their families. Many people had been forced out of their jobs; others were from other provinces.

When the children came for their holidays we once again went to Pretoria because they were keen to see their father. It was a very happy reunion, although they could see each other only through the usual wire mesh. The children returned to school at the end of July. Then, the State of Emergency was lifted at the end of August 1960, and all the detainees were released. It was only now, when my husband was home that I told him that I had 'got rid of the Devil' (his pass). He said that it had been a brilliant move I had taken, and we never spoke about it again. Neither the police nor the Superintendent asked for it again, but I knew, however, that, having destroyed my husband's pass, we had no chance of getting the receipt for a house. But we could do without the receipt, rather than to give information to the superintendent about ourselves, even though these superintendents had the right to expel anyone, just by branding him or her a 'trouble-maker'. So, Robert had to go around again as a passless person.

One morning, as I was at a garage, getting petrol for my car, a black Special Branch man stopped his car and came over to me. When he greeted me, I insulted him; I told him that I did not speak to people who spy on their own people. But he insisted that he wanted to tell me something. I was already in my car when he came over to the window and told me that I was lucky that the police had not found me at home, because a warrant had been issued for my arrest for not paying the £25 fine. Although I did not want to talk to the SB man, it clicked in my mind that my sister had told me twice that uniformed policemen had been looking for me. 'What a useful leak!' I said to myself.

The following day I left home very early for the Magistrate's Court in Johannesburg, to pay the fine. Robert had given me half of the money after I had told him what the SB man had said; the rest of the money I had saved up. In

Johannesburg, I went to the same office where we had gone the day we reported to go to Number Four (the Johannesburg Prison) to serve our sentences. I handed the money to the clerk, after telling him who I was and what the fine was being paid for. After checking in his books, he took the money and gave me a receipt. He then told me to go to the Newlands Police Station to show my receipt to the white man in charge there. When he said that, I asked him if I was not going to be arrested there. His reply was that it was for that reason that he was telling me to report to the Newlands Police Station — because they would not otherwise know that I had paid my fine. This I did. When the man at Newlands saw the receipt, he was hopping mad. 'You have only paid your fine today', he said. 'We have been looking for you for two whole weeks!' I looked right into his eyes, and said: 'Have you finished ?' His reply was 'I have got to look into this thing, why this woman was not arrested'.

I still do not know whether someone later lost his job, or was not promoted, because of this episode. I think, on the whole, I was a bit neglectful about this fine. I never put it as a priority in my mind. I think that, when one has been involved with the police, the courts, and prisons one becomes acclimatised to these things.

As I left the office, I passed through another big room, where there were between fifteen and twenty uniformed policemen, all of them black, sitting in rows, typing; they seemed to be very busy. All I could hear was the tapping of the machines; they seemed not to take any notice of anyone passing. But, just when I was at the door, one of them shouted: 'But Mrs Resha, why do you worry yourself with politics. You are an educated woman; you could lead a good life from your work, or be employed by the Government'. I was a bit amazed, because I knew none of these people. I half opened the door, but then turned back, and asked: 'Who said that ?' There was not a word from any of them. As if a ghost had asked the question. 'Cowards!' I said, and I walked out, leaving the door wide open, to register the contempt I had for the sick statement, which none of them was brave enough to own up to. Anyway, I had escaped by the skin of my teeth.

10

■

No Place to Hide

For the first few months in Mofolo I could say that we had relative calm, at least, from the nightly permit raids which had haunted us in Sophiatown. But the Special Branch did not take long to resume their visits to our house. This time, these visits were by African members of the SB. We had, by now, got used to their visits; we knew that they were visiting a lot of homes, especially the homes of ANC leaders. Where they made us fed up was that, when they found visitors in our house, they wanted to take their names. In other words, they were trying to stop people coming to our place for fear of their names being taken by the SB. So we always asked our visitors not to panic. We had been advised that the only information to give to the SB was your name and address, and nothing more. Sometimes, I would have heated exchanges of words with these men, telling them how they had sold their souls by getting money for spying on their own people. Some just walked away; others said they were working for their children.

One evening Robert had come home very late; he was very upset. He told me that the ANC wanted him to go abroad to reinforce the ANC Mission, headed by Oliver Tambo, who had been sent abroad in 1960, and who now had asked that more people were needed to help, because of pressure of work.

Robert did not want to go abroad. I remember that two of his friends, who were intending to, and later sought refuge abroad, had advised him to leave the country even before the Treason Trial had ended. But he refused. His friends thought that, because of his speeches during the removal of Sophiatown, and the speech he had made to the Volunteers (which had been secretly taped by the SB) that he might be convicted at the trial.

One of these friends had actually approached me first to try to persuade me to use my influence on Robert. Personally, I thought it was a monstrous idea, one tinged with cowardice. I told him that Robert would never do such a thing. The second friend approached Robert in our sitting-room. I was relaxing in our bedroom when I saw Robert opening the door; he stood there, before answering. I tried to tell him to close the door, but he stayed put and talked to his friend, standing there, and allowed me to overhear the conversation.

As Robert started to talk, I became completely confused over what the discussion was about, because of how he started his argument, which went something like this: 'In that most famous book, the Holy Bible, the Jews were promised that a Messiah would be born who would deliver them. But there is no book written in this world in which the African people are promised that someone will be born to liberate us from oppression. As such, it means that we must be prepared to die for our country. There may be few, or there may be millions, who will die. But we must be ready to make the sacrifice.' It was now that I knew that Robert was discussing something that he did not like, because I noticed that his eyelids started to become puffy and that his face started to change from being relaxed to being tense. Meantime, his friend was as quiet as a mouse. I am also certain that he must have noticed that Robert was, by now, quite angry.

After his friend had left, he said: 'You know Maggie, it is amazing that people can be colleagues, work together for years, yet they do not know each other. To run away from the trial because I might be convicted would be tantamount to stabbing my co-accused, as well as the ANC, in the back. If I have to die, or face imprisonment because I object to injustice against my people, then so be it.'

Still, the realisation that the speech that Robert had made had been secretly taped came like a bombshell, particularly since it had been made in the ANC office, where he had spoken to the Volunteers about discipline. Anyway, the three judges did not find any 'treason', not even with this speech; the Crown's hope to convict collapsed when Robert told the court what he had said, and why he had said it.

The prosecution team had kept this speech up their sleeves; they dramatically delivered it on the last day of the trial at the Drill Hall. Apparently, it was their intention to prove that the ANC were planning a violent revolution. But they quoted the speech that Robert had made out of context. The prosecution team highlighted the words 'murder', 'murder', 'murder', which Robert had used at the end of a phrase he had reiterated on the need for discipline.

I am not going to go into the Treason Trial and what happened in court daily at the Drill Hall and at the Pretoria Synagogue, because Helen Joseph, who was one of the accused, took notes of the case daily, from which she has written two detailed books: *If This Be Treason* (1963) and her autobiography, *Side By Side* (1986), except to say that although the Treason Trial finally collapsed, it did so only after inflicting enormous hardships on the accused and their families for nearly five years.

While there is no need to repeat the details of the trial, I would, nevertheless, like to highlight some of the events in court in which Robert was involved, as given in newspaper reports (some of them written by Robert himself). What is interesting for me, going over old newspapers of the time, is how scanty the reports were in the white daily press; for details the oppressed had to rely on radical weeklies like *New Age*, where, for instance, this report, written by Robert, appeared in the issue of 4 February, 1960:

Time is 10 a.m. There is an air of uneasiness surrounding the court. The accused are concerned about the Coalbrook tragedy where 440 miners have been trapped underground; also by the riot at Durban's Cato Manor. More than half of the accused are still reading the morning newspaper, where these incidents are reported.

There is a visible change in the Special Court. Apartheid in the witness box has been dispensed with. The "Non-Europeans Only" side of the witness box is no more. Next to the witness box there is a tape-recording machine and a microphone.

There are two loudspeakers, one behind the judges and the other in front of the 30 accused ... Advocate G. Hoexter (for the Crown) told the court that the Crown proposed to play back on the tape-recording machine certain statements taken by police officers ... Det. Sgt. Swanepoel of Durban played back tape-recorded speeches made at the conference of the Congress of the People held in Pietermaritzburg on December 5, 1954. Sgt. Swanepoel said that the conference was held at the Ridge Cinema. The people in the conference did not know he was there. He took a tape-recording of the speeches made.

The microphone opened with the singing of "Nkosi sikilel' iAfrika". This took the accused by surprise. Accused Nkampeni touched his head as if to take off his hat; accused Tshunungwa jerked forward to stand up but realised in time where he was. Before the accused knew what was happening, the microphone was switched off.

Cross-examined by Mr S. Kentridge (for the defence) Sgt. Swanepoel said that this was a private meeting, that was why he had concealed himself. He also said that his presence was unknown to the people in the conference.

Answering another question, he said that he had no reason to think that the notes he took at meetings would be used in a criminal charge.

The third witness to play back speeches ... was Det. Sgt. M.S. Diedricks. He was to replay a speech everyone had been waiting for. This was the meeting held in the Congress Hall, 37 West Street, Johannesburg, nine days before the 156 men and women were arrested at dawn on Dec. 5, 1956 on a charge of high treason.

The tape-recording machine went on: "War has been declared. The leaflets of the African National Congress say that the time has come!" The speech goes on to deal with what a Volunteer is. "A Volunteer is a person who is disciplined. That is the key of the Volunteer — discipline. When you are disciplined and you are told by the organization not to be violent, you must not be violent. If you are a true Volunteer and you are called upon to be violent, you must be absolutely violent, you must murder! murder! murder! That is all. Your leaders have told you that the government of this country, among other things, is planning to arrest 200 leaders and is attacking every day leaders of the people. My directions to you are, if the government in its madness does one day arrest 200 leaders, then 200,000 Congress members must emerge from those who are living in this country. You can only do that my friends if you are willing to kill your brother."

The part of the last sentence with the word "kill" has been played time and time again in court in order to ascertain whether the word was "kill" or "tell". After it had been played many times, Mr Justice Kennedy was of the opinion that the word was "tell". The interpreter plus some of the accused who have listened to the Sechwana translation uses the word "tell".

Again, in the issue of 9 September 1960, *New Age* reported that Trengrove, for the State, had suggested to Robert that it was part of the tactics of the ANC in the Western Areas of Johannesburg (which included Sophiatown, Western Native Township, Newclare and Albertsville) whether in connection with boycotts or anything else, to create a situation in which the police had to intervene in order to restore law and order 'and then you blame the police for the consequences'. The report went on to quote the following exchanges:

Trengrove: You exposed innocent people of the Western Areas to these conflicts between the police and subversive elements.
Resha: You don't know what you're talking about.

Trengrove then suggested that the Minister of Justice of the United Party government has praised the tact and restraint

185

of the police at the time of the 1946 Miners strike.

Resha: It would appear that the Crown and the Minister of Justice look at brutal assault and murder as restraint to be commended. Not I. If the Crown and the Minister of Justice are happy if the police baton charge.we condemn it. We differ.
Trengrove: You know full well that in the situation you were creating in the Western Areas it would need only a spark to start a conflagration.
Resha: We know that the government wanted to start a conflagration because it wanted to rob the people of their rights and threatens them with force. The government sent 2,000 troops into Sophiatown.
Trengrove: You regarded it as a victory?
Resha: Yes. Because 2,000 troops went away without shooting a person.

Asked why he had referred to the police as 'imbeciles, cowards and hooligans', Resha said that only hooligans would go to a peaceful meeting of the ANC to disrupt it, and only cowards would go fully armed to a peaceful meeting.

In the same issue *New Age* also carried a report that reveals a great deal about Robert's real nature and his attitude to the oppressor. The report tells that 'during the cross-examination of Mr Resha, Advocate Trengrove appealed to the court for the witness to be instructed to address their Lordships and not Mr Trengrove by name. Mr Justice Rumpff pointed out this might prevent the witness from concentrating upon his answer and urged Mr Trengrove not to take it amiss if he was addressed as 'Mr.Trengrove'.

Mr Trengrove: 'It would assist us because the difference will be that it would then keep the cross-examination on a proper level'.

Mr Justice Rumpff suggested that perhaps Mr Resha should not address anyone at all.

If that little interchange might be chalked up as game and set to my husband, the match was still far from over. Time and time again Trengrove returned to the explanation given by the defence for the 'murder! murder!' speech Robert had made. When it came to his turn to be examined on this point by Trengrove, *New Age* of 24 November 1960 reported that Robert point-blank refused to tell the court how many had been present at the meeting where he had made his speech. It also reported the following exchange between Trengrove and Mr Justice Bekker after the advocate had attacked another sentence in the speech, which stated that 'Every man, woman and child must put on his coat from which only death must from him part ...'

Mr Justice Bekker: Does he not say that it is metaphorical?
Trengrove: Everything has become metaphorical in this case when violence is mentioned. but when you have to meet the fascist beast, no.

The 16 February 1961 issue of *New Age* reported that Mr J de Vos, QC for the Crown, made the submission that Robert had conspired to propagate Marxist-Leninist doctrine and knew that violent revolution was a principle inherent in communism. This, he said, was based on the documents found in the possession of the accused. Among the documents was *The History of the Communist Party of the Soviet Union*. In this book, said Mr de Vos, there is reference in particular to the role of violence used in the course of the revolution in Russia.

Mr Justice Rumpff: Has he read the book?
Mr de Vos: The accused denied that he had read the book. But he was interested in the book and would have read the book if it was not seized by the police. His activities show consonance with this book.
Mr Justice Rumpff: Are you going to say that he read the book?
Mr de Vos: No, My Lord.
Mr Justice Rumpff: Then why do you refer to the book?
Mr de Vos: To give the total picture of this person's interest in Communism.
Mr Justice Kennedy: How would you suggest we deal with this book?

Mr de Vos: If the court will accept his evidence ...?
Mr Justice Kennedy: Then we should ignore it ...!
Mr de Vos: Yes, my Lord.

Later, still arguing about Robert's knowledge of communism, Mr de Vos said that, in his evidence, Robert had said that there was no communist country in the world yet, to which Mr Justice Kennedy had responded: 'I think that any student of politics knows that'. Despite rebuffs such as these from the judges, Mr de Vos apparently continued to fight gallantly, suggesting that Robert's remark should be of interest as an indication of his technical knowledge of communism.

I have quoted at some length to show the extent to which the regime went to try to convict our leaders, as well as the shambles they made of a case they realised almost immediately they could not make. I also want to show the militancy of our leaders in the face of this provocation on the part of the regime. I also want to emphasise, however, that we were never certain that we could win, right up to the end. I was in court on the day of the verdict, because we all knew in advance when that day was to be. The atmosphere was terribly tense: would the judgment go against the defence, despite the fact that dozens of prosecution witnesses, including that of the 'expert' on communism, Professor Andrew Murray of the University of Cape Town, had been discredited?

As Advocate Van Niekerk, the prosecution lawyer, dramatized the words 'murder! murder! murder! I felt this immense build-up of tension in my chest. My mind also began to wander: 'How could Robert have said those words?' I asked myself. Of course, everyone in the court (except the Crown, which chose not to do so) accepted that the speech had deliberately been taken out of context. While Robert had used it to illustrate the central importance of discipline to the Volunteers, the Crown presented the speech as if it was the administration of an oath, the issuing of an order. It was on this high-pitched note of emotional excess that the Crown got what it asked for — committal for trial to a higher court.

The pulse rates of many people must have shot up that day. I remember that I was wearing a black two-piece which had white flowers embroidered on the lapels at the top. Then, as soon as we came out of court, Lilian Ngoyi came to me and said in a firm voice: 'Maggie, you should not have put on that black attire today'. Although I did not reply to her remark, I inwardly interpreted her meaning as saying that it was a bad omen — that I was already wearing mourning clothes. So I pushed through the crowd to find Robert, in the hope of getting his reaction. However, since I found him deep in conversation with other comrades, I told him that I was off, back to Sophiatown.

Later, when Kepe and the others came home, as they usually did, I could see that they, too, were discussing the verdict: certainly, they were not making jokes, as they were used to doing. It seemed that some gloom had descended upon us.

When Robert came back I was very keen to get his reactions, especially about exactly what he had said. He immediately reassured me: 'Van Niekerk has the temerity', he said, 'to misquote me. They usurp our country and expect us to fold our arms and look up to the heavens for help, when the life expectancy of an African is 35 years as against 72 for whites.'

After he had reassured me, I began to think that the crown was celebrating prematurely. Soon we had our first, albeit partial, victory: 65 of the accused, including Chief Luthuli, were discharged. Despite the set-back that 91 were committed for trial, we decided that the acquittal of the others was a sufficient cause for celebration. It was January 1958 when we held our party at the home of Ruth and Joe Slovo. Once again the defence team went out of their way to reassure us that we should trust them because they would be willing to bring down mountains in defending our leaders.

The Party was fantastic, especially because many of us who were not the accused were seeing these wonderful people in silk gowns, our lawyers, at close range under quite different circumstances. Then whoops! without any warning, journalists from the most rightwing of Afrikaans newspapers, *Die Vaderland*, gatecrashed the party. Who had tipped them off I cannot tell, but despite the helter-skelter on the part of those who wished to hide to prevent their photographs being taken, these gate-crashers even jumped on top of tables in order to get better shots of this multi-racial gathering. I was told that the newspaper later had to pay about £300 in compensation to the Slovos for the damages done to their furniture by these reporters from a newspaper that had once been edited by Verwoerd.

Some two months passed after Robert had told me that he had been asked to go abroad. Then, one evening, he told me that the ANC leadership had told him that it was a matter of urgency, and that he should leave at once. That night Robert did not sleep. I always knew when he was asleep. Often he snored, especially when lying on his back. I, however, was a light sleeper — partly because of Robert's snoring, partly because of also waiting for night calls as a nurse. So, time and again, I had to poke him with my elbow, then ask him to turn over. Well, his usual defence for snoring was that 'a man who snored loved his wife deeply'. Although this was unscientific, it was a clever defence. Besides all women enjoy words of endearment from their husbands.

But, when I woke up in the early hours of that morning to find that he was lying on his back, and not snoring, I quietly said: 'So today you do not love your wife, because you haven't snored'. To that remark he responded, 'Darling, I can't sleep'. Then went on: 'If I refuse to go, it will be defying authority'. There was silence for a few minutes; then I said: 'How could the Deputy-Volunteer-in-Chief defy authority?'

'You are perfectly right', he said.

The word 'Volunteer' came into the ANC vocabulary during the Defiance Campaign of 1952. In the same way as the youth in South Africa today call each other 'Comrade', so the word 'Volunteer' (transformed into singular, *ivolontiya*, and plural, *amavoluntiya*) became very popular amongst the ranks of Congress youth in the Fifties: it was felt to be closely linked to the Xhosa word for Volunteer *Idelakufa* (plural, *amadelakufa*), which may be translated as 'one who is prepared for the highest sacrifice; one who is prepared to die'.

In 1952, Nelson Mandela was the National Volunteer-in-Chief for the Defiance Campaign. Each province had its own

190

Volunteer-in-Chief with a sequence going down the line to Chief Volunteer for each batch which was ready to defy. It was out of the success of this experience that, by the mid-Fifties, it had become Congress policy for the President-General of the ANC to be designated as Volunteer-in-Chief. Naturally, he had to have a deputy. It was into this role that Robert was elected — Deputy Volunteer-in-Chief. Of all the positions that he had filled in the ANC, this was the one about which he was most proud.

It was for this reason that Chief Luthuli was the first person to burn his pass in 1960, after which he called upon all men to do the same — he was exercising his duty as Volunteer-in-Chief. Earlier on (if memory serves me right, it was during the Congress of the People) the Chief had called for 10,000 Volunteers to be ready for action and for any call that the ANC might make or action it might decide to take. During the Treason Trial this call was interpreted as the call to launch a revolution in the country.

Soon after these events, the Volunteers started to be issued with khaki uniforms; the jackets worn by the men had high collars, which were called Mao Tse Tung. We all know that khaki is connected with soldiers, so in other words, the volunteers were the political soldiers of the ANC which during that time was conducting a militant, but non-violent, struggle to overthrow the regime. As with so many other major moments, a song was composed for the Volunteers; it went as follows:

Singa masocha ka Luthuli (repeated 4 times)
napi napi singayayo sibenga bafakazi (repeated twice)
(we are Luthuli's soldiers,
and wherever we go, we are witnesses.)

It was in the context of this history that Robert made his remark about the impossibility for him to defy authority; it was a characteristic feature in him, that of abiding by the authority of the leadership, that he faithfully kept till the end.

For the two weeks prior to his departure, Robert went into

191

hiding in one of the safe houses in Soweto. These were houses lived in by people who were not suspected or visited by
the SB. Time and again I dropped him clothes to change, or
he would sneak back home for a few minutes. One night,
before he left, I was on a night call in Dube, which is opposite Mofolo. The husband of the lady I was attending to came
in and told us that the SB were searching Patrick Molaoa's
place, which was opposite. It was about 3 am I suspected
that they might have been to our place as well, or would still
be going there; but I was not worried, because I knew that
they would not find Robert in.

I got back home about four o'clock in the morning. I was
freezing, because there was a lot of frost at that time of the
year. I knew that the SB had not been to our place because
my sister always heard the car and saw the lights in her
room. When I got back she did not wake up to report anything, but it was hardly forty-five minutes after I was in bed
that I heard the banging of the doors of the police car. There
was a knock at the door. As I got up to see who it was, there
were shouts: 'Open the door! We have a warrant to search
the house!'

By the light of the candle I had taken from my room I saw
two white SB men and one black one. While the latter
returned to the car, the two white men came straight into
my bedroom, gave me the warrant to read, and started to
search. They asked me where my husband was. I said that I
did not know. Then one of them said that they suspected
that I belonged to a banned organisation. When I asked
'which one?' I got no reply. So I got back into bed, and
watched them upsetting everything in the room.

The same SB man who had talked about banned organisations said: 'What surprises me is why these people work with
Indians'. I really loathed to talk at that ungodly hour, plus I
was freezing as there was no heating in the houses in
Soweto, so I just said: 'We like those who like us'. I answered
because he had made a statement, not asked me a question,
and I did not want him to get away with it.

They looked under the bed; but, strangely enough, they did
not go into the other rooms, or the kitchen. After some time

they went out. When I had heard the car move away, I took a torch to go and close the front door. As I walked, I complained aloud: 'These Boers; they come and get me out of bed in this cold, and they leave the door open'. But, as I got back into the lounge, I found the same man who had been talking about banned organisations standing in the middle of the room.

'What do you want here?' I asked him.

'I am waiting for the others to pick me up', he said.

'Well, you can wait for them outside,' I said.

'No, I can't go outside', he said.

'Show me the warrant which says you must wait in my house then, because I only saw the one for searching', I said.

'No; I have no warrant for that', he replied.

'Then, out you go, and I'll open for you if you still need to search.'

When he did not move, I became hysterical. 'You get out; you want that, when your friends come back, they arrest me and charge me of having broken the Immorality Act with you?' I was now screaming at the top of my voice. Immediately I mentioned the Immorality Act, (which dated from 1927, but which had been amended in 1967 in order to tighten up the definition, as well as the penalties for 'immorality' between whites and black people) he shot out of the house like a bullet from a gun. I banged the door shut after him. I could hear him going round the house, could see him flashing his torch on the windows. But I was left, thinking very hard about what the motive was for this exercise, and I came to the conclusion that they must have thought that Robert was in hiding nearby, or in one of the other rooms, that he might surface when the car had left, only to walk into a trap in his own house. After about twenty-five minutes the car came back. I could hear him say: '*Die vrou*' (That woman). I could not hear the rest; he was already in the car. It was now going on for six o'clock, but, because it was winter, it was still dark.

At about 7.45 am, Robert walked in. I think he came in through the kitchen door, because it was around that time that my sister usually started to make the fire. I was trying to coerce some sleep when I felt someone sitting on the bed. 'Hello Maggie', he greeted me, to which I replied, 'Hello Sonny'. Sonny was my brother's name, the one who had escaped from the quarry. I then immediately made a sign that he should not talk, then took out my note-book and informed him about the whole episode with the SB. I also wrote that I suspected that they might have left some bugging device in the house. Finally, I asked him to leave at once, in case they were still in the vicinity.

Robert wrote back in the note-book: 'I am leaving today! When I have crossed the border, someone will come to tell you, and also to fetch my clothes. Look after yourself and the children. If you have any problems, you can always approach Walter Sisulu.' I was still so shaken by the encounter with the SB that I was not interested to know which border he was to cross. Then Robert changed his clothes very quickly, and, when I came back from the window, from where I had been watching for the SB car, he just pointed at three suits he wanted to be sent to him. As he slipped out of the house, I noticed that he was not going towards the direction of the buses, but towards the open veld between Mofolo and Dube. As soon as he had disappeared, I rushed to the tap outside the house, soaked the sheet of paper on which we had been writing, and flushed it down the toilet.

On the second day, someone phoned to the shop where I used to get my calls and just said that everything was OK. So I knew that he had crossed the border. But which border? That was not discussed over the telephone. The day after that a friend came to fetch his clothes. On the fourth day, reporters from the newspaper *The World* came to tell me that they had heard that my husband was in Serowe, in Botswana. I pretended not to know anything about it, and thanked them for letting me know. Anyway, I was greatly relieved — at least he had managed to escape.

The black SB continued to check on our house every fortnight, even long after Robert had left. Then, all of a sudden, they disappeared for about two months. During that lull, I would see another SB man, called Masuka, pass on his scooter in front of the house. I was puzzled by this, until I realised that he was going into the house of a black police sergeant, Mkwanazi, whose house was behind ours, in the next row. Our toilets and taps were back to back to each other.

The second month the SB stopped coming to our place I told Walter Sisulu and some other friends about it; I thought that they had given up, because they knew that Robert was now abroad. This halt of the regular SB visits to my place had made me either naive, or complacent, or both. I honestly believed that I was no longer on their watch list. However, one month before I left South Africa, I got a rude shock, when I found out that my sergeant neighbour was also a member of the SB.

When I recalled the sequence of events later on, I realised that he must have been recruited at the time that the African SB, Masuka, used to pass by on his scooter to his house. Secondly, his permanent presence at his home, where he was always peeping through the front window, looking at my gate, which was directly opposite, should have alerted me. It all tallied with the time the SB stopped coming to my place. But not in the least did I suspect him.

It was now May 1962. The ANC leaders had hinted to me that they were thinking of sending me abroad to join my husband. However, the idea was at its preliminary stages, and I did not put it in my mind seriously; even Robert had not mentioned anything about it in his letters. Of course he wouldn't, otherwise he would be telling the SB, as letters were being opened. Then, in June, the children came home for their school holidays, which would last until the end of July. I had already bought their return tickets when I was told that we would leave in September; I was advised not to send them back to school, because that would create problems.

On 12 August 1962, the Federation of South African Women (which was not banned) held a meeting in the Gandhi Hall to celebrate August 9. The meeting was also to demonstrate solidarity with Nelson Mandela, who had been arrested earlier, after he had been in hiding after his trips abroad. The meeting was chaired by Mrs Winnie Mandela. Although she was under terrible strain, she acted very bravely and encouraged us all. Which woman could not be under strain when her husband was the big fish of the police catch? It was the first time I had heard her make a speech; I admired her and her bravery. The SB were at the meeting, in full force, seated on a bench near the door. At some stage during the meeting I turned round to look to the back. To my greatest surprise, my sergeant neighbour was sitting with the SB; he was wearing plain clothes and taking notes, just like the rest of them. At first I thought that I was mistaken. So I looked again, between the gaps of the participants' shoulders, and indeed, it was him. There could be no mistake. Certainly, he did not see me looking at him at that time, as he was taking notes.

At the interval, before we went out, I told Albertina Sisulu about him; she said that I should behave as if I had not seen him. When we came out of the hall, I looked for him, but he was nowhere to be seen, though the rest of the SB men were still present. From that moment on I was convinced that the sergeant had been spying on my place and on me for months. It was now nearly three months during which I had seen his car always parked outside his house. The first month I had thought that he was on holiday. Then, later, I thought that he might be off sick. But he was always peeping out of his front window, which was in line with our gate.

I now also recalled that, when I was on my way to the meeting, the other SB man, Masuka (who used to pass in front of my house on a scooter to visit the sergeant's place) passed me on the way. As he did so, he slackened his speed and said, jokingly: 'I'll be there before you!'. He knew that I was going to the meeting because I was wearing my ANC uniform. I just wondered why he was there, because I was a bit late for the meeting. It was only after I had seen the sergeant that I started to hook the puzzle together, and realised that he must have been waiting at the sergeant's house, watching for me to leave, and then followed me.

My greatest worry now was whether or not I would be able to leave in the next month, with the two SB watching me. Walter Sisulu had told me to take the two children away, to hide them. So, in July, the day on which the children were supposed to leave for Lesotho, I took them to a place outside Johannesburg, though anyone who saw us leave could have thought that I was taking them to the railway station, because I loaded their suitcases in the car in the usual manner of parents dealing with children going to school. The place to which I took them was an Institute. It had many orchards and trees, so I was happy that they would be able to play and not stay in the house the whole time. Anyway, I gave them very strict instructions not to tell anyone whose children they were, and that they should not answer to anyone about why they were not at school. They were very cooperative; the idea of them seeing their father in a few months' time, if they behaved, settled well into their minds. After all, they knew everything about the Special Branch visits and arrests.

From that time on it was hide and seek between me and the sergeant. But, I think that it was not easy for him, because a midwife goes out at any time, and several times as well. But I also think that he acted very clumsily at times because, if I suddenly appeared on his side, trying to play with my dog, he would stoop down from his window, to make as if he was not there. The corner of my eye saw him, although I did not look at him. We never spoke to each other, though our toilets and taps were separated only by the fence. Yet I was always talking over the fence with the family next door to him. One could never know what the SB man was after; perhaps he wanted to see if meetings were taking place at our house, as the ANC was now a banned organisation. Some days, especially in the evenings, I would keep myself busy in the garden, digging the beds and watering them as if preparing for new plants. But my aim was to make the SB man think that I was not going anywhere. In the end, I thoroughly enjoyed our hide-and-seek. If only he knew!

A week or so before we left I took a friend to the municipal office for him to be registered as a sub-tenant, so that he could keep the house during my absence. The ANC leaders had said that we would be leaving for six months, at the most for one year. This was the usual procedure. All those who left the country at that time were told the same thing as I was told — that we would be back within six months or a year. I recall that, when I left Dar-es-Salaam for Algiers, I was a bit upset when other comrades I had left there were saying that, by December 1962, they would be back home. The intention was that people who had been sent abroad would be able to re-enter the country as soon as possible after acquiring techniques for the continuation of the struggle.

There was no reason why we should not have believed it at that time, because Mandela had gone back, having spent a few months abroad. There were other leaders, like Ray Mhlaba, Elias Mlangeni, Wilton Mkwayi, who had also returned. Mthembu was also with them, although he had turned traitor, by giving evidence at the Rivonia trial. Of course, the wrath of the people caught up with him: he was killed! The Rivonia arrests in July 1963 were the biggest body-blow to the ANC; without doubt it was that which contributed to the drastic change in strategy.

Two days before we left my sister had moved the furniture to her place. This was done in the middle of the night. This was one time I appreciated the dark streets of Soweto, the absence of street lights. We had perfect camouflage during those critical days. Then, the next morning, I just took the remaining things, like the blankets I had slept on, since my sister had by then already taken the beds. I left the house dressed in my uniform, as if I was going to work, but drove straight to my starting-point. Later, we collected the children from the Institute. Then, the following morning I drove the car to the garage to which I had sold it, and a friend picked me up there. We were leaving that same evening for Botswana, which was at that time still a Protectorate.

Our starting place was a safe one: it was the same one in which Robert had been hiding for the two weeks before he left. The children were very co-operative even there. By this time I had already said my goodbyes to the Sisulus and to Lilian Ngoyi.

We left Soweto at about four o'clock. We stopped in the city in order to buy more provisions — cold drinks, bread, two more chickens. We then drove in the direction of Rustenburg, passing through many farms. There was really no traffic on the road once we were out of Johannesburg, and the sun had just set as we passed by these farmlands. I had no detailed idea of the route at all, but my friend, who knew the way, told me that we would be in Lobatsi towards morning. What made the long journey interesting was that the driver sometimes had to go slowly to allow wild animals to dash across the front of the car. The eyes of the wild animals looked fearful as the lights of the car shone on them; the animals dashed across the road in wild confusion — great care had to be taken not to hurt them.

We travelled for the whole night. During that trip, time and again I thought about being intercepted and what the consequences might be. But, under such circumstances, one was ruled by a little bit of courage and determination to do the best to succeed. When we arrived in Lobatsi the next morning it was still a bit dark. Well, there was a little relief. However, never shout before you are out of the wood! So says the proverb. The fact that I was going to pass through hostile territory, unknown to me, left nothing to be desired. The instructions that I had been given for the journey were so full of do's and don'ts that I was really scared. To leave the country without valid documents is a terrible thing. From the time you cross the border, the sense and feeling of statelessness immediately grips you; your life is filled with uncertainty, and you feel that you have lost your dignity and respect in the eyes of people whose country you are in. The feeling of going back home every day lives with you. It grows by the day, and you never feel settled.

When I was told that I would be going abroad, I was very unhappy, especially because of the childrens' education. I really saw no point in moving them from another country and then back again within a year. But, after Mandela had returned from abroad, I was told that the leadership had decided that ANC representatives abroad should be with their families. I then advanced another excuse: that my practice had picked up and that I thought I could manage to look after myself. I had so much hope that the leadership would drop the idea that we should leave the country that I bought the tickets for the children to return to school. But the last straw, which made me give up resisting any longer, was when I was told not to send the children back to Lesotho. It was only then that I told my sister, although we kept the secret between ourselves — I warned her that the children should be kept in the dark until the eve of their departure to the place where I was going to hide them.

I was particularly worried about the children knowing earlier, because they were friendly with the daughters of Mr Kazamula, as they were in the same school in Lesotho. Their first reaction, when I told them that they would not be going back to their school, was one of sadness. There was one Sister (the school was an Anglican convent) called Frangeni whom they both loved very much, so they asked: 'Mama, are we no more going to see Sister Frangeni?'

'No,' I replied, 'but if you behave well at the place where I will take you tomorrow, in about a month or two you will be seeing your Daddy.' This changed their mood immediately to one of jubilation. From there, I began to give them long lectures on how to keep the secret, because children, through no fault of theirs except that they are little innocents, cannot be relied upon in security matters. However, African children by that age already know a lot about police and arrests. Even in the rural areas children are always warned not to give information to strangers in return for sweets.

When we were teenagers we used to make jokes about why Xhosa children were good at keeping secrets. It was said that one should never pursue questioning them once they had answered *andazi* (I don't know!) because, when they were babies, it is said, they were swung two or three times over a flame of fire, with the word *andazi* repeated in the child's ear two or three times. Because of that process, it is said, the child never forgot the word, since it was one of the first he or she heard spoken.

Comments like that are very common amongst our people; they are not tribalistic, they do not cause offence in the way in which the disciples of apartheid would like us to believe. For instance, Xhosa children used to call us 'khomo ha e bone e boneloa ke motho', meaning that the Basotho are great lovers and eaters of meat. Yes, we like meat; some of us even eat horsemeat. I think that this idea was brought to Lesotho by the French missionaries. When I went to Algeria I was at first quite taken aback to find horsemeat at the butchers, until I remembered these histories that were told to us in school. Anyway, it was as I recalled these stories that among the many warnings I gave to my daughters was that they should just say 'andazi' to anyone who asked them questions at the place to which I was taking them.

The circle of people who knew about my going was limited to three, including those ones actively engaged in the preparations. I could neither write to my mother in Matatiele nor tell either my brother or my brother-in-law who both lived in Soweto. But, when I talked with other comrades in exile, who had left after me, I discovered that many did not even know the date on which they were to go, because later on the SB planted spies who alerted them. Many people were arrested before they were able to cross into Botswana, and in Botswana itself there were many spies who had infiltrated themselves in the ranks of the refugees already there. While it was still relatively safe and easy when I left in 1962, it became very difficult very soon afterwards, especially for those who had to avoid the border posts in order to cross by foot. It was because of this relative ease that I was able to take so many suitcases full of clothes. But, all the same, I was terribly worried. At first I had been told to take only one suitcase. Then, after I protested that there were three of us, I was allowed three — that is, one suitcase for each one of us. Then, a few days before we left I was allowed to take the blankets.

* * *

In Lobatsi we stayed for two days with old friends from our Sophiatown days. It was during our stay with them that I realized the difficulties of exiles. Our friends lived in a corrugated iron shack, which they had partitioned into two rooms: one was their bedroom, the other doubled as a sitting-room

201

and bedroom for guests. Cooking was done between two medium-sized stones outside the house, with firewood collected from a nearby hill. Water was fetched from a pit.

After breakfast on the day before our departure, my friend took me to see a number of people from South Africa who had already escaped into Botswana. These were people who had escaped from Zeerust after the anti-pass and Bantu Authorities disturbances of the late Fifties. I don't remember their names, but the five I saw were at the Pretoria march of 1956. From these people we bought two chickens. Later we bought two loaves of white bread for our provisions. Later still, the comrade who had driven us from home came to tell me to be ready by seven o'clock the next morning to be able to catch the eight o'clock train to Zimbabwe (then still Southern Rhodesia). He also brought me some Rhodesian currency.

I awoke at first light, and went on my knees for a short prayer, 'God walk before us, all the way to Tanganyika'. We each had a wash and I packed our provisions into the basket we had carried with us from home. Because of travelling with small children, I realized that the luggage was rather too heavy. So I decided to leave the blankets behind.

The train was already on the platform when we arrived and the comrade bought the tickets for us to Zambia (then Northern Rhodesia). We hurriedly put our luggage in the compartment, then all stood by the window to wave goodbye, after the announcement was made that the train was bound for Bulawayo.

As the train started to move again, a tall African man, whose face I had noticed in the next compartment, came and stood at the door of ours. He started to pester me with questions; he wanted to know where I came from and where I was going to. I said I came from Lobatsi. To my unease, he corrected my pronunciation of the name of the place. From the correction he made, I decided to give him the cold shoulder to stop him asking further questions. So I spoke to the children about how they should dress their hair, and was relieved when my questioner disappeared from the compartment door where he had been standing. Anyway, I did feel guilty, because the man might have been asking innocent questions. He must have been, because (apart from some hic-cups) the Gods of Africa carried me and my daughters on their broad shoulders.

One station before we reached Plumtree, two black police-men came into our apartment. They wrote something on papers that they carried, but never said a word to us. They puzzled me a bit, because I thought they were Immigration Officers, and that they should have communicated with us. 'Anyway, they know their job better than I do; why worry,' I said to myself. Then, when the train stopped at Plumtree, a white Immigration Officer came into the compartment. At that time I was peeping out through the window, watching the children. I had asked them to get down to buy some tea from a kiosk, as other people were doing. We had with us a flask and three plastic mugs, which we had carried with us from home.

The Immigration Officer asked me if I was travelling alone, and I told him that I was with two little girls. After he had himself peeped out through the window to have them pointed out to him, he asked where I was going, to which I replied: 'Northern Rhodesia'. He then asked if I was 'Coloured', to which I replied in the negative. 'See you', he said, and left, glancing at his watch, but when the train pulled out he had still not come back.

I don't remember what time the train came to Bulawayo, but it was still during the morning, and we had to wait for the train to Zambia, which was due in the evening, for the whole day. When we got off the train, all passengers were directed to the Customs. Two African officials, dressed in khaki shorts, were in attendance. I did not expect my lug-gage to be searched because I was in transit, so I told the official about that, but he said that everyone's luggage was searched, including that of those in transit.

I put my luggage on one of the trolleys, and we passed through to the other side of the building, to the platforms. There was nobody in sight, but I noticed there were a few benches placed at a distance of ten to twelve yards from each other. I quickly checked them all to see which were marked 'Europeans only', as was the practice at home. But they were all unmarked. Fortunately for me, I saw an African man coming out of one corner, carrying a broom — he was apparently a sweeper at the station. I asked him if we could occupy the benches, to which he replied yes. He also gave me information about our train to Zambia, and showed me where the toilets were. So we sat down, knowing very well that we were going to remain there for about eight hours.

Time after time I would get up to stretch my legs and read the newspaper posters. In one of these the death was reported of Dr Pararenyate, who was described as an official of Zapu. I was so sad to read this, because I knew Dr Pararenyate very well when he was a medical student at the University of the Witwatersrand, he used to visit his girlfriend, Sibongile, whom he later married, at the Bridgeman Memorial Hospital, where we were doing our midwifery training together in 1953.

According to the newspaper headlines, it was clear that Dr Pararenyate, who was Deputy President of Zapu, had died a violent death. There was also a picture of a wrecked car, reported to be the one in which he had been travelling when it was said that he had been knocked down by a train at a level crossing. But when I came to Dar-es-Salaam, I found the Nationalists from Zimbabwe very sad and angry about what they called the 'mysterious circumstances' of their leader's death. When I returned to Zimbabwe in 1981, I could not miss going back to the Bulawayo station. I also had the opportunity of touring the Pararenyate Hospital, which is one of the most modern in Southern Africa, originally built for whites only during Ian Smith's fifteen infamous years of UDI, but which was renamed since Zimbabwe's independence to honour the doctor's memory.

We arrived in Lusaka about eight o'clock in the evening. I was supposed to have gone to the UNIP office to get assistance, but that was impossible. First, because the luggage was too heavy for me; second, because the first person I inquired from about UNIP said that the office was closed. People, he said, were out in the rural areas, campaigning for elections for internal rule and self-rule. This was a great setback to me. Not knowing the place, I decided to spend the

204

night in Lusaka at the bus terminal, where I could see there were waiting-rooms, and where there were hundreds of people waiting for buses to take them to different places the following day. Buses were also lined up there, but there was no bus marked 'Mbeya', which was the one going to Tanganyika. Some women told me where the Mbeya bus stop was. They also told me that the bus did not leave until the next morning and they advised me to stay with them until that time.

As I was talking to these women, I could see that some people were already spreading sheets and blankets, preparing their bedding where they sat. When I inquired about going to the waiting-rooms, they told me that nobody slept there because the rooms were infested with bugs. Furthermore, they said, there were snatchers, who took away peoples' luggage in these waiting-rooms. 'What are these people talking about?' I said to myself. 'Spend the night in the open with small children?' But, indeed, that was it! What made matters worse for us was that I had left my suitcase with blankets in it in Lobatsi.

At NDuduma, all passengers got off the bus, and stood in a queue. I was watching what the other passengers were doing, and I realized that they all held documents in their hands. Two black policemen dressed in khaki shorts and wearing maroon keffiyehs on their heads, started to check passenger documents. My elder daughter whispered to me: 'Everybody is showing documents, and we have none, what are we going to do?' I reminded her that I had said that they should not utter a word during our journey. But all the same, the moment of truth had arrived. I observed that, after documents had been checked, passengers were passed to the right, behind the policeman. When they came to me, I said: 'I am a South African and I am asking for political asylum in Tanganyika'. The children simply gawped at me, because they now realized that during the journey I had been telling half-truths, dodging peoples' questions, and even telling outright lies.

The policemen spoke to each other in their language. Without addressing any word to me, one indicated to me with his hand to join the other passengers. The lady to whom I had been talking in the bus told me that all passengers passed to the right were allowed to enter Tanganyika; she then invited me to go to the office to change Rhodesian currency into Tanganyika currency. Before I followed her into the office, I told my daughters that it seemed that we were being allowed to enter Tanganyika, and not being turned back. I could see the expression of joy in their faces. I told them to wait while I went into the office.

There were two long desks in the Immigration Office; the one on the left was marked 'Northern Rhodesia' and the one on the right 'Tanganyika'. When my turn came, I handed my money to the Tanganyika immigration official. He stared at me and asked: 'Where do you come from, lady?'

'From South Africa; and I am asking for political asylum in Tanganyika', I said.

He then asked, 'How did you pass through the Rhodesias?'

'Well, by hook or by crook', I replied.

'Did you have travelling documents ?'

'Nothing. I left South Africa by the back door because I am a Freedom Fighter and I was running away from police persecution,' I said.

'You are the luckiest person on earth', he said. Then he continued, 'Tanganyika is a free country, and you are welcome to enter'. I was now beaming with joy, and I recalled the words of our national anthem, *"Nkosi Sikilel' iAfrika'*.

The Tanganyikan officer next pointed to the Rhodesia desk and said: 'I want you to go to that desk and tell them where you come from, and that you are going to Tanganyika'.

'Brother', I said, having discarded 'Sir', which I first used in addressing him, 'I think you see the seriousness of the matter if those people arrest me; it means five years of imprisonment for leaving the country without a passport. Moreover, I am travelling with two children'. To that he replied: 'If they try to arrest you, you must run back to me and once you reach the centre of the floor, I will grab you. I have police here, you know,' he said. He then went on: 'I want to show you that Tanganyika is under African rule, and that it will welcome all Africans'.

I really did not like this idea at all: it seemed that he wanted a show-down with the other side. So I asked him again what would happen if things did not go according to what he was telling me. But he insisted that he would not let me fall into the hands of the Rhodesians because he had already agreed to grant me asylum.

Meanwhile the other women had all already left the office; the only people left in that large building were the two of us and the African at the Northern Rhodesia desk. I started to blame myself: 'Why did I follow the other women to change money, because the policeman had already waved me to the side of those passing to Tanganyika'. I began to picture myself struggling in the centre of the floor with officials; I thought of the children waiting outside hopefully, only to be told to join their mother somewhere in a cell. 'Just when I am on the doorstep of my destination,' I thought. I started to shiver; I imagined myself in the dock in South Africa, answering a charge of leaving the country without a passport, with sergeant Mkwanazi as the chief state witness.

Reluctantly, I went to the Rhodesia desk. The African official asked to see my documents, and I told him that I had none. He then called for a white official, who was dressed in white, like the one I had seen in Plumtree. When this white official asked me where I came from, I told him I had come from Mafeking, which is the last town on the border between South Africa and Botswana, and which is now, as Mafikeng, part of the Bophutatswana 'homeland'. When he then asked me how I had got past Plumtree, I told him that the white official who had come to my compartment had said that he would come to see me, but that he had not returned. Strange enough, this white official also asked me if I was a 'Coloured', to which I gave the same negative answer. He then shook his head, keeping quiet the while. Meanwhile, I kept my cool, but watched him closely, thinking of what the Tanganyikan official had said that I should do if they tried to arrest me. The Rhodesian official now turned to the Tanganyikan desk. 'Gentlemen', he said, 'please take this woman. I am sick and tired of people who do not do their work properly. This woman should have been stopped at Plumtree.'

As he was saying these words, I was already taking a few steps backwards and in the direction of the Tanganyikan side. I actually turned my back on the Rhodesian, when I was about four yards from him. The Tanganyikan official started to fill in my entry visa there and then. I don't know how I managed to answer the questions he asked me in order to complete the form, because, spontaneously, I was reciting the twenty-third Psalm: 'The Lord is my Shepherd' in my heart. When he had finished everything for me, and had exchanged the currency, he accompanied me to the door; he was really so very happy, still telling me that Tanganyika was a free country, for all Africans.

When I came out of the office, the children told me that they had already identified our suitcases, which task was now complete for everyone proceeding further. I showed the girls the entry visa; they did not quite understand what it was, and one of them (I don't remember which one) asked if we were South Africans no longer. I replied that I would explain everything in the bus.

Mbeya was still very far away; we did not arrive there until towards evening. The roads were not at all good and the landscape still as hilly as it had been in Zambia. Time, and time again, the bus stopped at some road-houses for people to relieve themselves and also to get something to eat. It was the first time that we spoke about South Africa in the bus. We were so relaxed, knowing that there were no more borders to cross; it was then that I told the girls about the saga of the Immigration Office at NDunduma, and explained about the entry visa.

At Mbeya we took a taxi to the address we had been given in Botswana. We stayed at this address for two days, waiting for the day when there would be a bus going to Dar-es-Salaam. On the first evening, our hostess, who was one of twenty nurses who had been recruited by the ANC for the Tanganyika Government, phoned Dar-es-Salaam, to announce our arrival. The representative of the ANC, James Radebe, told the lady to call me to the telephone. To my delight and surprise, my husband's husky voice was on the line. I had not expected him to be in Dar; he had been globetrotting so much since going abroad, and our correspondence had not been regular.

James Radebe had been the Transvaal Provincial Secretary of the ANC in the late Fifties. A former teacher, he was a formidable organizer, who lived in Daveyton, Benoni, where he was an active member of his branch. I remember how his wit, in 1957 or 1958, deflected what might have resulted in an ugly situation at an ANC meeting. The SB, together with armed police, had invaded one of our meetings at the Trades Hall in Johannesburg. They had marched into the hall and then provocatively mounted on the stage and searched members of the Presidium body with their hands raised up (I think they gave the orders).

During the higgledy-piggledy, James, after being searched, moved to the front of the stage and started the freedom song, *'mayihambe le vangeli mayigqib'ilizwe lonke'* (Let this Gospel be Spread All Over the World). He was a tall man and, as he flung his hands like a Master of Music indicating to the Choir to go softly, softly, we all sat down and joined in the singing. James's action calmed tempers, and we all awaited directions from a leader. The police picked up all the documents of the meeting and then left. After that, we expected an announcement that the meeting was banned. But, to our delight and relief, Oliver Tambo, who was chairing the meeting, announced: 'I am still your Chairman'. The meeting then continued. I only heard that James was abroad when I was told that I would be going abroad.

The story of the 'twenty nurses' is a little-known but important example of how the ANC, since 1948 had developed a policy of forming links with 'progressive' political organizations in Africa as well as in the rest of the world; the South African struggle was seen as part of the loosely-defined 'African Revolution', and the ANC took part in PAFMECA (Pan African Movement for East and Central Africa), which later became PAFMECSA when it expanded its membership to include liberation organizations such as UNIP in Zambia; Zapu of Rhodesia; the BCP of Basutoland and the ANC. I am grateful to Mr Alfred Kgokong Mqota, who was a member of the National Executive and part of the team in Dar-es-Salaam at the time, for the details. According to him, the ANC had developed extremely close and cordial working relations with TANU (Tanganyika African National Union) — to such an extent that fraternal greetings to each other's annual conferences had become a regular pattern. So, when Tanganyika (now Tanzania) gained its independence in 1961, it decided to show its practical solidarity with the the South African liberation struggle by asking the ANC to send a contingent of qualified nurses to the newly-indepen- dent State. According to Mr Mqota, twenty-one nursing sis- ters from the different provinces of South Africa went in 1962.

The story of these nurses should be told in greater detail, since it is clearly a fascinating one. We know that some (Koleka Tunyiswa, Edith Ncwana; Sinha Jali) got married to Tanzanian citizens; others married men from other coun- tries: Phine Luke married a Zimbabwean, someone else mar- ried a Mr Swart from the Netherlands. Some of the nurses came to England, while others (like Sister Edna Mgabaza, who recently died in Zimbabwe, still faithfully supporting the ANC and the liberation struggle) went to other African States after their independence.

The morning before we left Mbeya, the Tanganyika Security came to see me, because the lady at whose place we were staying, had reported our arrival to them. They were very polite. They told me that I was the very first South African to get my entry visa at NDuduma. Yes, I really real- ized that Tanganyika was ruled by Africans; I was filled with pride for that.

After the Security men had left, we went to the market to get a chicken and fruits for our provisions. We were told that the journey to Dar-es-Salaam would take more than twelve hours, but that fortunately there would be no sleeping by the roadside. I was just too scared of insect-bites, whose marks were still visible on our skins. We baked some bread, roasted the chicken, and also bought some soft drinks for our jour- ney. In the evening our hostess gave each of us a quinine tablet to swallow, because, as she explained, we were in a malaria area. Oh heavens! this was another scare story. I knew about malaria, but only in theory, and I even suggest- ed that the rash might be due to it. But I was told that the first symptom of malaria was headache, and none of us had that.

The following morning a taxi dropped us at the bus stop at seven o'clock. We bought our bus tickets from a window hatch, then joined the queue for the identification of our luggage, so that it could be placed on the rack on top of the bus. From there we went to the front of the bus to get in, but we found that there was no queue — a group of people were struggling and pushing at the door and the bus looked already full. Our hostess told us not to worry; she said that the majority of the people who were seated in the bus were not going anywhere, they vacated the seats after the real passengers gave them tips. So she pushed her way into the bus and, after she had paid the tips, she shouted to me to come in. As we walked in, the chaps who had been tipped walked out. After we were seated, our hostess got off the bus. When the bus left, at about eight o'clock, there were many seats which were vacant after all the non-passengers had got off. I've never seen anything like that. But, as our proverb says: *Ho tsamaea ke hobona* (to travel is to see). Indeed, I saw.

The journey to Dar-es-Salaam was wonderful, despite the bumps of the untarred road. But who cares about bumps or untarred roads, or dust, when we knew that Robert was waiting for us at the end of our journey. We were all so happy all along the way that we hardly spoke about South Africa. It seemed as if we had been travelling in thick fog for many days, and that, at long last, it had dissipated when the sun rose. The verdure of tropical trees and bushes along the way was refreshing too.

At sunset, we came to a small town, which they said was Morogoro, which was the headquarters of the ANC before it transferred to Lusaka, Zambia. It was said that we were not very far from Dar. When the bus entered the tarred road, there were yellow electric lights on both sides of the road; they were really beautiful, and I envied that our dark townships back home could have such lights.

When we reached Dar it was already dark, but we could see people seated on the verandahs of their bungalows. On

211

the whole, the place looked quiet, with no semblance of township life. The first thing that surprised us, when we got off the bus at the terminus, was the heat. We had to take off our overcoats, which we had put on from Mbeya, because there it had been cold. At the terminus we waited for only a few minutes before Robert and two friends arrived to fetch us.

It was a happy reunion when we got to Dar-es-Salaam, one year and four months after Robert had left South Africa. Our colleagues all got a blood chill when I related to them the story of my journey. It was exactly two weeks to the day when I arrived in Dar-es-Salaam from the day that I had left Soweto; they said that it was a record. Actually, I was very lucky, as the Tanganyikan Immigration Officer had said, because the students who had been coming on after us were arrested in Rhodesia. It had been the intention that I should have left with them, but plans were changed at the last moment, and I was told to go alone, because I had the children with me. The students were put in police cells in Rhodesia, and they had to renounce South African citizenship in order to be freed. But it took them more than a month to reach Dar-es-Salaam. The twenty nurses I mentioned earlier on were stuck in Botswana; they did not arrive in Tanganyika until nearly three months later.

Two days later Robert gave me a priest's collar, and said that I should keep it as a souvenir. It was the collar which, he said, he wore when he left South Africa in 1961, disguised as a priest. I wanted to know how he had disguised his hands, which could easily have been identified because of his missing index finger — lost, as a result of an accident at Crown Mines, where he had worked in the Thirties. He said he wore gloves! I was amused, as I imagined him walking in the streets of Jo'burg, dressed as a priest. The collar had a dent in one side; he said that it must have been gnawed at by mice at the place he left it in in Dar. I still have the collar.

Two weeks after our arrival, Robert left for England. From there he was scheduled to go to Algeria to open the first office of the ANC. I remained in Dar for a few months, settling the children, and trying to find a school for them. They

212

first started school at St Joseph's day school; then Robert wrote to tell me that a sympathizer in our struggle had offered to pay for their fees at a boarding school. We were lucky to get them admitted to the Aga Khan Girls Boarding School. We were very grateful to this samaritan, whom I never got to know personally, though we did write to each other. But the offer enabled us to do full-time work for the organization at a time when the ANC was still short of personnel and funds.

All of us received our first travel documents from Tanganyika, in order to be able to travel to other countries, in order to carry out the work of the organization. To us, South Africans, finding refuge in free African countries like Tanganyika and Ghana, was the realization of the ideals of the foundling fathers and mothers of our organization; they saw the peoples of the continent of Africa as one; they saw how the colonial era had disinherited the people of Africa, how the brutal practice of slavery had affected the continent as a whole. It was for that reason that the ANC National Anthem was a clarion call to the people of Africa to fight together for the restoration of their land and their rights. The still colonized parts like South Africa and, until 1990, Namibia drew great inspiration from the liberated countries of Africa, and with their help, it is simply a matter of time before apartheid, too, is thrown into the dustbin of history.

11

■

The Small World

Once the children had been settled in a school in Tanzania, my next step was to move to Algiers to join my husband. I had spent five months in Tanzania.

I left Dar-es-Salaam on the same day as Moses Kotane; he had, with Duma Nokwe (who was, at that time, the Secretary-General of the ANC) been a recent arrival, having also left South Africa by clandestine means. It was my first time in an aeroplane. I sat near a window and, as the plane straightened up over the clouds, I looked down and thought: 'Umkhulu ANC' (ANC You Are Wonderful); the anxiety and risks of the first part of my journey to the North were over. I felt great, travelling with a document from a government that would protect me; yet in my own country I was a non-citizen and alien only because of the colour of my skin.

After supper, the lights inside the plane were dimmed. Some people took off their jackets in order to go to sleep. I was very sceptical about that; I was very stupidly thinking about a crash, and thought that it was unwise for these people to do what they did — they might die without their jackets on. (As if the jackets would stop the crash!) So, I did not sleep for the whole night, watching the 'fasten seat belt' sign, although the flight was smooth, except for a few air pocket dives. Malome (Moses Kotane) was sitting behind me, and I told him lies when I came back from the toilet and said that I had been asleep for half an hour.

We made one stop at Khartoum; it was about midnight. It was so hot that I felt I could catch the heat with my hands. Malome explained that it was because the line of the Equator passed through the Sudan.

By daybreak, I was feeling a bit sleepy. But now there was a new fascination — the Sahara desert. And, within a few minutes we could see the pyramids on the ground. I was so amazed — all that I had learnt at school was unfolding one after the other in front of my eyes. Within about an hour, the Captain announced that we would be landing at Cairo airport; that announcement was followed by the illumination of the 'Fasten Seat Belts' and 'No Smoking' signs. A few moments later the hostess passed sweets around to every passenger. I took one, and popped it into my mouth, as I had been told that chewing sweets helps to lessen the noise in the ears at take-off or descent.

The weather was fine. I looked out of the window, still somewhat bewildered by this flying steel house. Yes, indeed, there on the ground I could see buildings. Cairo looked really beautiful from the air — in fact, it looked a bit like Johannesburg, with its high-storey buildings. And the river Nile made a beautiful scene along its way, dividing the city in two. Hmm! Is this really Cairo, home of the ancient Pharaohs? Hmm! Is this really me in Cairo, when just a few months ago I was under the watchful eye of the South African SB? I kept shaking my head in disbelief.

Then, as we passed through the Customs, I was curious about the presence of so many coloured people wearing soldiers' uniforms. Thanks again to Malome, he explained that they were Arabs, and that the Algerians with whom I was going to stay looked exactly like Egyptians.

As soon as we passed the Customs, there were scores of taxis and touts; we followed one, and were relieved to get seated in it because of the noise they made. The taximan drove us to the city at a frightening speed. When he put on

215

his brakes at traffic lights, we were flung backwards and for-wards — I really felt that my last meal was coming back from my stomach. But what was the hurry for? Anyway, we never spoke to him until he delivered us to the address we had given him.

The ANC Representative in Cairo, Dr Mzwandile Piliso, had taken us to a transit hotel. This was another first; my first time in an hotel. He left us for a while, and then came back to tell me that he had sent a telegraph to Robert to meet me in Algiers the day after next. The following morn-ing the waiter brought me breakfast in my room. Later, when he fetched the tray, he said: 'Baksheesh!'. After I had told him that I could not understand his language, he showed me, in sign language, that he wanted money. I asked him what it was for and he said that it was because he had brought me my breakfast. So I gave him a few Egyptian coins, since we had changed some of our currency at the reception desk. After that, he gave me a bill to sign, after which he said another 'Baksheesh'. Again I asked him what that was for, and he said that it was for using his pen for signing the bill. I gave him a few more coins. When I later met Malome in the lounge I asked him if his waiters had asked for money, and he said 'no'. He had a good laugh when I told him of my episode with the waiter; in fact, I had never before seen him laugh so much. He was always one of the feared ANC leaders, always looking serious, but always kind and polite. After the laugh he said: 'By the way, Maggie, it is your first time out of South Africa'. He then warned me not to repeat what I had done. So, the following morning, I told the waiter to disappear when he again asked for 'Baksheesh'. I had become clever for him this time.

We finished our breakfast at about nine o'clock and then decided to take a little stroll not too far away from the hotel in order to stretch our legs. Dr Piliso had promised to come to the hotel at between half-past ten and eleven o'clock to take us sight-seeing. When we were walking, I tripped over something on the pavement, with the result that I nearly sprained my left ankle. Malome rushed to help me. While I checked to see if the heel of my shoe was still intact, he held

216

my handbag. 'Oh! Maggie,' he said, 'what on earth are you carrying in here that is so heavy? Are you carrying bloempots (flower pots) from Mofolo?' I blushed a bit, and then replied: 'No, Malome, it is not bloempots, but face creams, because Robert warned me that I might have difficulties in Algeria because of the language and of the different products.'

'What!' he said. Then he laughed again, 'Well, now I know that all women are the same'.

I blushed again, wishing that the subject should be changed, and I think he noticed that, because he started to ask me about some people who used to be members of the Sophiatown branch. What a relief! But this was the time that I realised that Moses Kotane knew about and cared for everyone in the organisation, even if they were known to him only as names. Many people he asked about I could never have imagined being known to him, a top leader, and one who had not been a member of the Sophiatown branch. But Malome knew many peoples' difficulties; he also knew those who took risks like going to the Reserves during the Bantu Authorities and Anti-Pass campaigns; he even asked me about the treatment I had received in prison in 1960. I was really amazed about his knowledge of names and his concern about everyone. I had always known him as a serious, devoted, and highly-principled leader, but during the thirty to forty minutes walk, I discovered other traits in his character, especially his fatherliness and benevolence. Moses Kotane died some years ago in Moscow after a long illness, and like many other of our pioneers in the struggle, he left a rich heritage and foundation.

Robert was not at the airport when I landed at Algiers; the telegram had not arrived. A big problem soon surfaced: I spoke neither Arabic nor French; nobody spoke English. One of the Immigration officials told me, in sign language, after I had identified my luggage, to stand aside. Then, after about half an hour to forty minutes, a tall Algerian, who could speak a little English, came to ask me who it was I was waiting for. When I told him my husband's name he replied: 'Oh! that is my brother; I'll take you there!'

217

We took the bus to the city. But, when we came to the place where he should have been, Robert was not in. The Algerian friend told me to wait on the steps, while he went to look for Robert. When Robert came back about an hour or so later, he was surprised to find me there. He had not received the telegram. Later, when I related to him the story of my sleeplessness on the plane, he was amused. That story reminded him about how Nelson Mandela had behaved on one plane trip while they were abroad, when they were flying over the Mediterranean Sea to meet Algerian leaders at one of their camps in Morocco. Robert said that, as the plane was flying over the sea, Nelson would say: 'Mtembu' (calling Robert by their clan name) 'this is what I do not like! I prefer flying over land'. Robert said that he could not convince Nelson that their chances of survival were better over the sea than over land.

To say that we settled in Algeria would be an understatement; we were at home! And, by the end of the second month after my arrival on the 18 March 1963, we were issued with Algerian passports. The country was now in the hands of people who had, themselves, been exiles only a year or two previously, and they understood our situation completely. So, besides the offices for the ANC, there were also offices for Frelimo from Mozambique, MPLA and GRAE/FNLA from Angola. The Algerian people were still very militant after the six bloody years of the war of independence that had claimed one and a half million Algerian lives. To us, who arrived at that time, it was like coming to the very fountain of revolutions. Yes, the Algerian people had sacrificed their lives for their independence.

Although we had difficulty with the language, scores of Algerians came to our office every day to tell us about their revolution. Some came out of curiosity — to see what South Africans look like: men and women would come and put their arms next to mine, and say: 'Soeur, meme chose' (Sister, the same). Where we really made a mess was with the telephone. We cut off several calls when we heard, but misunderstood, the phrase: 'ne quittez pas' — we thought 'ne pas' meant that the person we wanted to speak to was not there, until one day one official whose calls we had cut off several times asked us why we put the receiver down when the call was passed to him. When we told him that we had understood his secretary to have said that he was not there, that he explained the phrase to us: 'hold the line'. It was learning French the hard way. However, I seemed to be picking it up faster than Robert, although he had arrived four months before I did. Soon he was calling upon me to interpret whenever people came to visit. Robert's fault was that he was, by nature, a perfectionist; he did not want to make mistakes. So, my vocabulary increased rapidly because of tasks such as going to the shops and by inviting women friends to teach me the names of objects in each room, from kitchen to bathroom.

On Sunday afternoons, friends who knew some English, took us round the city to show us the scars of the revolution, which were not only on people, but also on buildings. For instance, part of the University of Algiers, which had been severely bombed, had not yet been repaired. Amongst the horrifying places we were shown was a place at the Casbah, where some of the revolutionaries had been trapped by the French army. The Casbah itself was depressing; it had dark and narrow streets, with slippery places from running water, and was a disgrace compared to the large and well-lighted houses where the French used to live. Yet this was the place where the Algerians were confined to during colonial occupations. One could see that there must have been terrible overcrowding.

As time passed, we could see that there was not a single family who had not been affected by the Revolution. For instance, there was a young girl called Jasmina Balcacem, who worked in the office of the Party as a typist and telephonist; when she was fifteen, she had been maimed in a bomb blast and had lost both her legs. She was an astonishingly brave woman. The thing that still made her angry when she related the story of her accident was that one Algerian, who had been a collaborator, came to mock her, telling her that since she had lost both her legs, there was nothing left for her in life; she had been, he said, misled by the FLN 'terrorists'. But Jasmina was sent to the USA for treatment, and, when she returned, she was taught typing and telephone operation. When I saw her, she moved about in a wheelchair, and had artificial legs fitted. Although Jasmina was maimed, she was an enormous asset to her country. Besides her normal work, she helped with interpreting and translating because she spoke excellent English.

Another woman whom I met had had her breasts disfigured — her ordeals during torture sessions was so terrible that it is too painful for me to relate. Time and again we were told the stories of martyrs like Ben M'hedi Larbi, Colonel Amerouch, Colonel Didouche Mourad and others. The streets of the capital bore the names of these great men. Indeed, our ANC office was in Rue Ben M'hedi Larbi. The office had been opened on 26 June 1963 by no less a person than President Ahmed ben Bella. This was a great honour, not only to the ANC, but also to the fighting people of South Africa. We learnt later that Walter Sisulu had made a radio broadcast about this event from the underground where they were in hiding in Rivonia. We also saw the prison in which prisoners had been detained, tortured, and hanged. And indeed, some people who were sentenced to death had been saved because the war had ended. The Arabic words of the Algerian National Anthem were translated for me. There was one verse which said that 'The People of Algeria have folded the mighty France like the leaves of a book'. I liked that very much indeed.

In July 1963, the ANC headquarters in Dar asked me to lead a delegation of the ANC Womens' League to the World Congress of Women in Moscow. This meant that I had to prepare a speech for that Congress. My husband suggested that I prepare the speech on my own, and that he would help me with the typing. I was shattered. I had never before written a speech; at home we usually addressed meetings off the cuff. But Robert encouraged me; he said that I should put down on paper everything that I did with other women in the ANC. It took two weeks for me to finish the draft, which Robert then typed. At first, I thought that Robert had been unreasonable in not wanting to write the speech for me. But I soon realised that he was right: we were not always moving together in our work.

220

In Moscow, it was wonderful to see and meet women of different races, colours and creeds working as equals, in great harmony. From their speeches I soon realised that other women had the same problems as ours. There were Freedom Fighters from Vietnam, Palestine, Zimbabwe, Namibia as well as from the former Portuguese territories; all of them were pledged the support of the women for their liberation struggles. The Soviet Womens Committee, which was hosting the Congress, invited several delegates to visit other Soviet Republics after the Congress had ended. I was one of those invited.

During our visit we were asked to address the people of the area about life in our countries. It was a wonderful experience, and one of the effects was that I started to gain confidence in myself and in my ability to write down what I was going to speak about. When I returned to Moscow, I was invited by the Chinese delegation to visit their country. That was wonderful. I visited Peking, Nanking and Shanghai. In each of these cities, I was asked to make speeches to trades unions, to womens groups and the like. What impressed me in these countries was their care for child health and education and for the conditions for working mothers.

I returned to Algiers after two months, feeling immensely enriched after my first visits to Europe and Asia. What was even more important to me was that I had established contacts with women from the vast African continent, since, in South Africa, we did not hear much about the women of Africa. The only woman I had heard about was Angie Brooks of Liberia, and it was only in Moscow that I met, for the first time, leaders of the Pan-African Women's Organisation, with whom I later worked very closely. Prominent amongst them were Mrs Ransome-Kuti, a powerful speaker and fighter for women's rights from Nigeria, and Mrs Aouwa Keita from Mali.

The Algerian government gave us many facilities. We were offered radio broadcasts once a week for our bulletins. The press also published our articles, and the ANC office was soon well-established. We held Press Conferences for our National Days, such as 26 June; South Africa Freedom Day;

221

South African Women's Day and Heroes Day. I also established contacts with the Union of Algerian Women. By this time Johnny Makatini and Joe Matlou had joined the Algiers office; later, Joe was asked to open an office in Ghana, so he left for Accra.

Then, in 1966, Robert was asked to move to London to do another job there. That job was to co-ordinate the work of the former Congress Alliance with that of the ANC. Several members of the Alliance had gone into exile, and most of them had settled in England. For that reason, the need arose for all these exiles to work together under the umbrella of the ANC to rouse international opinion against the apartheid regime. I did not follow my husband to London because we agreed that there was no particular role for me to play in the work there; I also felt that it was an advantage for me to remain in a French-speaking country, since the knowledge of another international language would not only benefit me, as a person, but also the organisation. Lastly, the ANC itself did not see the necessity for me to follow my husband. Instead, Duma Nokwe, the Secretary-General of the ANC, appointed me formally the Assistant Representative to Johnny Makatini. The children were now in the Soviet Union, having been awarded scholarships from the Soviet Womens' Committee: my eldest daughter studied fashion design, while the youngest studied pharmacy. When they came home for holidays, Robert would also try to hop to Algiers to see them.

* * *

As I am revising this, news comes of the death of Johnny Makatini, in Zambia on 3 March 1988 and it is to honour his memory that I want to write about him as I knew him. Johnstone Mfanafuthi Makatini (universally known as Johnny) was a modest sort of person, who did not want to be showered with praises — even when he had done something praiseworthy and there were many examples of those. He was hard-working, devoted and selfless; his enjoyment in his work was clearly dictated and guided by an inner sense of duty to his country and people. He was ready to pay the highest sacrifice in the fight against apartheid's tyranny, and he died during the course of that mission of restoring human dignity and self-determination for the oppressed black majority.

His Zulu name, Mfanafuthi, was given to him by his maternal grandmother because he had been born after another boy, and that is the meaning of the name. I did not know him at home, but time and time again I used to hear the Youth League leaders like Peter Ntite, Patrick Molaoa and others, talk of Johnny Makatini as a solid militant of the ANC in Durban.

Like all black children, Johnny grew up the hard way. By the age of six or seven he was already responsible for jobs like bringing water from the well and sweeping the lawns early in the morning. His mother, Johnny told us, struggled to educate and clothe her children. One of the effects was that he depended on clothes passed down to him from his elder brothers. These were never the correct size, but he had to make do with them throughout primary school. He got his first pair of shoes only when he went to the secondary school at Pholela Institution in Natal. There he met many students from Matatiele, whose behaviour left a bad impression on him about that place. They said that Matatiele was bigger than Pietermaritzburg, which it was not, and called it 'Sweet Matat — the place where Jesus was nearly born'. What eccentrics, I told Johnny. Matatiele was only a dorp with two streets and a railway line which received one train per day.

At one time he was employed in the Native Affairs or municipal offices in Durban. It was while working there that he observed the bureaucratic ways of the white officials which inflicted such untold sufferings upon black people. He was so resentful of this behaviour that he adopted a clandestine way of saving some of them by giving falsely translated replies to the many questions to which the white officials subjected the people.

Johnny eventually became a teacher. Later still, he taught at a primary school in the rural areas. Here, he had endless fights with the principal of the school, whom he saw as a real puppet of the regime. In order to register his resentment of that obsequiousness, he stopped clocking his name in, as was required of all staff. He also refused to teach gardening to the pupils. The result was endless stormy meetings with the principal, who, in a very pompous way, was trying to insist that a teacher should be an obedient servant to the authorities. In the end the principal was forced to clock in Johnny's name himself, because of his fear that the white inspector might come and find out that there was a teacher who was getting a salary, although he was never (according to the register) at school. The principal had another dilemma: how to get rid of the teacher whose classes produced the best results, yet who refused to take classes in gardening, which the children hated because they correctly believed that it was training them for jobs in servitude.

In the end Johnny left the school of his own accord to go to university. Later he studied law, and was left with two years to complete his course at the University of Natal when he went into exile at the direction of the ANC. This was in 1962. He had a short stop in Tanzania before passing on to Rabat in Morocco to open an ANC office. But there things did not go according to promises made by that government to the ANC leaders in exile. Johnny struggled so hard there that sometimes he would telephone Algiers to say: 'Robbie, I only live by drinking water'.

So, in 1964 Robert asked him to come to Algiers — Robert was then also in charge of external affairs of the ANC. There the first thing he had to do was to get a decent pair of shoes. Yes, exile has its horrors; to be in a foreign land with neither relatives nor people you know can be a painful experience. The only thing that made him strong in Morocco, Johnny used to say, was that there was no police harassing him for a pass. In South Africa he had had several encounters with police, and had been locked up, sometimes for several days at a time without food, in police cells.

The Algiers office of the ANC was one of the liveliest and busiest. Every day, when Robbie and Johnny came back from appointments either at government departments or embassies, as soon as they entered, one of them would say 'victory'. We would then all sit down around a table for an analysis of the report of what had been done. Sometimes, when we felt really homesick, we would all sing freedom songs and hymns, while we carried on with the compilation of bulletins and other office work. Johnny would sing bass in a very beautiful, deep voice, whilst Robert would sing tenor.

I recall the report they gave when they returned on one occasion from the Japanese embassy. They said that during their talk the ambassador had told them that he was not aware of race discrimination in South Africa. Johnny was thoroughly amused as he recounted how Robert had taken His Excellency to task by slowly and politely, but firmly, telling the story of the old man who had lost his donkey because he could not make up his mind. Finally, Johnny said, Robert asked the ambassador if he was aware that Japanese were classified in South Africa as 'honorary whites', whereas Chinese were classified as Asians. Apparently the ambassador did not know. He said he 'would raise the matter' with his government, but we never heard any further: Japan, like many Western countries, is one of the racist regime's biggest trading partners.

When Robert came to London in 1966, Johnny became Chief Representative in Algiers. In 1969, coming home from a conference held in the Palais des Nations in Algiers, he was involved in a terrible car accident in which his driver was killed on the spot. The doctors who attended him said that he escaped serious brain damage by a whisker. It was only after a long convalescence that he recovered completely, although he was unable to sleep regularly and was forgetful for a long time afterwards. But he was soon back in the mainstream of the ANC External Mission. He stayed in Algeria until 1975, when he became the ANC representative at the United Nations. By the time of his death he was in charge of External Affairs of the ANC.

* * *

In 1968, the Pan African Womens Organisation (PAWO) formerly known as the All Womens Conference (AAWC), which had been formed in Dar in 1962, held its first conference in Algiers. Its headquarters was also moved from the Republic of Mali to Algeria. PAWO had been formed two years after the unprecedented stampede to independence in several African countries; its formation followed upon the UN General Assembly resolution 1514, of 14 December 1960, on Decolonisation.

The Constitution of each of the newly-independent countries contained radical clauses setting out equality and full participation rights for all men and women in the political, social, economic and cultural life of their countries, as the basis for rapid development and prosperity for the continent as a whole. However, in practice, women (who usually made up at least half of the population of each of these countries) very often could not take up their rightful place. Disabilities, mainly inherited from the legacies of colonialism, marred their progress; their integration and development was seriously hampered. Women, themselves, recognised this.

It was to begin to solve these problems that the women of Africa met, for the first time, in Dar-es-Salaam in July 1962, to exchange experiences. They came together to work out how best they could improve themselves qualitatively in order to be a useful force in the eradication of the last vestiges of oppression, side by side with their menfolk. They saw their participation in all spheres in the life of their countries as a stepping stone to the harmonious emancipation of women; they wanted to work, in solidarity, with women all over the world, against male domination. They also wanted to be guardians of African culture, and to bring up their children in happiness and security. Last, but not least, the PAWO pledged to support women of the liberation movements in Africa morally as well as materially until their countries were freed from foreign and racist regimes.

Three liberation movements, namely the PAIGC of Guinea-Bissau, Swapo of Namibia and the ANC, were elected to the Secretariat. As a consequence, the ANC nominated me as its representative to the Secretariat. The work at the Secretariat was mainly administrative, but I found it a very challenging and interesting. But we also attended several international conferences in many parts of the world, including several African countries.

I think that PAWO was well received by African governments. Not only did all African governments agree to pay subscriptions for the womens' organisations from their countries, but they also invited and hosted conferences, seminars and training centres for the PAWO. Finally, in 1968, the OAU formally granted PAWO observer status. That same year, the PAWO, as a non-governmental organisation, also gained observer status at the United Nations and its specialised agencies. PAWO also developed close links with womens' organisations in Europe, Asia and Latin America. To the women of Africa, the PAWO, like the OAU, was a great sign of hope; the unity and strength of the continent lies in the continuous blossoming of organisations like these, no matter what obstructs their progress. There can be no rest until every inch of the continent has been returned to its rightful owners, and its vast resources used for the benefit of all its peoples.

At the 1968 conference in Algiers, Mrs Jeanne Martin Cisse of the Republic of Guinea was re-elected as Secretary-General. Since she was at that time a Member of Parliament in her country, she could not reside at the headquarters in Algiers. However, she shuttled between the two places, in between keeping up a 'hot line' between both. Later, she became Guinea's Ambassador to the United Nations, serving as chairperson of the Security Council for one year in the period that her country was elected as a member of that body. A former teacher, and a graduate of the University of Dakar, Mrs Cisse was a brilliant woman and a brilliant orator, full of wit. Most of us who worked with her, owe her much thanks for the manner in which she shared her knowledge, with great modesty, with others. Jeanne and I established close personal relationships, and kept in touch with each other even after both of us had left PAWO, but there has been a break in contact since the change of government in her country.

I left Algeria in 1975, coming to England in order to help our daughter, who had been so traumatised by the death of her father, about which I write in the next chapter, that I realised that it would be unwise not to be near her.

12

■

The Parting From A Companion

My younger daughter, Masechaba, who was staying with her father in London in 1973, where she was then a postgraduate student in pharmacology, sent me an urgent letter saying that Robert had been been admitted to hospital for tests. When we had last been together, in Cairo and in London in 1972, Robert had looked fit and well, so the letter from my daughter immediately made me feel very apprehensive. ever since we had got married, Robert had never been admitted to hospital. I came to London at once.

The evening I arrived in London, which was 18 November 1973, I went to the Hampstead Hospital to see him. That hospital no longer exists; it has now been replaced by the much larger and more modern Royal Free Hospital, at which I was to work later, when it was finished. Although Robert looked ill, he was still well enough to take us to the hospital gate. On the way, he would point out to me the new building being erected, and about the much larger numbers of people who would be able to get treatment there.

Then, six days after I arrived, the doctors decided that, having seen the results of all the tests, they had to operate. The doctor who broke the news to me said that there were two schools of thought among them: some thought that he could just have had a recurrence of a hydabid cyst he had had and that it could just be punctured and aspirated; others, including the chief surgeon, thought that it would be better to operate. But they had agreed that it would be a simple operation. How it became complicated I cannot explain. What still puzzles me to this day is that some people at home later wrote (as can be seen from the letter from Kathrada which I include later) and said that some South African newspapers had reported that Robert had died of cancer. The doctors never mentioned cancer to me, and I simply do not know who gave such information to the South African newspapers.

At the end of all these consultations, the Registrar told us that Robert would be well enough to be home for Christmas. The operation was done on 28 November. My daughter Masechaba joined me in waiting at the hospital. Then, at about seven o'clock, which was much later than the time the operation was expected to be over, Robert was returned to the ward. When we went in to see him, I realised at once that all was not well. One of the doctors called us to the waiting-room again; he told us that the operation had not gone well, and that they had made a decision to take Robert back to the theatre. According to what the doctor told us, it was to be an intensive operation. Then, as it was by now 9 p.m., he advised us that we might as well go home; he assured us that he would let us know as soon as Robert came back from the second operation. This was the beginning of an agonising period for me and my daughter.

When we got home, I asked my daughter to go to bed, since she had to go to university the next day. We then waited for the call from the hospital. Waiting with me were Mrs Maud Phillips and Joe Matlou, a colleague in the ANC of my husband since Sophiatown days; he had postponed his return to Africa until after Robert's operation. When there was still no call from the hospital by twelve midnight, I decided to enquire if Robert was still in theatre. The nurse who answered the call told me that they were about to call me to say that I should come over because Robert's condition was causing concern.

When we arrived, accompanied now by Joe Matlou and Maud Phillips, we were led to the recovery room. As soon as I saw Robert, I asked Joe to call for Canon Collins and for Oliver Tambo, who happened to be in London at the time. Canon Collins came immediately, accompanied by another priest; they were taken to the recovery room by a nurse, while we waited downstairs in a waiting room. Canon Collins told me afterwards that, after he had offered a prayer, Robert had called his name. Similarly, when I went up again, Robert called my name as well. I could see the relief on the faces of the nurses who were monitoring him — these were signs that the crisis was no longer acute. When we left the hospital at 4 am, Robert's condition was still critical, but at least it had stabilised.

For the next four days his condition continued to be promising; he could take fluids by mouth, and talk to us. And, even though he was critically ill, Robert was still thinking about Sophiatown: he asked me to remind him of the name of the old man who had given him the name of Makhonatsohle. After I had reminded him of his name, he said: 'I am still like that; and I will be with our people on that day'.

Because of the many treatments he was having, we could not finish our talk. It was only after he was gone that my mind recalled some of the critical times that the people of Sophiatown had gone through. I thought that perhaps Robert was trying to show me that his condition was as critical as the removal of Sophiatown; a comparison I could understand better. However, having been a nurse for many years, watching his condition now hour after hour, I waited for one of Christ's miracles. The doctors, including the chief, called me outside many times, to tell me that Robert was putting up a good fight. The nursing officer (matron) also came round to see him; after which she said that I must keep on praying. I must say that all of the nursing staff were wonderful, and that, after all these little encouragements, my hope was rising that Robert would pull through. Meanwhile, Canon Collins had been there on several occasions to see him. I also received a call from Father Huddleston, who had been informed that Robert was critically ill; he was very upset, but assured me that he was offering prayers.

Then, on the fifth day, his condition deteriorated. On the sixth day the Sister arranged that my daughter and I should sleep at the hospital. Robert died the following morning, 7 December.

Before he had the operation, we talked a lot because Robert was always analysing situations. He expressed much joy that our children had acquired their specialities. Our eldest daughter had completed her course in Fashion Design in the USSR and in the GDR, while our younger one was completing her doctorate in pharmacognosy in London. Robert expressed the wish that she should keep her maiden name if she decided to get married, because we did not have boys. We also spoke about the struggle, and he said that he would not worry if he died, because Umkhonto we Sizwe (Spear of the Nation, the military wing of the ANC) had been established and had gone into action during his lifetime.

Time and again, at home, we had talked about death. I recall Robert saying, on one occasion, that if he died before I did, I should not wear black clothes to mourn for him; he said that such practices had no meaning for us: our people, he said, had copied the wearing of black clothes from Europeans, yet in the Transkei there were millions of women who had lost their husbands, but who continued to put on their *umbaco* (Xhosa traditional wear). These women, he said, mourned properly and with dignity for their departed.

In 1954, when we were preparing for the formation of the Federation of South African Women, Robert had asked me to sew myself an umbaco; that request came shortly after he had returned from his home in Queenstown, and from a visit to the Eastern Cape. There, he said, he had found many women, like Mrs Baard, Mrs Njongwe, Mrs Matomela and many others putting on their traditional wear. At first I objected, because the traditional wear I had seen when I was in East London had been dyed in red ochre, which stained other peoples' clothes on touch. Robert then suggested that I

231

might buy a fast-dyed material; what was important was the style and beauty of it as a modernised version of traditional wear.

When the women of the Cape saw me wearing my dress on the opening day of the conference, they were amazed because they knew I did not come with them. But, after I was introduced to them, they said: 'Oh! it is Robert who did this!' from that moment on, women (especially in the Transvaal) stampeded to traditional wear. But what I liked best was when women put on any traditional wear, and not according to ethnic groups. For instance, the Basotho traditional wear called *seshoeshoe* became very popular. This return to traditional wear hit the pockets of the white traders: women were no longer buying expensive dresses and hats from department stores like John Orr and the like.

At first, some of the white liberals saw traditional wear as a revival of 'tribalism'. But they had never complained about the Indian sari or the kilt. Perhaps it showed their lack of knowledge of how people dressed in the rural areas. Gandhi had gone, we were told, to a party at Buckingham Palace, wearing a dhoti, when everyone was supposed to wear morning dress. His answer to his critics was that they should go and see how the Indian people dressed. Did he not help to lead his people to independence wearing his dhoti? Actually, we heard that when Gandhi was in South Africa, he had pointed out to the early leaders of the ANC that one of the effective weapons in the fight against colonial and oppressive rule is to stick to your country's culture.

Colonial mentality is as destructive as colonialism itself. As a result, when the colonists pack up and go, the leaders who take their power find themselves oppressing their own people, albeit unwittingly, the reason being that they have just stepped into the boots of the former colonialists in every respect. But, when Kwame Nkrumah went to the United Nations for the first time, after Ghana's independence in 1957, there was much comment that the Ghanaians entered the world's 'highest chamber' wearing their traditional kente cloth. One of the effects was that black Americans, who had not wanted to have any identification with Africa, because its people had been characterised as barbarians, wearers of beads and grass clothes, changed their attitudes; today many see themselves as African-Americans; they are proud of Africa, and we are proud of them: they are our brothers and sisters, whose fathers and mothers had been traded like cattle in the market. African people are reviving African personality, and women are taking the lead because they are the guardians of that culture. To know your roots provides you with the sense of stability and pride in yourself that makes you realise that you are somebody.

All these reflections remind me how much my husband and I had in common. The longer we stayed together, the more we discovered that we were not just husband and wife; we had become friends, comrades-in-arms, and — indeed — confidants, which is a normal thing between people who love and trust each other. That confidence and trust enabled us to overcome enormous difficulties. One wise man once said that 'Marriage was not a picnic'. How right he was! From having confidence in each other, we acquired tolerance towards each other. Thus we covered each other's weaknessess and found out that we were assets to each other, mutually supporting.

Of course we did use angry words at each other at times. But never in front of the children, or other people. When we saw that an argument was getting out of hand, we sat down and discussed it, because from the very first day we lived together, Robert said that he could not afford to have runaway wife. That openness helped us a great deal because we kept it to the letter — the one who was wrong found no shame in admitting his or her mistake and apologising.

Robert knew when I was angry, not only with him but with other people; that was when the wrong thing had been repeated more than three times. By nature I take long to get angry. Robert had studied that trait, and he exploited it to the full, and that worked for the good of our internal peace.

When the children got older, they used to ask me if I and their father had had physical fights; they recalled how other children used to tell them of physical fights between their parents, and how the children themselves had joined in those fights.

Sometimes I think the ANC also stabilised our marriage, because here we were, placed in positions of trust and responsibility by other people. How could we be trusted and given responsibility if we did not set an example? We had to work together, advise each other on many things concerning the organisation, and here I really appreciated Robert's resourceful mind. But time and again he praised me, in return, for one thing or the other. Neither of us was a paragon; we needed each other.

Robert was very tidy. He wanted to be smart-looking from Monday to Monday; he could not wear a jacket from the wardrobe without the pockets and sleeves being pressed. Of course, he wanted me and the children to look smart; he warned me when I left hospital work that I should look smart, just like he had first seen me there — no going without stockings, or discarding my make-up.

Because I was the house treasurer, he always reminded me about paying our annual subscription to the ANC. Robert would say about our subscriptions, that the branch was where a freedom-fighter's charity began; without the branch, he said, one had no roots or home and did not merit being an office-bearer. And without strong branches, he added, the whole organisation would not be able to blossom in order to fulfil the aspirations of the oppressed masses. The Sophiatown branch became one of the strongest branches of the ANC. Like all branches, it later played an important part in circumventing the machinations of the Africanists, who tried to wrest control from the leadership, and who later formed the PAC. Although I told the story earlier, I wish to recall here, incidentally, about my role that one of the comments that his brother made at the gathering after our wedding was: 'Robert, if you want peace in your house, don't keep money! This woman is your treasurer. The woman uses money only for the home and her clothes, whereas you could find yourself penniless for entertaining friends'.

Robert loved and respected his senior leaders and colleagues, but what was notable — though not surprising — was the number of close personal friends he had amongst those younger than himself. Even when he had reached the

234

top in the organisation, he was accessible to all. Obviously, as a former sports reporter and active sportsman, he knew many people. But his popularity increased particularly during the campaign against the removals, and then during his militancy under cross-examination in the Treason trial.

He was like that in ordinary situations as well. I recall an incident that took place one Sunday, when we were still living in Sophiatown and we were walking down Victoria Road, going towards Freedom Square. When we passed the bus rank, Robert suddenly grabbed a stick from one of the queue marshalls, who were responsible for keeping order and seeing to it that people did not jump the queue; they carried two or three sticks each (or sometimes a knobkerrie) to discipline those who caused trouble. With the stick he had grabbed, Robert challenged one of the queue marshalls, a man called Majola, to a fight, just like the herd-boys do in the rural areas to prove who is the stronger. After a good go at each other, that must have lasted some five minutes or so, Majola retreated and threw down his stick, then offered his hand to Robert to shake, saying: '*mfo ka Resha Ndiyazi ke ngoku ukuthi, ukulele ebuhlanti*' (Son of Resha, now I know you grew up in the cattle kraal). By this stage the other marshalls were cheering Robert, and saying to Majola: 'Don't judge a man by seeing him wearing a tie and shining shoes — this man is from the people; that is why he speaks the language of the people'.

This is how Robert mixed with the people. Mr Kwembu, who, I am told, used to be feared in the Western Areas, and Samson Dubaduba, who confessed to me in my house that he used to be a street fighter, respected and loved Robert. Dubaduba was well-known in the Western Areas: he was a bit too hefty for his age, but when he took the floor for a jive dance, he moved like a feather. So too Harry Mekela, who called himself the best-dressed man in Sophiatown or Johannesburg (he claimed that he had 22 suits) addressed my husband as Bhut'Robbie (brother Robbie). Harry was a great and well-known socialite, though a bit eccentric at times. When he returned from India, where he had gone on tour as a boxing manager, he wore a Sikh turban around his head and had started to call himself 'Maharajah'. During the Women's Anti-Pass Campaign arrests of 1958, Harry acted as an interpreter in the magistrate's courts: he seemed to be in everything. His wife was also a nurse; her name too was Maggie. We were personal friends.

It was therefore not astonishing to me that when Robert died, I received so many letters of sympathy from all over the world, not only from the famous, but particularly from ordinary people who told me how he had helped them in one way or another; some other letters were just from people who had just admired him for his courage and principled beliefs. Of course, like all human beings, Robert had those who did not like him, although those people were not necessarily enemies: there were genuine differences of political views.

Political differences within the ranks of the ANC have always been seen as a sign that democracy was being protected in our organisation. It is that which has enabled the ANC to grow from strength to strength, despite the systematic onslaughts against the organisation on the part of its enemies. In exile, however, there ensued a strange struggle for power that manifested itself in the most absurd and unorthodox methods that engulfed our organisation.

Perhaps the most important instance was that, soon after the 1969 Morogoro Consultative Conference, Robert was jettisoned. It was at that conference, held in Tanzania, with participants from each of the Congresses, that Robert, Duma Nokwe, Joe Matlou and others were made to resign from the NEC under duress. They were warned by those who had called the conference that their refusal to resign might lead to the possibility of bloodshed. Umkhonto, they said, had stated that it wanted new leaders. This assertion on their part can be refuted very simply. As early as the 1971 extended NEC meeting in Zambia, at which I was present, Robert had publicly complained that, throughout his period of exile, he had been kept away from Umkhonto. That this deliberate policy to isolate him was affecting his health can be shown from a note I found among his papers. Dated 16 May 1973, it reads: 'The time is 02.22 Wednesday. I'm still wide awake and yet my mind is vague, hence this funny thought: Mathematics of Life — V x V = L/D. In other words, virtue and vice constitute man's active life and inevitably leads to death. Thus life, however full, is a postponement of death by a day. To live longer, therefore, man must defy death and plan for the future.'

Perhaps his reluctance to go abroad was a premonition of what would transpire in exile. During these years of ordeal I still remember that one day he remarked: 'If my persecution by my colleagues will hasten the day of liberation for our people, I am ready to pay the price; and our people will know one day, that I could not take part in anything I saw as an action to weaken the ANC, or even perhaps destroy it'. What must be emphasised is that despite this isolation, Robert remained a steadfast, faithful, and disciplined member of the organisation until the moment of his untimely death. His patriotism cannot be doubted. Let him rest in peace!

To some, Robert was well-known as a 'quick to fight' person, willing to settle with fists what he could not settle with words. Personally, I think he was a man of no nonsense. An example is a story told to me by his elder brother. He reminded me that after Robert had left the mines in the late Thirties, he had taken up work as a bus conductor in the Western Areas. During those days there were a group of *tsotsis* who bullied the bus conductors, and who refused to pay their bus fares. One day, the most-feared of them, called Temba, together with a group of his lieutenants, was a passenger on Robert's bus. They all refused to pay their fares. Robert challenged Temba either to pay his fare or to get off the bus and fight him. That suggestion led to a rumbling of feet, and whistles of astonishment from Temba's mates. 'Slaan hom, man! (Beat him up, man!), they instructed their leader during a fight of considerable fierceness. At last, my brother-in-law told us, Robert knocked the *tsotsi* down. The sight of blood streaming from the nose, mouth and eyes of their leader terrified the rest, and the story of the event went round the townships so quickly that, from that day onwards, *tsotsis* paid their fares without murmur. Robert had cured an ill that had bedevilled all conductors, many of whom were not

237

only the victims of physical attack, but often of lost jobs or earnings because the bus company deducted the cost of missing tickets from their pay-packets.

When I asked Robert about the story, all he said was that Temba had been a good fighter, but that he had probably been a bit tired. Still, Robert said, once he had made the challenge, he had to carry on. Although Robert was known as a short-tempered and fighting person, he was a different one at home. My whole family, especially my mother, loved him for his gentleness and his respect for them. And he absolutely adored the children: after they had been dressed up on a Sunday morning, he would walk them to the meeting place, while I stayed behind to do the finishing touches at home. He often shared a lot of his experiences with us about his youth and when he first came to the mines.

Although we were not from the same group, there were no rules laid down about which language to use in the family. We spoke Xhosa as well as Sesotho, with the result that our children became fluent in both languages. In places like Sophiatown, where there was a mixture of people of all racial groups, we used any language that made it possible for us to communicate. We were equal partners in everything. When my elder daughter Nosipho was asked in marriage by the family of her husband, Robert told them that he could not give an answer without me. Indeed, in the end it was my decision, because I knew the family of the young man.

When Robert died, in my grief, I recaptured our life together, and the sweet memories filled the vacuum left by his departure. Then, as we had always said to each other during our discussions, life must go on; so I decided to wipe away my tears. The decision was greatly assisted by the messages of sympathy which flooded in from all over the world, from world leaders to ordinary people who had got to know my husband.

From all these, I have selected three: from Nelson Mandela, from Ahmed Kathrada, and from Helen Joseph. After receiving those letters, I felt very proud of my husband — because they had known him, had worked very closely

238

with him for several years in the movement, and had suffered the jackboot of the regime for their efforts.

The letter from Nelson Mandela, dated New Years Day 1974, and carrying the stamp of the prison censor on Robben Island, reads as follows:

Our dear Maggie, it seems that the old and stable world we once knew so well is beginning to crumble down, leaving us with nothing but painful memories. Veterans like A. J. [Luthuli], Z. K. [Matthews], [Nana] Sita, J. B. [Marks], A. L. [Arthur Letele] and Debi [Singh], the commanding figures who kept us together in difficult times, and who helped to show us the way forward, are no more. Vuyisile [Mini] and friends from the Eastern Cape, tried and dedicated comrades with tremendous reserves of inner strength and initiative, are gone for ever. Pat and young pioneers like Jacques, Gandi, Basil, Panga, Charles and others, once a source of strength and pride to us, remain Kwa Mashobane, far from the areas where they were born and beyond reach of their loved ones. We shall never again have the joy of being hugged by Molly [Fisher], or entertained by Amina [Pahad], nor of listening to the words of experience which the ageless Louis possessed. They were lifetime friends to whom we were connected by a thousand strings. Together we took solemn oaths, shared intimate secrets, suffered common set-backs and enjoyed the fruits of victory.

Today it is the death of Robbie, your darling, that we mourn and we write to give you our deepest sympathy; to let you know that you and the children are in our thoughts; to remind you that the battle for happiness is never won, that in the field defeat and victory, sorrow and joy, hope and despair, always go hand in hand. At no time did we get as much as a hint that Robbie was unwell and Joe's telegram reporting his death struck us like a flash of lightning. That telegram arrived on Dec. 10 and we now know the cause of death. The next day I telegraphed back to Joe our message of condolence, via Zami [Conco], which I hope you received. All of us, without exception, were deeply moved by the sad news. The following remarks from some of my colleagues will give you an idea of the wide measure of solidarity evoked by Robbie's death. I have deliber-

239

ately taken the liberty of mentioning certain names in the hope
that the knowledge that his loss stirred even people outside
our ranks will give you the courage to go through what is perhaps your greatest personal disaster to date. Xhamela [Sisulu]:
'Robbie was a dedicated, militant and energetic worker, and
eloquent speaker'. Fikile [Bam]: 'Robbie's death is a real loss to
us all'. He went on to recall the days in Sophiatown where he
(Fikile) grew up where Robbie was the central figure, and
ended with the observation that he had died in harness.
[Eddie] Daniels: 'The past deeds of men like Robbie will
encourage others'. Toivo [Ja Toivo of Swapo]: 'I have heard a
great deal about Robbie and his life will be remembered far
into the future. Pokela [former President of PAC] spoke of
Robbie as a sportsman and recalled a conversation when they
travelled together in the O. F. S. in '52. These were spontaneous and sincere sentiments from mature men whose own circumstances make them particularly sensitive to everything
they consider a set-back to the realisation of their ideals.
Distress tends to drive them closer and closer and to brush
aside the abstract issues which loomed large in our lives in the
days of bliss. All have asked me to convey to you and family
their condolences.

Someone has said that those who renounce self-interest and
who commit their lives to the pursuit of higher ideals should
not so much concern themselves with victory or defeat as such,
as to live behind a fine tradition. The world has produced many
outstanding men, some of whom are blessed with exceptional
abilities, men who in general are better known to history. But
few will deny that our Robbie was defender and victor in his
own right, a man who left behind an impressive record. I imagine that speakers at the graveside will have traced his history
from the mid-forties right through the D. C [Defiance
Campaign], in'52, the COP [Congress of the People], the TT
[Treason Trial], the Removal, Curries Fountain, Dec. 16, '61
and the days thereafter, his work in Africa and America. He
was a man capable of making great sacrifices and played a significant role in the development of the outlook which gives
direction to our dreams, and in the shaping of those means
which enable us to defend all that is dear to our hearts. He

240

belonged to that band of men who, since the dawn of time, have concerned themselves, first and foremost, with questions of economic well-being and self-fulfilment. It is men like these who make the human race move forward, who can educate, persuade, arouse and inspire, and without whom human progress would have been impossible.

In Jan' 62 I met him in Lagos and, together with OR [Tambo], Mzwayi [Piliso], Xola and Bokwe, we flew to Addis and thereafter to Cairo. From there Robbie and I travelled in North Africa for about 3 weeks. We were again together in Accra and London. For me the trip was an experience I am not likely to forget. For one thing there was the excitement of visiting new countries, talking to their people and seeing the so-called underdeveloped countries struggling to solve the problems brought by the colonial era. But what struck me most forcefully during the trip was the fantastic progress made by my own colleagues less than 36 months after coming into contact with the new environment. Opportunity to use their talents and the weight of greater responsibility had radically transformed them, and I found the gap between themselves and myself too wide. My travels with Robbie fully confirmed this impression; I learnt a great deal from all of them.

But Robbie's achievements would have been impossible without your love, inspiration and support. His confident and everbright disposition reflected a man whose main source of strength was to be found in a happy home, in a companion who tried hard and patiently to create the ideal atmosphere where her husband's talents could blossom out. Of course, your own courage and love of independence are matters of common knowledge. For the greater part of your professional career you were on your own and you refused to work for a master. We have also not forgotten that in Oct/Nov '58 you even spent two weeks in quarters close behind the General Hospital. Above all, you gave your darling the most precious present a woman can give a man — 2 beautiful daughters. You have done your duty to Robbie and to your country. By the way shortly before Robbie left the country, I happened to be travelling through Bholotwa, the village where Robbie grew up. But there was not a single soul in sight, and all the huts were either roofless or razed to the ground. Perhaps one day it will be possible for me

241

to tell the children the full story behind those ruins. In the meantime, we like you to know that tomorrow we hope to gather the rich harvest of laurels planted by all those who have gone before us. When that great day comes we will count Robbie as being one of those who played a key role in this regard. He lives in our hearts. Once again our deep sympathy. We expect a report on his illness and on the funeral, as well as on the progress of the children as soon as you can. Did Matlala receive my letter of January '73 ? May '74 bring you and the children health, good fortune and many happy days. I miss the refreshments which you used to prepare so well and which you served so warmly. Love and fondest regards from all of us.

Sincerely, Nel.

The letter from Ahmed Kathrada, at that time also serving a life sentence on 'the Island' and also with the stamp of the prison censor, is dated 29 December 1973. It goes as follows:

My Dear Maggie, in all these years I never imagined I would have to write a letter of condolence to you. We were stunned when we learnt from Joe's cable to Nelson that Robbie was no more. At the time there was no information as to the cause of death, and we speculated that it might have been an accident or a heart attack. For Robbie was such a healthy man, and we had never heard that he had been ill. It was another shock when we later came to know that he had died as a result of cancer of the lungs. How very cut-off we are from the world outside the prison walls! Not to be aware of grave illnesses that have stricken dear friends until death snatches them away. Ever since we arrived on the Island, in 1964, we have been living from one shock to another. We were hardly here a few weeks when we heard of Molly's [Fisher] death. Then in September Baba [Saloojee] died so tragically. Then Arthur Letele; Prof [Matthews]; Chief; Mini [Vuyisile]; Mrs Pahad; Mrs Moulvi; Debi Singh; Uncle J. B. [Marks]; Pat; Hutch [Alfred Hutchinson, the novelist] — and so many other dear colleagues and relatives. And now Robbie. What a painful and harsh procession of death! In their living days we came to respect, honour, and love them all. So much that in the death of each one of them I felt as if a little bit of me had died with them. How true the words of John Donne: 'Every man's death diminishes ... For I'm of mankind'. How much truer when one as close to me as Robbie was, dies. I don't need to remind you that our friendship dated back to the late Forties. Since then we have been together through so much: turbulent times as well as peaceful, pleasant times and sad. It is too much to recall in a short letter. I remember how unhappy he was about going abroad. But as a dutiful son he obeyed. My last direct contact with him was when he phoned me one morning from SanTiago where he had been attending the FIFA soccer gathering. I shall always cherish the memory of that call. And can I ever forget our Sophtown days! Especially the Sundays after finishing our work at Victoria Street. The memories come flooding in, but I have'nt the space. How far away from home, and how far away from one another, they have died! Mrs Pahad and Mrs Moulvi in India; Hutch in England; Arthur in Lesotho; Prof in Botswana; Chief in Stanger; Babla in Jhb; Pat's blood was spilt in southern Africa; and J. B., Robbie! Yet, only a decade ago we were all together. Everywhere, in the foreign lands there is a little bit of South Africa where they lie buried.

Today we listened to [a] record of Belafonte and Miriam Makeba, and again I thought of Robbie. A few years ago we read a magazine article dealing with SA and it mentioned and had photos of Robby, Miriam, Stokeley, Raymond and others.

Over the years I've often thought of writing to him, but postponed it each time. Now alas it is too late. I hope you will find the time to write to me. Otherwise get one of the children to do so. Of course they will not remember me. They were so small when they left ...

Let me end by condoling with you and all the other who have been hit by Robbie's death. May the days ahead help to heal the wound and bring back some sunshine in the darkness that has enveloped your lives.

I'm getting on well. So are Walter [Sisulu], Nelson [Mandela], Ray [Mhlaba], Govan [Mbeki], Wilton [Mkwayi] and all the others. The first four have all got blood pressure but it is under control. After you acknowledge this I shall write again and tell you a little more about us. Keep well. My love to you and the children, to Joe, Cwanini, Tiny and to each and everyone of our friends. All the best for the new year, from

Your dear friend

A. M. Kathrada.

The first of two letters from Helen Joseph was short. Dated 8 December, it says simply:

My dear Maggie, This morning I heard from Lilian Ngoyi about Robert — I can't find the proper words to tell you how grieved I am that he has gone & will never now come back to South Africa. Indeed South Africa has lost one of her finest sons, but as his wife I know how proud you will be of his memory, & that this will help you to overcome your sorrow at the passing of your husband, a leader of your people in our struggle for freedom.

I send you my love and sympathy, to you and to your daughters. I am glad you have them to comfort you.

These sentiments reminded me of a poem that had been written and dedicated to the two of us by our younger daughter, Masechaba, when she was nineteen years of age and studying in the Soviet Union. It contained the following note: 'Mama — This poem is on all 4 of us but mostly for you and Tata. I only hope you do understand what I'm trying to explain. Really Mama, you and Tata are my real heroes. The poem goes like this:

Working Together Are My Heroes
The first day I came to town, I met them.
They were new to me, and yet already so dear
Too many for a go, they were three of them.
My father, my mother and my sister.

They made me one of them so easily.
I felt I was at home with talking and playing to do.
But work. Oh yes, there was a lot of it.
Father would go early to work, mother in a white starched
    uniform,
Sister and me up to school.

244

By the way we were born black and surely will die black
Because of that we lived through hard and frightening
    days and nights
Father hurled from bed from mama's side just to be taken
    behind the cold bars.
Sometimes mama taken.
And alas! both are now behind bars.
That left sister and me crying from not understanding our
    kind of life.

Time allowed us to dig the whole situation
We're oppressed: no work, no food, no place to live.
There was another type of work for my dears.
And that's work of the African National Congress.

And so we had to leave our beloved Motherland.
Surely the world is so big and friends so many
But we had to part to find work and studies.
Time and again there's that get-together my heroes
    arrange
Not knowing they are.

Far away from home, from relatives, even from their own
    children
Father and mother are going on.
Father so strong and full of anger. They labelled him
    terrorist.
Mother keeping up, knowing that she's not alone.

They look so good, so jolly, so young and beautiful
It surprises and thrills me at the same time.
My heroes are never tired, their way is the hard way
And they know it.
And working together, they are my heroes, they keep each
    other's morale so high.
When we received this poem, Robert and I were very
proud, and deeply touched; it aroused in us a discernment of
how apartheid cruelly violates the childhood of black chil-

dren — this essential period in the moulding process. All parents feel guilty for the inability to provide security, health and happiness for their children; but how gratifying it is to find out that our children are the heirs and heiresses of the struggle — for only through the struggle will freedom be restored.

* * *

Robert was laid to rest on 14 December 1973. His death had come as a great shock and surprise to many people: the majority of people had not even known that he had had an operation, or indeed, that he had been ill. But, when they heard, as is our custom, many people came to the house of Maud and James Phillips (who died in London in 1988) from whom Robert had rented two rooms to observe the night vigil. Many people made speeches about how they knew Robert, and about his work.

The funeral on the day of the service started from the house. Alfred Temba Mqota, his former colleague, who had been elected with Robert to the ANC NEC at home in 1955, was Master of Ceremonies; he read a selection of messages of condolence — it was impossible to read them all, because of their sheer volume, and because we were chasing time to get to the church. The late David Sibeko, who was the PAC representative in London, also spoke briefly at this time.

The church service was held in St. Paul's Cathedral, and was conducted by Canon John Collins, assisted by another priest. At the church, Oliver Tambo and Joe Matlou were the two speakers; both having worked with Robert for many years, spoke of what they knew about him.

Robert's coffin, which was draped with an ANC flag, had been carried shoulder-high in and out of the church by members of Umkonto we Sizwe. People who had been living in London for a long time said afterwards that this was the first funeral in their experience to which people had come in such large numbers, and from so many walks of life, and that despite the fact that it was on a Friday, which is a working day.

* * *

After Robert's death, and since 1975, I have resided in London in order to enable my younger daughter to continue with her studies. Because of grief and shock she got after, she felt it was time for her to leave everything and start working. But, remembering my husband's last wish about her, I decided to be nearer her in order to give her moral and material support. So I applied for a nursing job, and when I had got it, I moved from Algiers to London. The job was at the Samaritan Hospital, which specialises in gynaecological cases. I worked there for seven years and seven months. The first night I went to work (I preferred to do night duty) the night Sister gave me some forms and told me that I had to join a Trades Union. I was very shocked; I thought that she was trapping me, because, as I have said earlier, in South Africa nurses are not allowed to join unions. So, when she had gone, I asked the nurse who was on duty with me, about it: she said that everyone belonged. So I joined.

Well, I liked the hospital, but the work was heavy, especially when you find yourself in charge of a ward containing twenty-four patients, most of whom had come for major operations. But the work helped me to forget my grief, because I love nursing.

After I had lived in England for four years, I received a letter from the Home Office, telling me that my restrictions had been lifted: I no longer had to report to the police once a year. So, in my fifth year, I applied for naturalisation, and, when that was granted, I applied for a British passport, which I received in 1983.

The greatest problem I had was in getting accommodation when I came to England. At first I stayed in a bed-sitter. For the year and seven months I stayed here it cost me £100 per month; that figure did not include electricity. Not only was this very expensive, but the place was also too small and too hot because of the cooking. Furthermore, I had to share one toilet with five other tenants, and that can be difficult at times because people have visitors. Then, during weekends, when some tenants held parties, it was terrible. My daughter had meantime left her hostel at Chelsea College, where she was studying, to come to live with me, but we soon realised that that was an impossible situation: she could not study under such conditions, so she moved back to the hostel, from where she would come to visit me at weekends, when we would visit Robert's grave. Her stipend, which was £90 per month, at that time, allowed her to buy only the essentials and the bare necessities, but I was able to help her to get clothes to be able to look like other young people of her age. Later, through friends who had themselves been helped by my husband when they had first arrived here from South Africa, I was able to get a two bedroom flat; that was in 1976. Although it was a bit dilapidated, it was a good flat, in a convenient situation, and I was thankful to be able to move out of the bedsitter.

My daughter, who had moved into the flat with me, because she wanted to be near me, was awarded her doctorate in Science from the University of London in 1977; she specialised in Pharmacognosy, and the subject of her thesis was: 'The Alkaloids of Mitragyna Speciosa Korth'. When she got married in 1979, she went to live in Cambridge with her husband, Dr Mkwananzi; he was from Zimbabwe, and doing research in Immunology. In the same year I accompanied her and her husband to the Royal Albert Hall, for her graduation ceremony, and that was one of the happiest days of my life: happy because I knew that my husband's dearest wish had been fulfilled; throughout the ceremony I felt that Robert was there, sharing our joy.

This was another first time for me. Proud parents were walking around with their children in their graduation gowns. White women (there were hardly any black women) were proudly introducing their children to anyone who looked at them: 'This is my son so-and-so ...' or 'This is my daughter ...'

So I also joined in: 'This is my daughter ...' The children were just looking at us; we were behaving like real peacocks; I even thought to myself that if we were in South Africa now, the women would be ululating like hell. It was a very exciting day, and later, when I recalled the events, I said to myself that these women were right because it is not every parent who gets the joy of sharing in the success of their children. Education is the key to a person's progress in life; all parents strive hard to give that to their children, but it is not every child who gets there. And what about our black children in South Africa? Their chances of getting access to that key are deliberately being denied because of the colour of their skin. Apartheid is the greatest shame of the twentieth century.

My eldest daughter had, meanwhile joined her husband in Cairo, where he was doing an advanced course in Statistics. He had originally been a student at the Turfloop University in South Africa, where he had been a member of the PAC. In Cairo, to where he had been posted, he defected to the ANC, after which he went to the German Democratic Republic, where he obtained his original qualifications. He was now trying to complete his doctorate. Somehow, for reasons I do not know, he did not complete, although he was brilliant in Mathematics, and a very good chap: he had given lessons to many of our boys in Umkhonto we Sizwe, many of whom had never been to school at home. At some stage, he had also helped in the Liberation committee offices in Dar-es-Salaam with J. B. Marks.

After Cairo, he went to Lesotho, to work there for the government; his parents had come from before they went to live in Matatiele. Then, in 1981, he was reported missing. In 1982, a year after my daughter and the family had been searching for him, his mother wrote to me to say that they had just received a death certificate from a Bloemfontein hospital, which stated that he had died there the previous year: the cause of death was given as poisoning. From what we could reconstruct later on, he had been brought to the hospital by people who had lured him into South Africa. Although these people claimed to be his relatives, they had given false names. It was only much later that it was established that these people, who had known my son-in-law in Dar-es-Salaam, were deserters from Umkhonto we Sizwe who had become agents of the white regime. So my son-in-

249

law was one of the first victims of the South African hit squads. Naturally, my daughter took this very hard; she is still shocked and grieving. But she has two wonderful children — a boy and a girl.

I finally retired in 1983. Although I could have carried on for a few more years, my health has not been good and I am under regular medical supervision.

So, here I am, like many other of my colleagues and fellow exiles, stuck here in London, and (like many others in other parts of the world) unable to return while the regime is in power. However, some of us are lucky because we are in touch with our families — there are many exiles whose family contacts have broken down, but that is what happens in every revolution and in every war. But while England offers many opportunities for the elderly, and while I am busily occupied doing lots of things, I can now see that the day is not too far distant when the apartheid regime will be no more.

Appendix I:

Speeches at the Funeral of Robert Resha

For the record, and because in later years there has been some argument as to exactly who said what at the church and at the graveside on the day that the tombsone was unveiled on 19 July 1975, I include word-for-word the speeches that were made at both places; these are taken from a tape that was made for me of the ceremony.

The first part of the service took place at St. Paul's and St. Luke's Parish Church, (with the African Methodist Episcopal Church), Camden Square, London. After the congregation had sung the first two verses of a popular Xhosa hymn by Tiyo Soga: *'Liza lisidinga lako, Tixo Nkosi Yenyaniso* (Fulfill your promise Lord God of Truth), the Rev. Mabona read from Ecclesiasticus, Chapter 44: Let Us Now Praise Famous Men.

After the conclusion of a short address by the Rev. Mabona, the Chairman of the proceedings Joe Matlou spoke as follows:

Thank you, Rev. Mabona, thank you for guiding us by showing the relationship between the work of God and the work which we are engaged in to deliver ourselves and our people from oppression.

I'll proceed to make a few remarks, and they will be very few indeed. For that I am very sorry; I am sorry that my position to chair this occasion deprives me of an opportunity to speak all that I know about my dear brother Robert Resha.

I knew Robert Resha in the mid-forties. At that time, I distinctly remember, he was a sports columnist for *Umteteli wa Bantu*, one of the newspapers which pretended to cater for African opinion in South Africa. I knew him as man of great interest in sport. But our friendship developed more when we found that we had similar interests politically. We were members of the Youth League — the African National Congress Youth League — when it started. I still distinctly remember that its earliest meetings were held at 58 Commissioner Street

252

— that is, Barclay Arcade. I still remember all our colleagues; we worked together, built up the Youth League, and the Youth League which later on became a real force in resuscitating the ANC, which, in the Thirties perhaps had become poor in its activities. Many of the Youth Leaguers of that period have distinguished themselves in the struggle for freedom. Robert Resha has particularly laid impressive footprints on the road towards freedom of the African people. Robert Resha was a devoted man, a selfless man who devoted all his life to the struggle of his people. In the African National Congress there is today a vacant chair, a vacant chair which Robert Resha had for many years occupied. Robert Resha distinguished himself particularly by his display of courage, by the manner in which he faced very difficult occasions in the struggle, without flinching. I worked with Robert Resha especially on the campaigns against the removal of the Western Areas of Johannesburg. We worked very closely indeed, and not only were we political colleagues, but we were brothers: we shared political views; we shared various other aspects of life which bring two people together. I have discovered that I was associated, truly, with a man of integrity, as Rev. Mabona put it. The struggle for the liberation of the African people of South Africa will forever miss the contribution of Robert Resha.

I am not a speaker on this occasion; there are speakers who will bear witness to the work of Robert Resha: they will do it better. I am only feeling very proud that I have been able to be here today to be able to attend this occasion. Eighteen months ago we laid down the body of Robert Resha; today we are going to unveil the tombstone. All of us must join our hearts in looking forward to carry out the work which Robert Resha had carried out. I have no doubt that many of us are determined to further this course of liberation of South Africa to the very end. With those remarks, I declare this latter part of the occasion open, and therefore I proceed to call upon His Excellency, Mr Lakhdar Ibrahimi, The Ambassador of Algeria, to make a few remarks on this occasion.

After commencing by thanking the chairman, the Ambassador continued:

253

When I was asked to come and participate in this occasion, I had absolutely no hesitation in accepting. Although I have known Robert for probably a much shorter period than most of the people who are in this room, I had so much regard and admiration and friendship for him that is, for me, a duty and a very good occasion to remember Robert in a few words in front of you.

We met about fifteen years ago, and in those days we were both exiles, representing Liberation Movements from our respective countries. Although we met mostly on African soil, mostly in Cairo, still we were both exiled. Soon after that, after Algeria became independent, Robert came and — as a matter of fact — got, I think, to Algiers before I did, and he opened the first office for the ANC in Algeria.

I remember very very well when we used to go to see him in Rue Larbi ben M'hedi, as his wife and many other people here will remember, we used to discuss always the same subject. We used to discuss the question of what aggression is, and I think in a gathering like this, it is perhaps not very important to talk about this, because everybody I think, agrees with us. But what I would like you to do, what I would like us to do, is to go out from this room to tell the people we know that Robert Resha and people like him, who died away from South Africa, of natural causes, have been killed by the South African regime; they are the victims of the permanent aggression of the South African regime as surely as if they were hanged in a prison inside South Africa. This is what we want the outside world to understand; this is what we want, in particular, the Western world to understand: that the aggression a country like South Africa is victim of, is something that is happening every minute, every day, and is directed against everybody in South Africa, whether they are actually inside South Africa or abroad. All the exiles, all the people who are in this room who come from South Africa, are the victims of permanent aggression. I think this is the point we were very often discussing with Robert Resha, this is what we tried together, and what he has always tried to do in England, in Africa, in Latin America, in Asia, everywhere he went — that is the point he wanted to get across to people, and that is what we must go on trying to

254

bring home to people in the Western world, who think, you see, that the evil of apartheid is something which you can piously condemn on your way to work or on your way from work. It is something which has to be destroyed; it is something which has to be destroyed by all means at the disposal of every man, of every woman, and of every community. This is what Robert Resha died for; this is what killed Robert Resha, and we have got to stop this system which kills people like Robert Resha. I think this is the best way, really, and the best manner for me to pay my tribute to Robert Resha and to remember him on this occasion. It is not ... not ... I mean, you all know him ... everybody who is here is here because they know him ... he was ... he was a very very good man ... I am sorry ...

This was a very poignant moment in the proceedings for all of us, because the Ambassador, overcome by the solemnity of the occasion, now broke down. Thankfully, the other priest, Rev. Sepula immediately launched into the third verse of the earlier hymn: *Laula Laula Nkosi Yesu* (Rule, Rule, Lord Jesus), which was taken up and sung feelingly by the audience.

The chairman now called upon someone whom he described as 'one of Robbie's best friends in this world', Rev. Canon John Collins, of St. Paul's Cathedral. I wish I could convey the beauty of the tone of voice, the emphasis he put on certain words and phrases, the pauses etc. to gain their effect, but these are the words Canon Collins spoke:

Maggie, and Friends: I think I can say almost everything that I want to say by the words that come to my head: Robbie was a faithful, a loving, and a beloved friend, and it is very difficult to speak of him without getting a sense that I can say nothing because my heart is too full.

I got to know him very, very well all the time he was in London, and we became the closest possible of friends. He was a man of ... I think, if I can just briefly sum up my impressions of him ... a man of great integrity and honesty and giving of himself to the utmost, to the utmost power that he had, of giving the whole of himself to the cause of freedom for his fellow

South Africans who are oppressed. His whole life was devoted to this, and yet I think of him — each day almost I wait for him to come and for us to have a talk together — I think of him as a man, whatever other qualities he may or may not have had — as a man that you could trust completely, whether you agreed or disagreed with him. Of course, he was a politician to the fingertips and, I think, an exceedingly good one. But he was basically ... basically ... a great African. Every inch of him. And that's what I think of Robbie. And I think probably the nicest tribute I can pay today, because we shall all say a lot of the same things, who knew him.

If you will allow me to let you share with me in an experience which only, in my capacity as a priest, I was able to have, the last time I saw Robbie. He was — what can I say? — still the few words he could say, he was thinking of "Free South Africa!" But... he had few words left, to say, and I knew that he had been brought up, and knew ... close to and knew Father Trevor Huddleston, and I said to him: "The Lord is My Shepherd ... " And Robbie very quietly continued the psalm, until he came to "... though I walk through the Valley of the Shadow of Death ... " and he stopped. "John", he said, "am I dying. " Now, any of you will know what a question to a man that is when you know that he is. So I said, "Robbie, you are very, very, very ill, but we all want you with us. Africa is not yet free. " And, with the sweetest possible smile, he said: "John, I shall be with you, and I shall be with all who fight for South African freedom, when the day comes that it is free. And, whatever our views may be, religiously, Robbie is not gone; Robbie is still with us, and he will be there, with us, on that great day when the flags of the African National Congress and the other freedom movements, the flag of African South Africa, is flying. He will be there, rejoicing, with all who are there.

The next speaker was Mr Peter Katjavivi of Swapo, who spoke on behalf of all the Southern Africa Liberation Movements; he made the following intervention:

Friends: I have been thinking, for the last two days, what I

256

should be saying on this occasion, in paying tribute to a friend, to a colleague, Robert Resha. It is not easy, for there is so much in what one can say by tracing his life, his work, up to the last day. But I would like to be brief; I would like to be brief by saying that, what I think is important for us here to remember is that here we had a friend, a brother, who dedicated his life from the early days of his childhood; he fought along with all the comrades, but, due to circumstances under which we live, conditions we are subjected under, he left us. But his work, the job of liberation South Africa, remains our main task. I think the best tribute to his life is for us to rededicate ourselves, is for us to finish the job of liberation of South Africa.

During his life, Robbie shared so many things with people not necessarily from his own country; he was a close friend of our people, of our organisation, and many others in Africa and beyond Africa. I think he was a man of great courage, who showed tremendous capacity and influence which had inspired many of us. We remember him as a man who committed himself fully to the cause of freedom, not only in South Africa, but I think in the rest of Africa. His work is well-known to many. I think many of you will always remember him as a very inspiring and moving figure within his own organisation, and also among people and those who have shown interests in helping the ANC, in helping the forces for the liberation of South Africa. As I said, we on our part, within Namibia — and I am sure, I believe, this goes for the friends in Zimbabwe and elsewhere — our tribute in continuing his work is to intensify, is to shape up the liberation struggle in our respective areas. We will fulfil his dreams, his hopes, by intensifying our efforts. And, above all, we will fulfil the dreams of millions of Africans in Africa by narrowing the gap between the forces for liberation. Unity is Strength! And I am sure this is one of Robbie's main hopes; he had a lot to say about this during his days ... the need for us to forge together, irrespective of areas we happen to come from. I think I have no doubt that many of us will always remember him, and work hand-in-hand, until South Africa is liberated. I think this is all I can say, by adding my voice to those who have spoken here. Thank you.

The next speaker was Ambrose Makiwane. He started by singing a verse from the Freedom Song: *Umtomnyama Emhlaben 'ifun' inkululeko* (A Black Man Wants Freedom in the World) in which the audience joined him. He then continued:

Friends — I am going to make no apologies whatsoever about what I am going to say about my leader, the leader of the African people, Robert Resha. I have chosen to write my speech, so that I assume full responsibility for what I'm saying, and so that I'm not misquoted or misrepresented.

Today, according to custom, we have gathered to bring Robbie back, to talk about his inspiring deeds in order to arouse that deep sense of patriotism without which we cannot hope to free South Africa. Robbie was known to all of us; we know how pleasant he was, how an injustice done to him or another person would immediately arouse his righteous and revolutionary anger. We remember his wit, his astuteness, his accessibility to all and sundry. We know how generous Robbie was. Robbie gave all his life, and he was prepared to give all his blood, to the service of the oppressed and exploited people of South Africa. We are bringing (back) a man back who had fought bravely; but, above all, who knew how to die. Robbie died being the same defiant, unyielding, proud Robbie.

Isolation: Robbie died in isolation. Isolation. And, by the way, also, isolation is one of the instruments various successive regimes in South Africa have used, but they have had no effect on Robbie. This weapon of oppressive regimes was used against this gallant son of Africa. Yes, Robbie died in London, having fallen under enemy hands. Imagine the tears of the African women in South Africa, when they think back and remember how they, in agony and blood, (mourn?) for those who have fallen under enemy hands, for those who are languishing on Robben Island, and greater is the wrath of these mothers, of every African, young and old, when, in spite of this, the enemy is not properly identified. And worse still, the ANC has been hijacked by non-Africans. Robbie fought tooth and nail against this treachery, and, like the warrior he was, died fighting.

The late Robbie was a former member of the National

258

Executive of the ANC and was a former Deputy Volunteer-in-Chief; he was (a) Foundation Member of the African National Congress Youth League. Robbie was a staunch patriot, and a man of action, and remained true to the aims and objects of the African National Congress. The ANC was founded to build the unity of the African people, and nationalism was to be the instrument to achieve this objective. Robbie threw himself into tasks with all his heart; he understood well that the African National Congress was Africa-oriented. This is shown in the ANC anthem: God Bless Africa.

From earliest times, the African people of South Africa were viewing the South African situation in the broad context of colonised Africa. Their nationalism, their urge for freedom and unity, was not limited to the narrow confines of their national boundaries; to them, their struggle was the struggle of the whole of Africa and (of) all the African people languishing abroad under the yoke of colonialism. The ANC flag symbolises this, and the fact that the Anthem and the flag have been embraced by some African countries is a tribute to the far-sightedness of the Founding Fathers of the African National Congress. Further, Africa and the world do realise that, until South Africa is free, the Continent is not free. Detente will not free South Africa, nor any counter-revolutionary arrangements between Vorster and people listening to Vorster. Detente can only be effective when there is direct consultation with the leaders of the African people, and not through intermediaries.

Revolutionary struggle and armed struggle are instruments of the African people, with which to attain the goal of independence, the goal of freedom. In this revolutionary struggle, all people opposed to apartheid, irrespective of colour, race, or creed, have a part to play. The non-violent pressure by students, workers, churches and social organisations, have one objective. The people of South Africa have to be organised, under the objective of fighting the system of racialism on which the government is based, and this system has to be replaced with a system of equality and political independence, where merit (and merit alone) shall be the criterion of individual advancement.

The trouble the African people have at present is that our

strategy and tactics are in the hands, and dominated by, a small non-African clique. This is the result of the disastrous Morogoro Conference of 1969, which opened membership of the ANC to non-Africans. At this conference, Robbie opposed this, on the grounds that that was a violation of the policy of the ANC. But all that was in vain. Robbie went to his grave, having not submitted to the humiliation of the African by this small clique, whose actions have brought a terrible set-back to our struggle. This small clique quickly consolidated itself, reorganised representation of External Missions to suit its aims, and carefully selected delegations to conferences so that they acted robot-fashion. Nationalism is pooh-poohed; those who espouse it are either isolated, or branded as racists. The label of "racist", which the non-African clique uses, is against all Africans who oppose the control and manipulation of the ANC by non-Africans, is an anomalous one. It is anomalous because Africans suffer from the jackboot of white racism from the cradle to the grave: in their own country they are made aliens.

Now, this cruel form of white racism is extended, albeit covertly, to the Africans' own national organisation, whereby opposition to non-African domination of the ANC carries heavy political penalties, like isolation and character-assassination and alienation. Since 1969, the Executive Committee of the ANC has never functioned with [a] full complement: either some of its members are dead, sick or in full employment, and the remainder are attending all international conferences, of course, under the Argus eye of this small clique, for visiting certain countries, whilst others are taboo. The resultant effect of this has been the estrangement of the ANC with many countries and many organisations, and on its dependence for support on [a] few countries. In 1971, an External Executive meeting of the ANC was convened in Zambia. Amongst other things, the meeting, having observed the stagnation that had set in [in] the ANC, decided on the establishment of a National Secretariat, whose task would have been to revamp the organisation. Robbie was a member of this Secretariat, together with other leading members of the ANC. At the insistence of the non-African clique, the Secretariat was dissolved.

Robbie never accepted the dilution of African leadership of

the ANC: this is the view of the African members. He died, championing and correctly reflecting the views of the African people. The realities of the South African situation reflect this. This is so because South Africa is an African country. The African is the most oppressed; he suffers worst deprivation and exploitation. This is not being racialist; it is a fact, it is an objective reality. If the African people are to achieve their independence, they have to unite. Robbie believed in unity. Robbie fought and died for unity — the unity of the African people. The manner with which we can cherish the memory of so dedicated a leader of our people, is to do the best that we can to build this unity.

The African people can not be expected to wait indefinitely, on the fringes of their organisation, whilst non-Africans exercise a leadership function, though unable to accept the responsibility for the consequences of their actions. If nothing else, the radically changed situation in southern Africa now favouring the struggling masses of South Africa, calls for fundamental changes in the manner in which the ANC operates abroad. The ANC must be redirected to its true nationalist cause, and the first step is for the members of the African National Congress to press, relentlessly, for a representative conference of the ANC, with a view to putting its own house in order. Amongst the first things to be done in that conference is to cauterize the small non-African clique. If this small non-African clique claims to be non-racial, it should, from now, acknowledge that the essence of non-racialism lies in accepting the dignity of the African and the fight for freedom from domination, from control from all sides — both inside South Africa, as well as outside of South Africa. The Africans hate the domination of the Communist Party of South Africa.

Finally, I appeal to all people who want the overthrow of the system of apartheid, to support the African cause: its triumph will make possible the triumph of democratic ideals [and] the ushering [in] of an era of social advancement, peace, brotherhood, and friendship among all the people of South Africa

After thanking the speaker for his remarks, which he observed would be 'well noted', the chairman called upon Mr

261

Mqota to read a few of the very large number of letters and cables that had been received. Among these, Mr Mqota singled out, first, a message from the Rev. Gawe, who had been a Treason Trialist with my husband. The message informed us that the Rev. Gawe had held a memorial service in Robert's honour in the Church of the Israelites in Queenstown location. Mr Mqota reminded the congregation that this was the Church from where the ANC had sent its volunteers during the Defiance Campaign and all other campaigns. Again, for the record, I quote, word-for-word, the message from the Rev. Gawe, as told to the congregation by Mr Mqota:

According to Rev. Gawe, a hymn was sung, and it was Xa umhlaba upitizela. Then, Mr Mbhengo — again, those who are familiar with important people, African leaders in the ANC, will know Mbhengo — made an address, giving Robbie's history. I should say that he is also a cousin of Robbie. Rev. Gawe says [that] in his sermon, he touched on certain characteristics that he had observed in Robert from Robbie's youth, and he says [that] he seemed to be interested in things beyond the understanding of an average child; he gives a very difficult rhyme, which Robbie knew very well:

Kuqhunkq' ukuqweb' amaqhinga,
Ngeqoqo lamaquth' aseqaco,
Liqwebe loqola likuqwele —
Leqonce lokuquthiswa qho.

Now, summarized, this little rhyme (which, I am sure, you are aware is full of clicks) simply means: "don't undermine the authority of the people", and Rev. Gawe based his sermon on the authority of the people, and how Robert was a servant of those people.

Because it was now becoming urgent that we vacate the church, where the next service was imminent, Mr Mqota read out only the following cables.

First, one from Helen Joseph, which said: 'To the memory of a brave man. We shall remember him. Among other cables read out were from: from Gert Sibande, from Swaziland: 'All with you, this day of remembrance of a dear colleague and fellow leader. Amandla!'; from Miriam Makeba and Stokely Carmichael; 'Doubly sorry unable to be with you physically. We must, however, salute this great son of Africa. The struggle continues'; from the Solidarity Human rights Committee in Johannesburg: 'The Human Rights Committee salutes the memory of Robert Resha.'

The meeting at the church finished with the congregation observing a one- minute silence. After that, we all proceeded to the Great Northern London Cemetery for the unveiling of the tombstone.

At the graveside, people who had arrived ahead of Robert's brother, sang Freedom Songs while they waited. These included: *Lihambile lihambile iqhawe la maqhawe uRobert Resha* (Robert Resha, hero of heroes, is gone); *Malibongwe malibongwe igama la mavoluntiya malibongwe* (Let the names of the Volunteers be praised); *Hamba kahle iqhawe la maqhawe hamba kahle* (Hero of Heroes, Go Well!) and other freedom songs.

The service at the graveside, which was conducted by Rev. Sipula, who had replaced Rev. Mabona, began with the hymn: *Ndikokele kuyehova ndingumhambi nkosi yam* (I am a Pilgrim leading to Jehovah my Lord). After that, the priest continued the proceedings with a short address, followed by a prayer. Then Robert's elder brother, Bhut' William, cut the tape to unveil the tombstone.

The unveiling of the tombstone took place on 19 July 1975. I started to make plans early to see that my brother-in-law should come over; he had been unable to come to the funeral because of failing health, and seeing that it was winter in England, it appeared unwise. It took a long time to get him a passport, but eventually it was issued and he came; he was by now very old. Indeed, he died about a year after he returned home.

'To live in the hearts of those you leave behind, is not to die. *Lala Ngoxolo MThembu Omhle*' (Rest in Peace, Beautiful Mtembu). These are the words my daughters and I chose to be engraved on my husband's tombstone in the Great Northern London Cemetery, which was unveiled in July 1975.

Having completed that task, my brother-in-law, spoke about his reasons for coming to England to take part in the ceremony; he had come to make certain that his brother was indeed here. Having satisfied himself of that, he concluded: 'We Reshas are agreed — a man's grave is by the wayside! and here he lies today. Sleep, Robert. And remember me!'

After that farewell, followed by the blessing of the grave by the Rev. Mabona, the ceremony concluded with the singing of the National Anthem and with our daughter Masechaba laying a wreath on the grave.

Memorial services were held in many other countries, including several in Africa. At a meeting in the United Nations chapel in New York, Thami Mhlambiso, the ANC Representative at the United Nations, paid tribute to Robert, calling him a hero of his people; he also paid tribute to two South Africans who had been killed by parcel bombs sent by the agents of the regime. They were Boy Mvemve (also called John Dube), then deputy representative of the ANC in Lusaka, and Abraham Tiyo, former president of the South African Students Association, killed by a bomb in Botswana.

African National Congress

Award of Merit

This award is conferred upon

MAGDELENE RESHA

in the name of the oppressed people of
South Africa
for
outstanding service given in a spirit of
selflessness and courage in resisting
oppression on the occasion of

ANTI–PASS CAMPAIGN

By this service the day of liberation
from oppression has been brought closer

Nokwe

SECRETARY-GENERAL

Nutuli

PRESIDENT-GENERAL

Royal 559

265

Appendix II: *Family Tree of Tsiu*

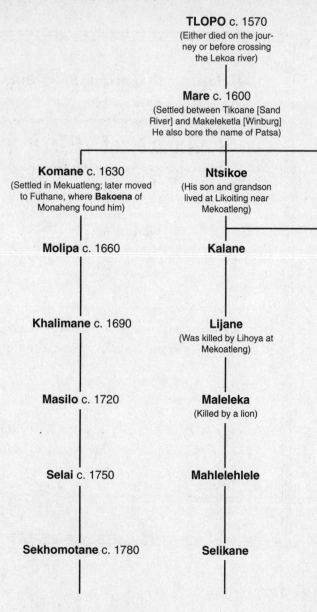

TLOPO c. 1570
(Either died on the journey or before crossing the Lekoa river)

|

Mare c. 1600
(Settled between Tikoane [Sand River] and Makeleketla [Winburg] He also bore the name of Patsa)

Komane c. 1630
(Settled in Mekuatleng; later moved to Futhane, where **Bakoena** of Monaheng found him)

Ntsikoe
(His son and grandson lived at Likoiting near Mekoatleng)

Molipa c. 1660

Kalane

Khalimane c. 1690

Lijane
(Was killed by Lihoya at Mekoatleng)

Masilo c. 1720

Maleleka
(Killed by a lion)

Selai c. 1750

Mahlelehlele

Sekhomotane c. 1780

Selikane

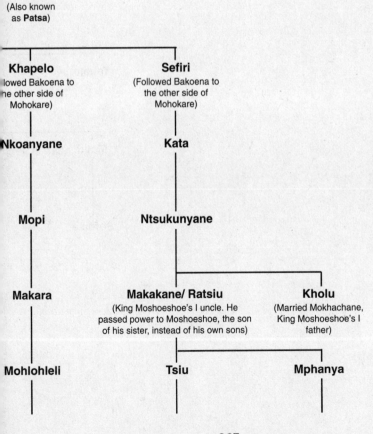

Mangole
(Also known as **Patsa**)

Khapelo
lowed Bakoena to
he other side of
Mohokare)

Sefiri
(Followed Bakoena to
the other side of
Mohokare)

Nkoanyane

Kata

Mopi

Ntsukunyane

Makara

Makakane/ Ratsiu
(King Moshoeshoe's I uncle. He
passed power to Moshoeshoe, the son
of his sister, instead of his own sons)

Kholu
(Married Mokhachane,
King Moshoeshoe's I
father)

Mohlohleli

Tsiu

Mphanya

267

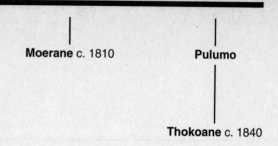

Moerane c. 1810   **Pulumo**

Thokoane c. 1840

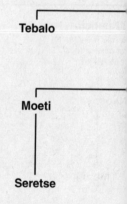

Tebalo

Moeti

Seretse

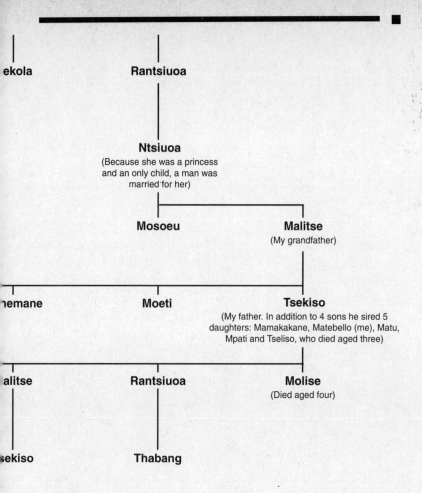

ekola   Rantsiuoa

Ntsiuoa
(Because she was a princess
and an only child, a man was
married for her)

Mosoeu   Malitse
(My grandfather)

hemane   Moeti   Tsekiso
(My father. In addition to 4 sons he sired 5
daughters: Mamakakane, Matebello (me), Matu,
Mpati and Tseliso, who died aged three)

alitse   Rantsiuoa   Molise
(Died aged four)

ekiso   Thabang

269